Frank O'Hara and MoMA

Frank O'Hara and MoMA

New York Poet, Global Curator

Matthew Holman

BLOOMSBURY VISUAL ARTS
LONDON · NEW YORK · OXFORD · NEW DELHI · SYDNEY

BLOOMSBURY VISUAL ARTS
Bloomsbury Publishing Plc, 50 Bedford Square, London, WC1B 3DP, UK
Bloomsbury Publishing Inc, 1359 Broadway, New York, NY 10018, USA
Bloomsbury Publishing Ireland, 29 Earlsfort Terrace, Dublin 2, D02 AY28, Ireland

BLOOMSBURY, BLOOMSBURY VISUAL ARTS and the Diana logo are trademarks of
Bloomsbury Publishing Plc

First published in Great Britain 2025

Reprinted 2025

Cover design: Elena Durey
Cover image: Larry Rivers, *Double Portrait of Frank O'Hara*, 1955. Oil on canvas.
15 1/4 x 25 1/8" (38.4 x 63.6 cm). The Museum of Modern Art, New York.
© Estate of Larry Rivers/VAGA at ARS, NY and DACS, London 2024.

Bloomsbury Publishing Plc does not have any control over, or responsibility for, any third-party websites
referred to or in this book. All internet addresses given in this book were correct at the time of going to
press. The author and publisher regret any inconvenience caused if addresses have changed or sites
have ceased to exist, but can accept no responsibility for any such changes.

A catalogue record for this book is available from the British Library.

A catalog record for this book is available from the Library of Congress.

ISBN: HB: 978-1-3503-9859-7
       PB: 978-1-3503-9863-4
       ePDF: 978-1-3503-9860-3
       eBook: 978-1-3503-9861-0

Typeset by RefineCatch Limited, Bungay, Suffolk
Printed and bound in Great Britain

For product safety related questions contact productsafety@bloomsbury.com.

To find out more about our authors and books visit www.bloomsbury.com
and sign up for our newsletters.

For A. H. J. B.

CONTENTS

LIST OF ILLUSTRATIONS

ACKNOWLEDGEMENTS

Frank O'Hara and MoMA took a long time to write, and I have found doing so joyous and torturous in turn. With that said, to this writer at least, it is hard to imagine a more enduringly exciting subject than Frank O'Hara, whose wit, poetic imagination and unrelenting vim for life has been continually inspiring. I first became infatuated with O'Hara's work as a nineteen-year-old Erasmus student at the Free University of Amsterdam, when I persuaded Diederik Oostdijk to let me take his Masters course on American poetry. This book is, in many ways, the culmination of nearly fifteen years of research on O'Hara and therefore requires thanking many people who have helped me write it.

Over the course of writing this book, I was lucky to spend time in many archives and university collections in Europe and the United States. I was particularly fortunate to have worked with such receptive, knowledgeable, and above all patient ambassadors for artistic legacies and scholarship. Among those who have not tired, or have not made their tiredness explicit, of my repeated requests for scans and permissions, and who have offered insight and expertise, are Valentina Bandelloni (SCALA, Florence), Andrew Beccone and Laura Morris (The Joan Mitchell Foundation), Sarah Haug and Grady O'Connor (Helen Frankenthaler Foundation), Lena Kühnel (*documenta*), Monica McTighe (The Dedalus Foundation), Jacquline Protka (Hirshhorn Library), Josie Shenoy (DACS), Elizabeth Thomas (MoMA Archives), Melissa Watterworth Batt (University of Connecticut), as well as Alexander Nemerov, who provided valued counsel in the final stages of the project. Rowland Hughes at The University of Hertfordshire, where I now teach, helped secure funding to reproduce important reproductions of archival treasures. To the anonymous readers and editors at Bloomsbury, I appreciated your comments and suggestions, especially on the history of modernist thought and the institutional machinations of MoMA. Thanks to Ross Fraser-Smith and Alexander Highfield, my editors at Bloomsbury. My sincere thanks to Maureen O'Hara, executrix of Frank O'Hara's estate, for permission to generously reprint extracts from O'Hara's poetry and unpublished letters, and for a particularly memorable seafood lunch in Stamford, Connecticut.

This book was borne out of my doctoral dissertation, completed over five years at University College London, which was generously funded by the

London Arts and Humanities Partnership. Mark Ford and Hugh Stevens, my brilliant supervisors, read countless drafts and helped me shape my often-laborious prose into, I hope, something more readable. The shrewd feedback of Robert Hampson and Rod Mengham, my thesis examiners, showed me what kind of monograph this book would become. I would like to thank Lara Choksey, Elsa Court, Jess Cotton, Hugh Foley, Dai George, Matthew Ingleby, Matthew Sperling and Christopher Webb for making Foster Court a home from home. During my PhD, I spent an exceptional autumn at Yale University, and am thankful to Rebecca Birrell, Sam Buchan-Watts, Emily Burns, Francesca Kaes, Mae Losasso, Hannah Lyons, Brandon Mencke, Rosie Ram, Rachel Stratton and Edward Town for their stimulating conversation and enduring friendship, as well as to Langdon Hammer for his stellar supervisions. The Leverhulme Trust funded a year's long winter in Berlin, at the John F. Kennedy Institute for North American Studies, and several comrades – Larne Abse Gogarty, Sean Bonney, James Hutton, Siofra McSherry, among them – ensured that year was ultimately one of light.

I am particularly indebted to Alex J. Taylor, my referee and a model for the kind of scholar I want to be, and the Terra Foundation for American Art, who supported three transformational gifts during the writing of this book: a residency fellowship in Giverny, in the project's earliest stages; a travel grant to New York and Washington DC, to conduct essential archival research; and a postdoctoral fellowship at The Courtauld Institute of Art, during which I completed the manuscript. I learnt a lot on that long hot summer in Giverny, adjacent to Monet's waterlilies and so close to where Joan Mitchell painted her magnificent *La Grande Vallée* series, and want to thank Przemek Branas, J.V. Decemvirale, José Joaquin Figueroa, Carolin Görgen and Levi Prombaum for their friendship and exuberance; my tutors Alan Braddock, Simon Faithfull and Tanya Sheehan for their formative feedback on O'Hara and American art; as well as Veerle Thielemans and Alessandro Gallicchio for taking such good care of us. In New York, I benefited from many interactions with the friends and relatives of those who knew O'Hara intimately, especially Elizabeth Hazan and John Yau, and navigated the city and found new life in O'Hara's old haunts, thanks to Megan Kincaid and Molly Taylor. For my brief but greatly valued period at The Courtauld, I am grateful to Jo Applin, Lucy Bradnock, and David Peters Corbett for their candid advice and guidance.

A huge debt of gratitude is owed to my parents, to whom this book is dedicated, as well as to my sisters Catherine and Rebecca, and brother Mark, for opening me up to the stakes of art, politics and ideas in what felt like, at least at the time, a small world. I am incredibly grateful to the dear friends and superior scholars who have provided incisive suggestions, encouragement and much-needed distractions along the way, including Mathias Arguimbau, Noah Beyene, Eleanor Careless, Fabienne Collignon, Rona Cran, Sophie Godwin, Patrick Grimmer, Chloë Julius, Sam Ladkin,

Adonis Leboho, Catherine Levi, Jack Mann, Orlando Reade, Filippa Ronquist, Megan Rooney and Colin Roth.

Finally, thank you to Adrienne Buller, whose love has always made life seem beautiful, interesting, and modern – O'Hara's cherished trinity – and without whom this book would not have been written. You are the best of all my days.

ABBREVIATIONS

MoMA: The Museum of Modern Art, New York

IP: The International Program of the Museum of Modern Art, New York

RBF: Rockefeller Brothers Fund

CIAA: Coordinator for Inter-American Affairs

Introduction | Curating Modern Life

I. Taking Over the Galleria Umberto from the Milanese

It is late November in Belgrade. Outside, the ancient city is cloaked in a thick winter mist, illuminated only by pockets of ghostly iridescent lamps. Frank O'Hara lights a Drava cigarette, collects his papers, and sits down to write a letter to his friend Joe LeSueur, who is back in New York and eager for news. From the vantage point of his plaster-panelled hotel room, looking out of his window onto the blackened streets below, the nightmarish vista reminded O'Hara of a Franz Kafka novel. In his letter, which reads partly like a camp aristocratic diary entry and partly like an eight-page boast, O'Hara enthusiastically filled LeSueur in, detailing all the fun that he had been having travelling across Europe: the parties, the cities, the young men and, most of all, the art. He was now towards the end of what can only be described as a grand tour that had already included stopovers in Amsterdam, Rome, Turin, Antwerp, Paris, Milan, Copenhagen, Stockholm and Zagreb. The poet had developed a taste for a glamorous, if exhausting, life as a curator thousands of miles from New York.

O'Hara was particularly enamoured by the Swedish capital, where he stayed at the Grand Hôtel beside the Kungsträdgården favoured by Nobel Prize Laureates. He proposed to LeSueur that 'if you're game for a quick year in Stockholm, I think I could make that quite nicely', gloating that he knew 'just where it would be nice to find an apartment'.[1] O'Hara longed for a quietly productive spell writing 'in the brilliant northern lights' and resolved, simply, that 'in the snow it would be heaven'.[2] Even more than Stockholm, O'Hara fell in love with Zagreb, 'which fits its landscape beautifully and whose sunset is marvelous and whose mists stream through the city glamorously feeling very cool and moist and refreshing', and where all the cars seem to suddenly disappear entirely from the streets as they fill with people, 'as if Orson Welles in one of his more malevolent moments had taken over the Galleria Umberto from the Milanese.'[3] O'Hara lusted after the Yugoslavian men, who brooded with an 'adolescent discontent in their faces that could keep one busy for the next fifty years if one were so inclined', he wrote, which apparently he was.[4]

The purpose of this trip in the autumn of 1963, however, was business. O'Hara travelled officially as a curator with The Museum of Modern Art's International Program. His schedule as an ambassador for American modern art was unrelenting. O'Hara noted how three days in Zagreb felt like a week in New York as he met with two museum directors, saw three museums, visited five artists' studios, went to an opening, had dinner with one of the museum directors and received a tour of the Old Town – describing it as 'ravishing' – all without working out whether there was even a queer bar in the city.[5] Earlier, O'Hara had visited Rome and it was there that he played *La Dolce Vita* with the artist Cy Twombly, his glamourous aristocratic wife Tatia, and his dealer Plinio; all in all, a 'perfectly marvelous time'.[6] At a party hosted by Twombly, O'Hara was photographed by a charming marquis called Durazzo, who was just about to 'create the beginning of the world in abstract technicolor for the forthcoming production of *The Bible* in America'.[7] O'Hara was even very nearly persuaded to change careers by a 'great camp named Guidarino Guidi', the casting director for Federico Fellini's *8 ½* (1963), who accosted him at a party and promised to make him 'famous in Italy' as a movie star.[8] The next stopping points on his journey were equally thrilling. He gave up on the idea of going to Warsaw because of a show of Polish art that he disliked at the museum, but O'Hara looked forward to three days each in Vienna and Prague, before regrettably flying back to New York for Thanksgiving. 'And you wonder why I've stayed so long in Europe', he quipped.[9] From Amsterdam, O'Hara joked in a letter to Lawrence Ferlinghetti that 'one of the ironies of my "life" is that the only time I'm not broke is when they send me somewhere and I have a per diem'.[10]

I read O'Hara's Belgrade letter on a dull spring afternoon in suburban Connecticut, as listless rain drizzled down the window of the cramped archive room. By the time I was back in New York, the showers had passed, and the Manhattan sun's warm light flickered on the wet steps of the fire escapes. The beautiful people were walking up and down University Place. After getting lost thinking about O'Hara prancing around scenes of art and exhibition-making on either side of the Iron Curtain – which was drawn across Cold War Europe during the period of the John F. Kennedy Presidency (Kennedy died between O'Hara writing his letter and LeSueur opening it) – I suddenly remembered why he has often been remembered as *the* poet of New York. Backlit by those much-mythologized days at the Cedar Tavern, his friend John Ashbery's introduction to the *Collected Poems* celebrates O'Hara's invention of a 'vernacular corresponding to the creatively messy New York environment', with its 'scent of garbage, patchouli and carbon monoxide'.[11] Grubby and chaotic, certainly, but alive to the thrills of a teeming centre, irrepressibly on the move. That ever-shifting kaleidoscope of urban life – the carousel of billboards, parkways, loft parties, neon signs,

Robert Moses' grid, fast food, and railroads to East Hampton – is so unavoidably O'Hara's subject that taking him out of New York may seem an unnecessary, and even unwelcome, task. It is precisely because those networks of relations are so excitingly multiform, apparently possible only in a metropolis the size and scale of New York City, that we allow this peripatetic poet to be demarcated there: as readers, and as critics, we have found few virtues in situating O'Hara elsewhere, but his curatorial career, with displays engineered in São Paulo, Venice and Kassel, demonstrates more extensive geographical networks of affinity.

Academic criticism and an increasingly visible corpus of popular and journalistic writing on O'Hara has maintained his position as perhaps the most locally committed of all the New York School poets, which included Ashbery, James Schuyler, Kenneth Koch, and Barbara Guest.[12] The art critic and poet John Yau has said simply: 'New York was Frank O'Hara's city more than any other postwar poet's.'[13] The major critical anthology on his work was published a little over a decade ago and entitled *Frank O'Hara Now: New Essays on the New York Poet* (2010). While a useful resource for O'Hara scholars, just two of the fifteen essays in the collection allow O'Hara to venture outside of New York, and none foregrounded his work as a curator in any depth.[14] Earlier, the selection of O'Hara's art writing and published ephemera was entitled *Standing Still and Walking in New York* (1983), a reference to his favoured pastime as he strolled 'through the noisy splintered glare of a Manhattan noon' on his lunch break from the museum.[15] In 1990, Jim Ellidge edited a collection of reviews and essays, *Frank O'Hara: To be True to a City*, requiring no explanation as to which city he was devoted to. O'Hara's verse is now even part of the topography of New York itself, as his blissful paean, 'One need never leave the confines of New York to get all the greenery one wishes', from 'Meditations in an Emergency' (1957), can be seen inscribed in bronze lettering on a harbour-side steel railing of the World Financial Center Plaza in Lower Manhattan, overlooking the Hudson River alongside words from Walt Whitman's *City of Ships*.[16] Put simply, it is O'Hara the poet, and even more so O'Hara the poet of New York, who has been remembered.

Just under three years after his atmospheric trip to Belgrade, in July 1966, O'Hara died in an accident on a beach in Fire Island. It was the early hours, around 3am, not yet cold in the high summer. O'Hara had joined his friend J. J. Mitchell to get a taxi back to Morris Golde's Water Island home after a night out in the Pines, and piled into a White Taxi Company cab with several others until the cabbie blew a tire. The group were stranded. Across the sand, Ken Ruzicka, a young plumber and star of the Patchogue Raiders football team, drove towards them in his red 1944 Jeep. Ruzicka gave the broken-down cab a wide berth, crossing over the soft sand of a ridge with rickety lights flashing in the darkness, when suddenly, he was blinded by the cab's headlights and crashed into O'Hara, who stood waiting outside the car. It was a tragic accident and O'Hara died the next day from a ruptured liver, on 25 July. The *New York Times* obituary ran with the headline: 'Frank O'Hara, 40, Museum Curator / Exhibitions Aide at Modern Art Died – Also a Poet.'[17] O'Hara was remembered as a distinguished curator of international modernism, as though his poetry were merely an avocation lazily pursued in the Olivetti typewriter showroom on those mythologized lunch breaks from his desk at the Museum of Modern Art (MoMA) on 53rd Street. Of course, obituaries can often be a misleading marker of their subject's legacy. The following month, Peter Schjeldahl's commemoration in *The Village Voice* was closer to the ground, describing O'Hara as the 'universal energy source in the lives of the few hundred most creative people in America', and stressed how the *Times* had overlooked dance critic Edwin Denby's remark that O'Hara had been 'America's greatest living poet'.[18]

O'Hara's ekphrastic poems are some of his most anthologized and regularly feature – often audaciously – in his critical studies on artists, such as 'Digression on *Number 1, 1948*' in his *Jackson Pollock* monograph (1959), the first on the artist. His art criticism, primarily for *Art News* magazine and the George Braziller publishing house, has been defended as a more discursive counterpoint to the dominance of material formalism in the print criticism of the period. T. J. Clark, another major critic of Pollock who, in his study of High Modernist aesthetics *Farewell to an Idea* (1999), identified O'Hara along with other prominent queer critics of Pollock as being 'clearly part – sometimes, I have said, a central part – of any defensible history of the New York School'.[19] It has become a truism widely repeated: O'Hara was an important figure in the Abstract Expressionist movement of the 1950s, 'a Fred Astaire with the whole art community as his Ginger Rogers' as composer Morton Feldman put it, who allowed his art criticism to bristle with the abstractions and flourishes of poetry.[20] By any reasonable measure, O'Hara's contribution to poetry in New York has engineered a reversal of the *Times* obituary's descriptor: today, we might say that he was 'also a curator'. But that would be a mistake.

II. A Somber and Joyful Art

O'Hara's professional career as a curator of art remains under-researched, rarely mentioned beyond historical texture for the New York poems. This is a surprising blind spot. Literary critics have neglected the influence that O'Hara's curatorship played on his poetic output, not least by underestimating how important those international milieus, in which he researched the European avant-garde and staged important exhibitions of contemporary painting, were to the development of his writing. Art historians, too, have miscalculated the role played by individual curators, as MoMA brought travelling exhibitions to Europe during the Cold War. Critics like Lytle Shaw, perhaps the most accomplished on his work, have suggested that 'O'Hara himself [. . .] had a direct role in changing the meaning of artistic gesture in

Europe', but no one has yet substantiated this claim.[21] Shaw's emphasis on O'Hara and artistic gesture in Europe is particularly important. The overwhelming majority of O'Hara's curatorial projects were presented in Europe, with the one major exception of the Reuben Nakian retrospective in 1966, which was commissioned for display behind what he called the 'heavenly glass doors' of MoMA only.[22] Most often, although not exclusively, O'Hara's exhibitions represented Abstract Expressionism in its painterly and sculptural forms, at biennales and international expositions, as well as in directed single-artist retrospectives and group surveys. O'Hara took special interest in the most recent developments of postwar European painting, especially on the second École de Paris (see Chapter Three) and the Spanish *Informalismo* artists (see Chapter Five). He was also an outspoken advocate for the more figurative styles of those friends to whom he was closest socially, such as Jane Freilicher, or more peripheral acquaintances, like Allan D'Arcangelo, both of whom were shown in *Recent Landscapes by Nine Americans* at the *Festival of Two Worlds* in Spoleto in 1965, the curator's penultimate commission.

There have been few single-curator studies of any nationality and any period.[23] The goal of this study is to bring the circulation and display of postwar American and European art alive through O'Hara's unapologetically personal approach to curatorial practice by focusing on the research, organization and reception of important exhibitions as cultural texts. As such, this book aims to contribute to art historical scholarship by examining the relationship between MoMA and the individuals who worked there, which has been neglected in favour of an institutional critique that imagines a byzantine and often self-contradictory organization as monolithically committed to a particular approach or ideology. I will advance our understanding of O'Hara among literary critics (for whom his status and broad appeal has never been higher) into his important and overlooked international contexts, and to integrate the study of his work into transatlantic curatorial history.

The story of O'Hara as a major curator and organizer of international exhibitions in the postwar period remains relatively unknown. While some critics have naturally focused on his relationships with the New York School artists – with Jackson Pollock, for example, and therefore lightly referenced his curation of the travelling exhibition *Jackson Pollock 1912–1956* (1958–59) – no published monograph or peer-reviewed journal article has examined this important element of his professional life as its primary focus.[24] The origins of O'Hara's career at MoMA, though, are well-rehearsed: a meteoric rise from selling postcards as a sales clerk on the front-desk to jet-setting envoy for the major Abstract Expressionists is probably what most know about O'Hara's life, if anything at all. But we understand so little about what he achieved on the ground at the host institutions of his exhibitions, or about his instrumental role in establishing transnational networks of artistic exchange. His physical presence in certain cities fostered collaboration between MoMA, recognized as a global centre for the display and collection of modern art, and emergent arts spaces – such as the Moderna Museet in Stockholm, the Kröller-Müller Museum in Otterlo, and the Musée des Beaux-Arts in Laon – which supported the widespread distribution of 'advanced art' during the Cold War.

The lack of research into O'Hara's curatorial career can be largely attributed to the fact that archival collections have not been fully appraised in relation to this work, especially those outside of the United States. To the best of my knowledge, this study has consulted more archives and research libraries in more countries than any other book directly focused on O'Hara to date.[25] The methodology of this book is therefore much indebted to these collections, which have shed new light on O'Hara's curatorial career, as well as on the ways in which the international travel made possible by his work for MoMA influenced and affected his life and poetry. The story told herein is principally led by primary materials, be they personal and professional letters, curatorial documents and work-texts, or the doodles that O'Hara

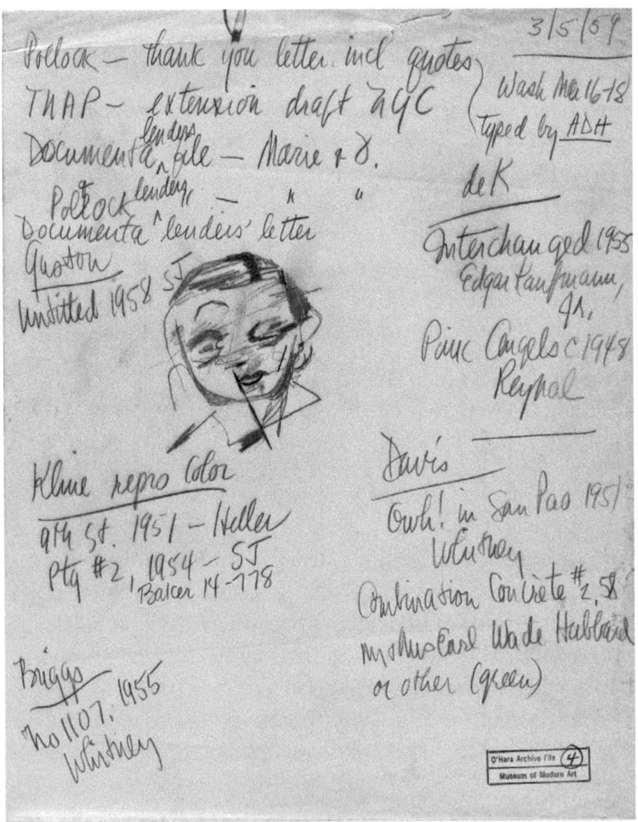

FIGURE 0.1 One page of handwritten notes on the *documenta 2* exhibition including a self portrait, n.d. Pencil on paper, 11 × 8 3/8' (27.9 × 21.3 cm).

liked to make at his desk. These documents have been particularly illuminating and include sketched meditations on the heated debates between abstraction and figuration, on emerging Yugoslav sculptors (handsome or otherwise), and the often-arduous ploys of persuasion to secure loans from cautious collectors.[26] One of my favourite discoveries at the MoMA Archives is a sketched self-portrait that O'Hara drew next to important preparatory notes for his selection of the American representation at *documenta* 2 in 1959 (Figure 0.1). The expression is at once louche and focused, as though performing his own assessment of the merits of an untitled canvas by Philip Guston, or how he can best thank lenders to the Pollock selection in Kassel. Much like O'Hara's poetics, and much like his curated exhibitions and catalogue texts, the drawing is both digressionary and attentive.[27]

Curatorship has come a long way since O'Hara's tenure at MoMA between 1956 and 1966, but not as far as we might think. Today, 'curation', or the verb 'to curate', now defines a plethora of organized objects or methodological ideas in our lives: we might find ourselves consulting a 'curated list' of art-house international films or critically acclaimed jazz albums by genre, or perhaps scanning a menu that has 'curated' the best local and artisanal produce. The word's overuse has, it can often feel, left it devoid of meaning. In March 2020, the independent gallery curator Lou Stoppard wrote an article called 'Everyone's a Curator Now' for The *New York Times*, in which she asked: 'When everything is "curated", what does the word even mean?'[28] Being a museum curator, never mind a curator of the kind who might categorize and display mid-century Danish furniture on a high street or English wine, is often considered to be a new profession, or at least one that emerged in the second half of the twentieth-century with the proliferation of public museum programmes. The spirit of the actions and activities that 'the curator' combines can be traced to ancient Rome and its Latin etymological root: 'curare', or 'to take care of'. During the early years of the Roman Empire, the *Curator Aquarum Censors*, such as Marcus Agrippa, lieutenant to the Roman Emperor Augustus, were civil servants far from the field of art, and managed important civic projects like the building of aqueducts and the maintenance of sewage systems. By the medieval period, *curare* transmuted into the noun *curate*, which equates to a parish priest or clerical assistant who is invested with the spiritual care or *cura* of souls in a locality. By the eighteenth century, *curator* came close to being defined as we see the role today: as a custodian of a museum or collection. It was only by the first decade of the twentieth century that the curator's role bifurcated into a 'collections curator' or an 'exhibitions curator'. In all its various derivations, though, the root of the word has been constant: to take care of something. 'The curator's task is not only the safeguarding, analysis and presentation of a cultural heritage', Bruce W. Ferguson, Reesa Greenberg and Sandy Nairne wrote: 'it includes enriching it, principally through the acquisition of contemporary works—a function which confers upon the curator a role in the art market by the selection of objects and names and similarly calls upon him or her to resist the times or fashion.'[29] The curator of contemporary art, especially one who does not work in a *kunsthalle* tradition in which their main task is the business of exhibitions and not collecting for the institution, is seen to be responsible to their broader community and success measured by their choices which could become hostages to fortune in the long arc of art history. In many ways, though, it feels appropriate that O'Hara's professional title stems from the act of caring.[30] O'Hara cared passionately about many things but especially his friends, whom he championed as a curator. His exhibitions were animated by the earliest definition of care within the practice of curation, and which spoke back to the art that was displayed as though the artwork and the viewer were each bound by a co-dependent responsibility to the other, as he wrote in 'Art Chronicle I' (1964):

> Underlying, and indeed burgeoning within, every great work of the Abstract Expressionists, whether subjectively lyrical as in Gorky, publicly explosive as in De Kooning, or hieratical as in Newman, exists the traumatic consciousness of emergency and crisis experienced as personal event, the artist assuming responsibility for being, however accidentally, alive here and now. Their gift was for a somber and joyful art: somber because it does not merely reflect but sees what is about it, and joyful because it is able to exist. It is just as possible for art to look out at the world as it is for the world to look at art.[31]

This book is structured into six chapters, each of which deal with one or more of O'Hara's exhibitions, whether survey, biennale, monographic or group, and travel between New York, Paris, Venice, Kassel, Madrid, Barcelona, Turin and Otterlo. Chapter One, 'This is All Living Art', introduces O'Hara's professional career as a curator, in New York and in a transnational context, including O'Hara's highly individuated approach to curatorial practice and the anomalous place he held at MoMA at a time when the figure of the individual curator was yet to become clearly defined. I then use O'Hara's 1957 funding application to the Ford Foundation to contextualize the role and purpose of MoMA's International Program, identifying its aims, objectives and its contested place in art history given the question of American cultural imperialism. The title of Chapter Two, 'The Bar Américain Continues to be French', moves beyond the 'American in Paris' image of O'Hara that is briefly acknowledged in the existing literature by analysing three exhibitions that he was involved in curating in France for the International Program in the late 1950s: *Salute to France* (1955), *Recent American Watercolors* (1956), and *Jackson Pollock 1912–1956* (1959). *Salute to France* was a major diplomatic offensive, held in the summer of 1955 in Paris, and betraying many of the stereotypes of American and French art at a time when many believed the United States was emerging from a cultural backwater into becoming a leader of cosmopolitan modes of art-making.[32] *Recent American Watercolors*, O'Hara's first solo-organized show, travelled not to Paris but to regional cities in France, and allowed him to recuperate the watercolour mode by celebrating the emergence of 'brevity, wit, freshness, the intimacy of the occasional' in new American artworks – qualities that without doubt he saw as the strengths of his own poetic style.[33] *Jackson Pollock 1912–1956*, the memorial exhibition to Pollock that travelled to seven European cities, was arguably O'Hara's greatest curatorial achievement.

Chapter Three, entitled 'In Favor of One's Time', is comprised of two case studies of the international perennial exhibition format that became prevalent in the 1950s. First, the section begins with the *29th Venice Biennale* in 1958, when O'Hara curated the American Pavilion with selections on Seymour Lipton and Mark Tobey, who became the first American since James McNeill Whistler to be awarded the International Prize for Painting. Second, it concludes with a case study on *documenta 2* (1959), which crystallizes my discussion of an international language of gestural abstraction, as well as O'Hara's non-objective approach to curatorial research, selection and historicization. Chapter Four, 'Blue Territory', addresses O'Hara's major 1960 retrospective on Helen Frankenthaler at the Jewish Museum, the first on the artist. This exhibition embodied, for O'Hara, Frankenthaler's extraordinary capacity for risk-taking, not only in the material development of her 'soak-stain' technique but also in the exuberant way the artist conceived of each painting as a 'personal event', or her willingness 'to risk the big gesture, to employ huge formats so that her essentially intimate revelations may be more fully explored and delineated', as O'Hara put it in the exhibition catalogue.[34] I chart the way the exhibition inaugurated new chapters in the lives of both painter and curator as O'Hara moved increasingly towards monographic exhibitions in the 1960s and Frankenthaler took on an even more embodied approach to gestural landscape painting after her immensely productive decade as a young artist in New York.

Chapter Five, entitled 'Make it New, Make it Over', looks at O'Hara's work organizing the *New Spanish Painting and Sculpture* exhibition, held at MoMA in 1960, and the strategies he used to overcome many of the institutional challenges that faced him during the period of Franco's cultural liberalization programme. As Spain emerged out of its debilitating shadow as a European nation formerly aligned with the defeated Axis powers and continental fascism itself within nascent efforts towards European unification and the transatlantic alliance, two groups of avant-garde artists – *Dau al Set* in Barcelona, and *El Paso* in Madrid – achieved international recognition. O'Hara was tasked with putting together a major survey exhibition of these artists, and in doing so became embroiled in Falangist cultural politics, wrote fierce elegies for Republican martyrs of the Civil War, and became obsessed by the dark violence of Francisco Goya's 'Black Paintings' at the

Prado. The final and sixth chapter, 'The Slightest Loss of Attention Leads to Death', is broken up into two parts, both dealing with O'Hara's conception of the exhibition space as a kind of elegy. The first examines the Franz Kline memorial retrospective that travelled from Amsterdam to Turin in 1963, and enabled O'Hara to ingratiate himself with the nascent Dutch avant-garde and to discover curatorial craftmanship in the City of Four Rivers. The second half of this final chapter focuses on the last exhibition that O'Hara completed before his death: *David Smith 1902–1965* at the Kröller-Müller Museum in the Netherlands. While reflecting on his friendship with Smith in his late-career poetry, art criticism, and in an elegiac vernissage speech, as well as while melancholically repainting one of the sculptures damaged by rain, O'Hara makes a series of profound statements on his internationalist and personally committed approach to curatorial practice.

III. Lunchtime Poet

In October 2019, as part of its renovation and refurbishment of its Midtown premises, MoMA organized for Room 407 to be rehung and named 'Frank O'Hara, Lunchtime Poet' (see Figure 0.2). The room featured the twenty-one preparatory drawings made by artists close to O'Hara for the posthumous 1967 volume *In Memory of My Feelings*; a screening of the 1966 public television film that saw O'Hara conduct a studio visit at Al Leslie's loft; and a make-shift library of two armchairs and a coffee table with *Lunch Poems* casually placed on top. On the opposite wall, Motherwell's *Elegy to the Spanish Republic, 54* (1957–61) was displayed, one of only two from the

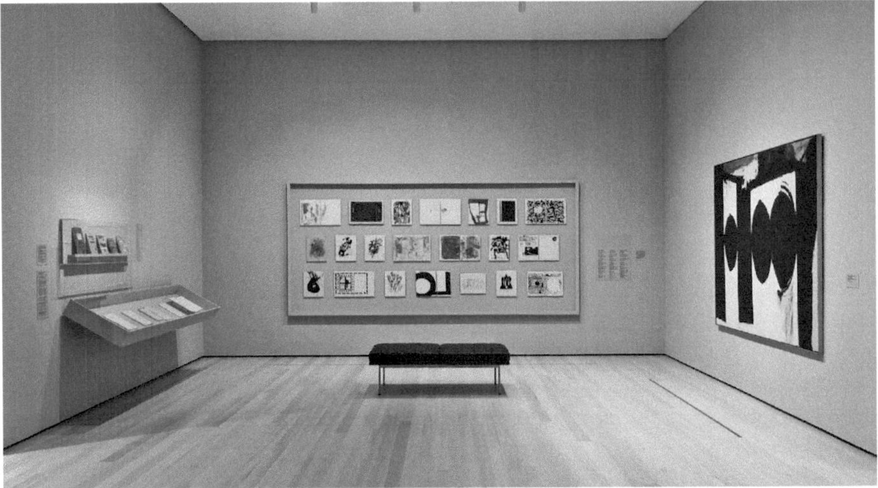

FIGURE 0.2 Installation view of the gallery room 'Frank O'Hara, Lunchtime Poet' in the exhibition 'Collection 1940s–1970s'. MoMA, NY, 21 October 2019–11 July 2021.

series held by MoMA. O'Hara had helped support this particular painting's installation in *Art in a Changing World: 1884–1964* (1964), and the *Elegies* series was important for O'Hara as an expression of internationalist solidarity with the Spanish Republican movement, as explained in Chapter Five. An early draft of a travel poem, 'Now That I am in Madrid and Can Think' (with the variant title, 'Now That Iberia Has Landed me Here in Madrid and I can Think') addressed to his then boyfriend, Vincent Warren, was also featured (see Figure 0.3). In his review of the installation on Floor 4 of the David Geffen Galleries, the literary critic Andrew Epstein remarked that despite the wondrous little details of 'the tightly packed room' in which the poet-curator has now received 'this somewhat belated recognition within its hallowed

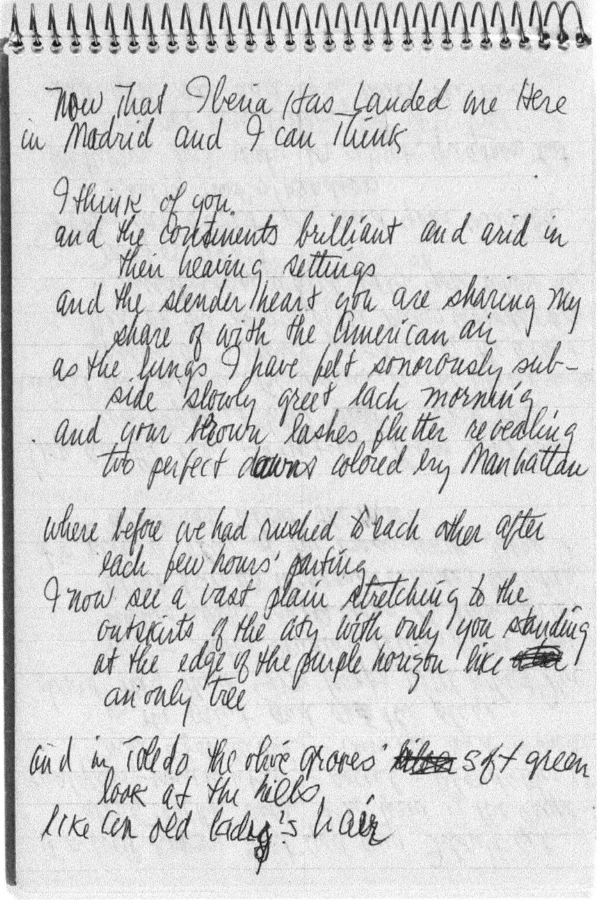

FIGURE 0.3 Frank O'Hara's notebook for 'New Spanish Painting and Sculpture' [MoMA Exh. #668, 20 July–28 September 1960], including a draft of his poem 'Now That Iberia Has Landed me Here in Madrid and I can Think' [Now That I am in Madrid and Can Think], c. 1960 Cover: 8 7/8 × 6 in. (22.5 × 15.2 cm).

halls', it would have been welcome 'to have received a fuller sense of O'Hara's complex, sometimes controversial, role as curator, art critic, and friend to the artists whose work he helped enshrine in the museum'.[35] This book addresses that glaring absence in the scholarship to date.

Most of all, though, this is a book about one curator's joy in art. O'Hara lived and breathed the painting and sculpture that he curated, and often wrote poems about, and this was partly because they were made by people he loved. 'I have to say right here, that the whole room of "Lunchtime [Poet]" feels like love', wrote the incomparable scholar and art critic Mary Ann Caws after she visited MoMA just before the Covid-19 lockdown in New York, 'and that when I went out onto 54th Street, the whole street felt like that.'[36] As we spend time with O'Hara's exhibitions, I hope that they too will spur a reaction like love spilling out onto the streets.

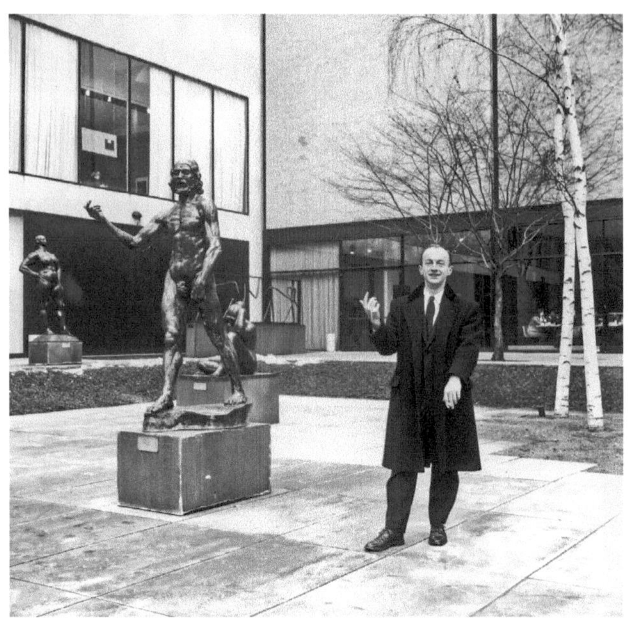

FIGURE 1.1 Portrait of American poet and museum curator Frank O'Hara (1926–1966) strikes a pose similar to that of Auguste Rodin's 'St. John the Baptist Preaching' in the Museum of Modern Art garden, New York, 20 January 1960.

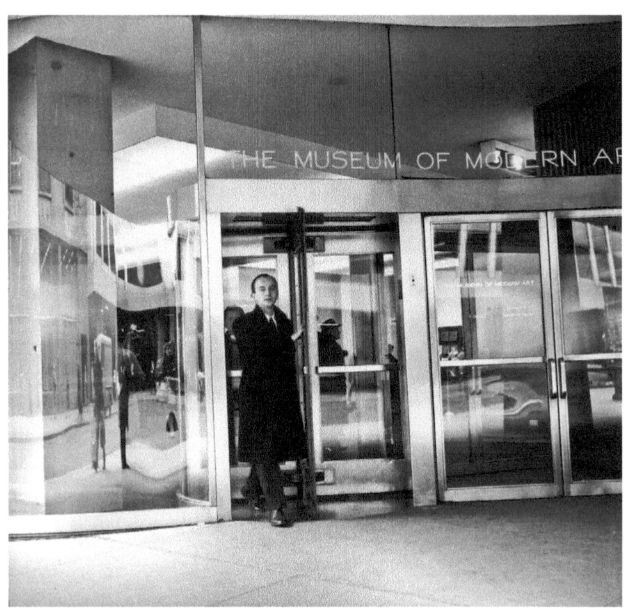

FIGURE 1.2 American poet and museum curator Frank O'Hara (1926–1966) walks through a revolving as he walks out of the Museum of Modern Art, New York, 20 January 1960.

One | This is All Living Art

I. Young Cherry Trees and Persian Jackets

'I first worked there in 1951 and 2', O'Hara recalled of his employment at MoMA, 'because they needed some extra people because they were having an Henri Matisse retrospective and it was so mobbed that they didn't have a big enough staff.'[1] *Henri Matisse* was curated by Alfred H. Barr Jr., the bespeckled Harvard graduate and founding Director of MoMA, which he helped establish with the so-called 'adamantine ladies' – Abby Aldrich Rockefeller, wife of John D. Rockefeller Jr., and two of her friends, Lillie P. Bliss and Mary Quinn Sullivan – nine days after the Wall Street Crash in November 1929. Despite his fussy and diminutive scholarly appearance, Barr was a fierce, card-carrying modernist. In MoMA's early years, his strategy was to bridge the distances between the European avant-garde and 53rd Street, and his curation of seminal retrospectives of Pablo Picasso, Vincent van Gogh, and the Bauhaus were some of the first on the western side of the Atlantic. Barr was twenty-seven in 1926 when Paul J. Sachs offered him the directorship; O'Hara twenty-five in 1952, brought in to sell postcards on the front desk. 'Frank had idols (many)', reflected James Schuyler, 'and if Matisse was one, so was Alfred Barr and remained so during Frank's association with the Museum.'[2]

O'Hara trudged through administrative duties on the front desk but found pockets of time to write – and observe the human carnival that stepped across the threshold from Midtown to the Museum and back again. James Schuyler noted that he once found his friend writing a poem called 'It's the Blue!' and another time leafing through a translation of André Breton's *Young Cherry Trees Secured Against Hares* while waiting to sell tickets to visitors. Around the same time, O'Hara became intimate with the Downtown artists who discussed philosophy at The Club on 8th Street, established by Philip Pavia as an informal gathering for dozens of painters and sculptors who all had art studios in Lower Manhattan across First and Sixth Avenues during the late 1940s and early 1950s, and then drank at the Cedar Tavern at 24 University Place in Greenwich Village. O'Hara participated in several of the panel discussions at The Club, and became friends with Helen Frankenthaler,

Edwin Denby, Joan Mitchell, Michael Goldberg, and many others. John Ashbery introduced O'Hara to Larry Rivers, Nell Blaine, and Grace Hartigan, for whom O'Hara served as an informal advance scout and envoy. On 18 April 1953, the last day of Hartigan's third solo exhibition at the Tibor de Nagy, O'Hara – who was ever-attentive to the entrance that opened onto 53rd Street – reported back with palpable excitement: 'Barr and Dorothy Miller have just come through the revolving doors with [Hartigan's painting] *The Persian Jacket* under their arms.'[3] Hartigan's large painting, at 1.46 × 1.22 metres, depicts a seated woman whose ostentatious burnt orange and red jacket is figured in bright relief against her frail hands. Her deadened face is obscured by a flurry of grey brushstrokes. When struggling for inspiration, Hartigan could be found wandering the vast corridors of the Metropolitan Museum of Art. She was so struck by El Greco's *Cardinal Fernando Niño de Guevara* (ca. 1600), with its withdrawn figure gripping the chair while wearing extraordinarily flamboyant clothing, that she modelled *The Persian Jacket* on it. In focusing on the shoes, Saul Nelson wrote that the sitter embodied the 'high street, . . . desirable, off-the-shelf, ready-to-wear . . . In fashion terms it is pure New York.'[4] O'Hara's excitement about the Hartigan purchase was not only down to an unapologetic enthusiasm for his friends, which defined his professional work as a curator and poet for his whole career. Rather, at this stage in the early fifties, Barr and the purchasing committee were broadly preoccupied with a much broader strategy of acquisition, especially of European artists and especially those who had been in exile in New York since the Fall of Paris in 1941, and had not yet specifically focused on collecting works on the Abstract Expressionists as such.[5] So the Hartigan moment was a significant one.

The purchasing of contemporary works for the collection was a foundational mission since MoMA was founded in 1929. Since the earliest days of his directorship, Barr believed that if the Museum was to remain a torchbearer for advanced art, then it must only collect works, give or take, from the preceding fifty years. After that, arrangements would be made to sell marquee paintings and sculpture to the Metropolitan Museum of Art once they passed that threshold. The inspiration for this model was Parisian, like much of the art that was collected in its first two decades: the Musée du Luxembourg, which was committed to the works of living artists, especially by the luminaries of the École de Paris, would pass on works from their collection to the Louvre, if they were deemed to have passed the test of time.[6] Forcibly putting MoMA at a remove from 'other museums with more retrospective collections', Barr knew that works like *The Persian Jacket* would bolster this ambition.[7] After all, here was a painting that was raw, gestural, by an American, and, as Hartigan put it, containing all she had 'learned so far from the masters'.[8]

O'Hara staffed the front desk for more than two and a half years before leaving MoMA to work in various temporary positions. He took on a position as editorial associate at *Art News*, for whom he contributed regular reviews on contemporary painting and occasional articles, developing a conversational parlance that was at once often intimate and cryptic. He had some of his early experimental plays performed by the Arists' Theater, acted in the Living Theater's production of Picasso's *Desire Caught by the Tail* at the Cherry Lane, and even had a stint as a secretary to society photographer Cecil Beaton. Beaton had recently used Pollock's *Autumn Rhythm* and *Lavender Mist* as backdrops in a fashion shoot for *Vogue* which, for Louis Menand, 'raised the question of whether they belong to the category of the decorative rather than the artistic, whether they are avant-garde art objects or very expensive wallpaper, whether they are noble or vulgar'.[9] These questions were also asked of any aspiring curator: how do you make the work *fit* when it is hung on the wall? How do you maintain some of the experimental or avant-garde vitality that the artist has spilled across the canvas when it is lent an institutional nod? At a time when the value of the art of the day was up for grabs, how do you distinguish between the noble and the vulgar?

O'Hara returned to MoMA shortly thereafter, although in an altogether more auspicious role, when Porter McCray, Director of the recently inaugurated International Program, drafted him in to support exhibitions.[10] McCray appointed O'Hara partly on the basis that he associated with the 'young artists, particularly the Tibor de Nagy group' and so had the 'respect [of] [Willem] de Kooning and [Jackson] Pollock and all the others'; he was often tardy but was 'an intelligent person with a good deal of taste and brains, a very useful person in the program'.[11] Waldo Rasmussen, who ran the Department of Circulating Exhibitions at MoMA from 1962, noted colleagues' anxieties about O'Hara's lack of professional accreditation, and that in his 'early years' at MoMA he was 'under suspicion as a gifted amateur' and his 'very closeness to the artists was questioned as a danger to critical objectivity'.[12] The critic Irving Sandler, himself someone who wrestled with critical distance, saw this as an advantage:

> Frank's contribution in both jobs [*Art News* and MoMA] was substantial, such was his taste and knowledge of art, but what was really important about his public role was that it augmented his private role, that of the friend of the artists. He had the ability to focus in on someone he liked so intensely that one could only feel like Frank's best friend – and he had the generosity to have had dozens of close attachments, as Larry Rivers said. His attention was of vital significance to artists, literally sustaining them. Morton Feldman wrote that 'what really matters is to have someone like Frank O'Hara standing behind you. That's what keeps you going. Without that your life in art is not worth a damn.'[13]

It is worth dwelling on these assessments from the outset because they reveal much about O'Hara's sense of style in relation to his curatorial practice and how that disrupted assumptions of 'critical objectivity' on matters related to selection and display. The curator, even more so than the critic, was expected to keep their distance. While it was commonplace for artists and others close to them to organize exhibitions featuring their friends and compatriots, such as the D-I-Y 9th Street Art Exhibition in summer 1951, a curator directly employed by an institution, indeed the premier institution for the display of modern art in the United States, could not avoid considerable scrutiny if he or she preferred or promoted artists on any basis except quality. With that said, O'Hara was not alone in blurring the distinctions between friendship and whatever new conventions or procedures were being set by a nascent curatorial profession. For instance, Henry Geldzahler and Walter Hopps, two verbose and eccentric curators, arrived on the scene at a similar time. Geldzahler joined the staff at the Metropolitan Museum of Art in New York at the age of 25 in 1960, and counted Andy Warhol and David Hockney among his closest friends; Hopps became the youngest museum director in the United States when he took the reins of the Pasadena Art Museum at age 31 in 1964, and would pick up artists like Frank Lobdell for exhibition openings high on speed. While this book makes a case for O'Hara as a curator who blurred the boundaries between life and the four walls of the exhibition space, and between the enthusiasms that one might feel for a friend on their birthday and a painting still wet on the easel, he was part of a generation of curators who had arrived in influential roles at major American institutions young, inexperienced, and resistant to the policing of boundaries.

Like all those who are perceived to have access, earned or not, O'Hara's personal proximity to the artists proved to be a hindrance as much as an advantage. While it enabled him access to recent developments through unguarded conversation and late-night studio visits, it also left him vulnerable to accusations of nepotism. It was not unusual for him to curate exhibitions featuring works that he owned and had received as gifts from friends, or to show paintings that were conceived as homages to him through their titles or dedications. This left him doubly exposed throughout the decade he served as a curator. Fascinated by the relationship between art and life, and between the biography of the artist and the work that they made, O'Hara refused any idea of the role of the curator, such that it may have been defined, as an objective arbiter of an artworks' quality.

O'Hara never set out a manifesto for his curatorial work in the way that he did for his poetry. 'Personism' (1959) was his broadside against the New Critical obsessions that then dominated academic literary criticism. O'Hara wrote: 'It seems to me that in the 30s and 40s there were an awful lot of dicta laid down by everybody, about what was good and what was bad without any consideration of what is valuable.'[14] In condemning critics who separated off fixed and stable criteria for the assessment of literature from what was worthy of attention but perhaps did not fit some form of teleological formula, O'Hara could have just as easily been referring to the dangers of formalist art criticism. His discursive essay 'Art Chronicle' was as close as he came to a curatorial manifesto. O'Hara's essay was a review of the *American Abstract Expressionists and Imagists* at the Solomon R. Guggenheim Museum, that 'controversial thing' designed by Frank Lloyd Wright, that had recently reopened its doors after 15 years of construction and featured a six-storey helical ramp which extends along the main gallery's perimeter, under a central ceiling skylight.[15] In calling attention to the ways that Al Held or Joan Mitchell 'will absorb the imagination of one season', and Michael Goldberg or Robert Motherwell another, O'Hara stresses the personal contingency of seeing work in a museum space based on the embodied subjectivity of the viewer. It all matters who you are and where you are standing. In turn, it was the responsibility of the museum to avoid becoming a well-designed sepulcher:

> This is all living art and the show reflects the living situation [. . .] It depends on what you see and when it's shown and it keeps you fresh for looking and for the excitement of art. A lot of people would like art to be dead and sure, but you don't see them up at The Cloisters reading Latin.[16]

When displaying contemporary art, O'Hara felt it important to never allow the work to be hung in such a way as to fix it for posterity or hold it in place as something only to be spoken about in the past tense. After all, the only art that was worth seeing, he felt, was being made right now, there in New York. Unlike a curator of Abstract Expressionism today, there is no benefit of hindsight. Everything was subject to change from one season to the next. It was a shot in the dark. Instead of depending on formalist criteria that could provide a sense of historical continuity and rupture, O'Hara's philosophy of art was alive, present, necessarily adaptable to the singularities of the works themselves. This was directly informed by the intimate knowledge that he had gained of how paintings were made because he was an insider trader with the artists themselves. After all, O'Hara might say, what good is an art that is 'dead and sure' at a moment when the modes of painterly experimentation were becoming so fiercely transformed, and being changed, in turn, by the demands that the world placed on artists? As he continued in 'Art Chronicle', again explicitly on the Cedar Tavern set: 'some artists maintain their vitality, others look terribly dull, younger members zoom to the fore [. . .] so no images are toppled permanently'.[17]

According to the *New York Times* obituary, when O'Hara 'posed frontally clad and only in shoes and socks' for Larry Rivers' *O'Hara Nude with Boots* (1954) (Figure 1.3), and the painting was exhibited at the Jewish Museum in the artist's first major survey in 1965, the 'issue' over whether the unavoidable subject of homosexual desire in the portrait was 'offensive' remained '[un]resolved'.[18] But the painting was scandalous for another reason. As the poet Eileen Myles has pointed out, 'you couldn't have somebody who was working at the museum have a nude portrait of themselves'.[19] The title acts as an ironic commentary on the usual anonymity of the nude model, but also because the boots in the portrait draw attention

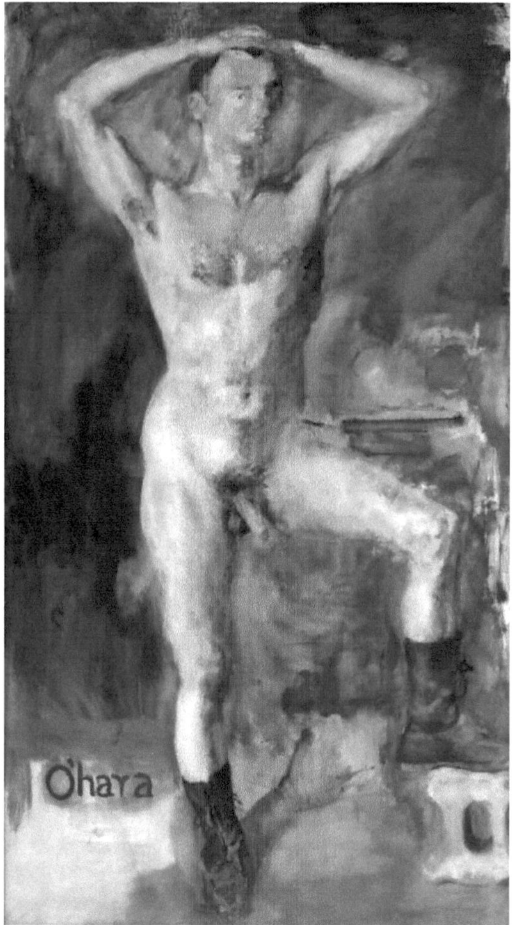

FIGURE 1.3 Larry Rivers, *O'Hara Nude with Boots*, 1954, 246.4 × 134.6 cm.

to the model as a connoisseur of style and as someone controlling his image rather than simply being observed by the painter and viewer of the painting. O'Hara emerged at a time before widespread professionalization and when the figure of the individual curator was still to be determined, yet there was nevertheless a sense that the role required critical distance, and that taking one's clothes off in front of artists foreclosed that. John Yau characterizes this dilemma well:

Can you imagine someone wanting to be hired by a museum deciding to pose nude, exposing himself for all to see? O'Hara's most egregious sin is his intimacy. Curators aren't supposed to be involved in art making, they are paid to keep their distance and observe. They aren't supposed to remove their clothes in front of artists. How could they maintain their critical objectivity?[20]

Yau's provocation sets the terms for this book. O'Hara's refusal to participate with the demands of 'critical objectivity' as he curated and circulated exhibitions meant he saw the purpose of the exhibition differently to those who wanted the display of art to be 'dead and sure', to be fixed and static, forever unchanged by each successive visitor who paid close attention to the impasto of a Joan Mitchell landscape, or felt something in Mark Rothko's rectangles that they could not explain. This attitude helped him to define the role of the individual curator at mid-century, and to shape the way that American art was received overseas. O'Hara was forced to atone for the original 'sin' of 'intimacy' in all kinds of ways, not least as a field ambassador for American art abroad, almost always in an 'official' capacity, as well as within the social politics of his Cedar coterie back home.[21] O'Hara's unapologetic interdisciplinarity – writing art criticism with the flourishes of a poet, directing professional exhibitions with a friend's subjectivities, and approaching his museum position, as Bill Berkson once joked, 'as an imaginative composite of salons at the court of Louis XVI and the 1930s Warners' lot' – was seen as a threat to the grand narratives of medium purity that supported the Greenbergian trajectory of postwar art.[22] His dovetailing careers as curator, critic, and poet were not mutually exclusive but rather closely enmeshed and mutually productive. But O'Hara did not curate in a vacuum. By its very nature, curating takes place in rooms that are often institutions, and institutions that have their own agendas and priorities. This was particularly so during the cultural Cold War. Before asking how and in what contexts O'Hara curated the artworks themselves, it is essential to begin by outlining the institutional framework of MoMA, and especially its controversial International Program, and show how Cold War ideologies framed the extent of that department's supposed internationalist allegiances.

II. The Marshall Plan in the Field of Ideas

In April 1952, MoMA established the International Program with a five-year grant of $125,000 from the Rockefeller Brothers Fund (RBF). The International Program was the brainchild of Nelson Aldrich Rockefeller, treasurer of the RBF and then President of MoMA, which his mother had helped found and whose family, to a large extent, still controlled.[23] Its purpose was to organize and circulate exhibitions abroad, predominantly but not exclusively curated by its own staff, on recent developments in American art, as an effective instrument for implementing a programme of international cultural exchange. That mission has since been understood as coexistent with an effort on the part of the United States to advance the prestige of American culture in Western bloc countries, where it was often seen as an artistic backwater, with Rockefeller acting as an intermediary between the national political establishment, receptive artists, and predominantly East Coast elite art institutions. Frances Stonor Saunders has detailed the 'various covert operations' led by Rockefeller, as demonstrated by his earlier leadership of the Office of the Coordinator for Inter-American Affairs (CIAA), from which the leaders of the International Program were sourced.[24] Established as a cultural exchange mission by President Franklin D. Roosevelt to spread 'material to Latin American press and radio, exchange scholarships, motion pictures, good-will tours, concerts, and art exhibitions', the CIAA was the first official (although not Congressional) monetary programme supported for the purposes of American propaganda abroad.[25] The CIAA sought to strengthen continental relationships, and Rockefeller oil reserves, against the perceived vulnerability of communist takeovers within the region. Two figures who would come to take on leadership positions at MoMA were associated with the CIAA. The first, René d'Harnoncourt, the six-foot-six Austrian aristocrat with European courtly manners who had originally trained for a career in the chemical industries but had reinvented himself as a Mexican arts and crafts expert, headed up CIAA's art section. He became MoMA's second Director in 1949. Second, the steely pragmatist Porter McCray, who had advised d'Harnoncourt in Latin America and was groomed by Rockefeller for several years to be the ambitious founding Director of the International Program. McCray, previously an up-and-coming curator within MoMA's Department of Circulating Exhibitions, was widely known for his ambassadorial skills and had extensive experience in national and international cultural initiatives and projects, not only through those headed by Rockefeller, but also as an attaché in the United States Foreign Service where he would become Deputy Chief of Presentations and Publications in the European Headquarters of the Economic Cooperation Administration. Bound by unwavering passions for modern art, this was nevertheless a diplomatic corps who knew what was at stake in the Cold War.

O'Hara quickly became close with McCray, both personally and professionally. Having fostered a reputation for giving opportunities to younger administrators and curators, McCray brought O'Hara into the International Program fold in January 1955, in line with his mission to privilege fewer 'graduate degrees in art history' and more individuals who could work with ease and conviction with international partners.[26] 'The Europeans, I think, developed great respect for someone like Frank O'Hara', reflected McCray, 'and younger people who were coming into the Program.'[27] In terms of recruitment, this was a time before modern museums underwent a crisis of expansion in the wake of the proliferation of the number of curatorial posts (and managerial and administrative roles in the museum, public and private) and what Nathalie Heinich and Michael Pollak have characterized as a correlative crisis, 'brought about by the widening of recruitment criteria and the opening up of entry routes into the profession'.[28] McCray had identified in O'Hara something that he admired in himself, and something certainly coveted by hiring committees in curatorial posts today: the oblique skill of 'networking'. But McCray also saw potential in a curator who had positioned himself in the thick of the Downtown action, who had the ear of the artists, and who had a demonstrable passion for contemporary American art and not only the European masters. The work that O'Hara completed during this first period was far from glamorous, as his biographer Brad Gooch notes: 'O'Hara's job (at eighty-five dollars a week [around $1000, adjusted for inflation in 2024]) consisted mostly of paperwork – writing business letters to lenders and paying attention to the minute organizational details. Deceivingly organized, O'Hara was able to [. . .] sail through the first assignment and prove his administrative abilities.'[29]

In 1957, after the initial funding for the International Program had elapsed, Rockefeller looked to like-minded philanthropists and elite businessmen to continue what supporters and detractors alike have called 'a Marshall Plan in the field of ideas'.[30] To help fund the Program, O'Hara was tasked with writing a grant proposal to the Ford Foundation.[31] The purpose of the application letter was to request additional funds to support the mission and present 'certain aspects of American culture that are little known or frequently misunderstood abroad'.[32] O'Hara acknowledged that while the 'technical achievements' and 'literature' of the United States were 'highly regarded' abroad, its contribution in the visual arts was seen to lack the vitality of its European counterparts, especially in the field of modernism.[33] This attitude was echoed in European criticism on American art. Fritz Nemitz, in his essay 'Is there Such a Thing as American Painting?' in the *Frankfurter Allegmeine Zeitung* in 1951, asked: 'Does anything resembling a specific American identity emerge from the examples on show? Is there a Whitman, a Hemingway, a Thomas Wolfe, or a Steinbeck of art? It is certainly not possible to identify a collective concept susceptible of being labeled "America." '[34]

The International Program was never intended to be a permanent fixture of MoMA's overseas projects; it was very costly, and the RBF had many (although sometimes overlapping) funding priorities. The original desire was for it to be so successful that it would push the government into establishing a programme of this kind on its own.[35] The United States government did establish a comparative organization, and at a strikingly proximate moment: The United States Information Agency (USIA, later the USIS), inaugurated in 1953 at the behest of President Dwight D. Eisenhower. As the Acting Director of the USIA put it, which serves as a middlebrow or expressly populist *modus operandi* and oppositional to the International Program's more modernist tastes: '[A] government is by its very nature against experimental art. We want to show the artistic nature and achievement of America in ways that all peoples abroad can understand.'[36] If the public did not understand it, there was no incentive for the government to fund it. But this also had strategic costs. O'Hara argued that the unforgiving perception of the United States as a materialist nation overshadowed its cultural achievements, a view only exacerbated by European economic dependency on the United States after the Second World War. This attitude could be overcome, O'Hara argued, through strategic exhibitions committed to showcasing shared artistic traditions. The International Program had been inaugurated shortly before the expiry of the European Recovery Program (ERP), or Marshall Plan, which was implemented between 1948 and 1952 with an extensive funding package of $13 billion. The ERP sought to weaken interstate barriers and deregulate business practices to strengthen western Europe against communism. State actors and multi-national companies sought to modernize European industrial policies and upskill its workforce. Significantly, it laid the groundwork for the integrative ambitions of the European Economic Community in 1957 and, with it, redoubled efforts towards continental unification with a strong transatlantic partnership. By the end of the decade, these institutional models, relationships and transnational identities were officially advanced by those same bodies in the cultural sphere, too, as we will see at the *29th Venice Biennale* in 1958 when the Council of Europe strategically promoted a progressive 'Idea of Europe' theme for contributors.

O'Hara contended that the crisis of the American cultural image was not just about an aversion to the work of its 'national' artists. 'While the best of our films are also recognized as a distinctive American contribution', O'Hara continued, 'on the whole we are apt to be judged unfavourably by the far more numerous run-of-the-mill films.'[37] O'Hara, known as an unapologetic celebrant of mass-produced Hollywood visual culture in his poetry (such as 'To the Film Industry in Crisis' and 'Poem [Lana Turner has collapsed!]'), wore a different hat as he composed the proposal. Likely, he was referring not only to questions of taste and quality but to the distribution models of American films that, as in the Blum-Byrnes accord of 1946 in relation to France, flooded the market to ease the country's debt to the United States. For many French critics, the influx of inexpensive American products that undercut local labour, combined with what O'Hara generally described as 'advertising and mass media', had resulted in the strategic weakening of national cultures and languages, despite efforts to fill protectionist quotas and currency export controls.[38] This bolstered what O'Hara called simply 'the unfavourable stereotype of America'.[39] In contrast, O'Hara conceded that American 'achievements in the visual arts' had been 'virtually unknown until the past few years' when, standing in for the absence of official governmental initiatives, the International Program sent over the course of this five-year period some 35 exhibitions to 22 countries abroad and facilitated 80 exhibitions from other countries to be shown in the United States. O'Hara stressed that the examples of travelling exhibitions 'have been warmly welcomed, and in one sense, the program has been too successful, for it has resulted in increasing requests for further shows from areas that have thus begun to be familiar with American art'.[40] With European museum directors knocking at the door, exhibitions were presented as invited, often collaborative productions with host institutions and not the result of unilateral decision-making. O'Hara stressed that, at the time of writing, the 'demands far outstrip the present capacity of existing government and private organizations to fulfil'.[41] Widely reproduced on press releases and promotional materials, the distinction between the two is significant: governmental institutions, rather than orchestrating over-zealous soft power strategies, have been unwilling or unable to supply the demand needed for meaningful international interventions and it would be up to initiatives sponsored by private capital that must seize the initiative.

For much of the 1950s private cultural institutions in the United States picked up the slack from the Federal Government, which largely forewent responsibility for the funding and facilitation of cultural exchange programmes that were then efficiently and quickly established by Allied nations after the Second World War, especially in the field of modern art.[42] Philistine and anti-modernist McCarthyite campaigns scapegoated cultural elites in his hearings of 1950–55, adding pressure against taxpayer-funded initiatives – most loudly denounced by Michigan Republican George Dondero, who pronounced on the Senate floor that 'all modern art is communistic'.[43] Incredulous, Barr responded to Donerdo and his ilk: 'Those who assert or imply that modern art is a subversive instrument of the Kremlin are guilty of fantastic falsehoods.'[44] But for all of Barr's protestations in the popular press, there was a distinct sense that modern art was peculiarly un-American, bolstered by the view that many of the principal vanguard artists were foreign-born and leftist sympathizers (such as Willem de Kooning and Arshile Gorky), who had grown up on support from the Works Progress Administration in the 1930s.[45] Barr, then an advisory director to MoMA, addressed this climate in a 1952 letter to the President of the American Federation of the Arts regarding the selection for the forthcoming Venice Biennale later that year:

> McCarthyism may have thrown light on a few subversive characters, but it has done us immense damage among European liberals, especially within that very influential and important body of European intellectuals and artists who are anti-communist or neutral ... Our talk of freedom does not jibe with our willingness to tolerate its unnecessary suppression. We ought, therefore, for political effectiveness to send abroad exhibitions which are not only as good in quality as we can possibly make them, but which will also demonstrate our tolerance of self-criticism and diversity of social attitudes.[46]

Ever the hard-headed pragmatist, Barr was an 'enlightened' Cold Warrior who was eager to promote the benefits of representative democracy and multilateral liberalism – of the kind outlined by Arthur M. Schlesinger Jr. in his foundational text *The Vital Center* (1949). Barr and others were also sensitive to the fact that the Soviet Union were outspending the United States at an alarming rate. Implicit in Barr's language of 'tolerance' and 'diversity' is the view that only under a free market and liberal democracy can dissent be admissible and even outwardly celebrated. Any artistic critique of capitalism only demonstrates the permissibility of dissent in a free society.

It was extraordinary how this discourse straddled the ideological spectrum within the American intelligentsia at this time. Irving Howe argued in an essay entitled 'The Problem of US Power' in the left-wing journal *Dissent* from 1954 that 'America needs a more socialist image abroad [. . .] American power multiplies – but the power to dispose of it creatively, with human warmth and intelligence, has never seemed smaller than today'.[47] It is difficult to gauge the extent to which O'Hara personally supported this position, assuming as we should that he may have held a different view outside of his administrative duties for MoMA. With characteristic humour, however, we do know from a 1959 issue of *It Is* that O'Hara felt strongly about the status (or lack thereof) of American vanguard artists within the national imaginary, as well as the opportunities that the state had hitherto missed in presenting their work during the Cold War:

> few Americans consider a great artist a source of national pride, and certainly the government is not going to reward him. [. . .] There is more for the artist to do here, and I believe more is being done, than anywhere else in the world at present. The State Department wouldn't be so upset about satellites if it knew more about art, which will after all stay "up" longer than any of the projects planned by scientists to date. If any of us do get into the future, it will not be by means of a lot of spheres and tank suits.[48]

All these factors – government indifference or open hostility to the promotion of American modernism overseas; the desire to rectify the perception of the United States as a purely materialist nation among the western European intelligentsia (especially those on the non-aligned left); and cultural diplomacy's ability to affect changing Cold War political relations – had underpinned the establishment of the International Program and its mission for the first five-year period. In a distinctly cultural diplomatic voice, O'Hara concludes the Ford Foundation proposal:

> On the evidence of the reactions to the initial efforts of the Museum's International Program, it is apparent that an extensive program of this sort in the field of American art would provide a particularly effective means of presenting certain aspects of American culture that are little known or frequently misunderstood abroad, and could also do much to correct the distorted picture of the United States that has been so harmful to our entire pattern of official and informal international relations.[49]

Since at least the publication in *Artforum* of Max Kozloff's essay 'American Painting During the Cold War' (1973), the strategy outlined in O'Hara's

Ford Foundation letter has come under considerable scrutiny. The ambitions that underpin the proposal fit squarely within the narrative that Cold War ideology was adopted uniformly by institutions committed to modernist art, especially by MoMA. American abstraction, it has often been argued, was used as propaganda for the United States in the culture war to win over the European non-aligned left. 'Never for one moment did American art became a conscious mouthpiece for any agency as was, say, the Voice of America', argued Kozloff, but 'it did lend itself to be treated as a form of benevolent propaganda for foreign intelligentsia'.[50] *Artforum* went on to publish more essays claiming that Abstract Expressionism was mobilized as a political instrument, a view developed by Eve Cockroft's 1974 essay 'Abstract Expressionism, Weapon of the Cold War', in which she argued that 'Rockefeller, through Barr and others at the Museum [. . .] consciously used Abstract Expressionism, "the symbol of freedom", for political ends'.[51] Freed from the kinds of pressure of unsubtle red-baiting and super-jingoism that often characterized official exchange programmes, such as the Voice of America, the International Program relied on its cultivation as an institution which was independent of government but founded on expertise to gain the support of European hosts.[52] Serge Guilbaut offered the first book-length contribution to this 'revisionist' history, *How New York Stole the Idea of Modern Art* (1983), in which MoMA is represented as a 'recreation center for soldiers, a symbol of free expression and a place to mount military exhibitions for propaganda purposes'.[53] Guilbaut noted that while Barr, Rockefeller and those in leadership positions at MoMA defended modern art from certain accusations by the right that it was a Communist plot to eradicate Western democratic cultural life, Abstract Expressionism (which Barr characterized as 'artistic free enterprise') instead symbolized the radical freedom of the individual under capitalism.[54] O'Hara is one of the few Guilbaut identified by name as one of the 'friends, promoters and admirers of the abstract expressionist artists' who represent this 'great tragedy of art history'.[55] While productive in shifting the scholarship on American gestural painting to look at the socio-political culture of New York and the de-Marxization of its intelligentsia, these 'revisionist' studies often imagine cumbersome and complex cultural institutions as monolithic entities, and individuals within them merely as conduits for the articulation of institutionally dominant ideologies.

Michael Kimmelmann led a rear-guard response in 1994 when his article 'Revisiting the Revisionists: The Modern, Its Critics, and the Cold War' was published in an edited collection by MoMA itself. In it, Kimmelmann argued that Guilbaut's claim that MoMA was some kind of quasi-military institution with a thoroughly top-down policy was a fallacy, and such a reading oversimplifies 'the byzantine cultural politics of the era'.[56] More recent scholars like Nancy Jachec and Hiroko Ikegami have expanded the discourse around the rise of American art by examining exhibitions, artistic communities and critics in countries that hosted initiatives of modernism from the United States, privileging instead the complexity of these historical phenomena from a European or global perspective, which has destabilized the revisionists' methodological focus on American institutions. Jachec has questioned some of the biases prevalent in the scholarship on international cultural relations in the immediate postwar period, which has 'privileged American over intra-European and European-led initiatives'.[57] This scholarship brings 'a policy-specific approach to this subject in order to challenge the dominant interpretation of Euro-American cultural relations from this period as a largely one-way process of Americanisation'.[58] As we will see in countless examples, from the art hung by the winding canals at the Venice Biennale to the provincial art utopia of *documenta,* as well as the controversial exhibitions of Spanish abstraction held at MoMA, displays were always mediated by complex processes of competing priorities, negotiation, and mutual benefit.

In a similar way, and through the prism of the transnational possibilities for Robert Rauschenberg's art, Ikegami argued that 'revisionist' accounts are limited not only because they lack positive proof from their institutions, but 'also and more fundamentally because they were written within a framework of a "national" art history – even though their subject matter was the international transport of art'.[59] While 'revisionist' critics Kozloff and Cockroft censured the supposedly colossal and impenetrable campaign of American cultural imperialism, many remained ironically fixated on the conditions of the United States and only belatedly considered the forces of cultural distribution from a European perspective. My own study, like Ikegami's, focuses on an important figure in postwar American art but directs attention to the content and reception of their work within intercity networks that in turn produced complex and important transnational avant-garde art communities. Each of these processes played a significant role in what Ikegami characterizes as 'the global rise of American art', and I argue that O'Hara was a major figure within those processes.[60]

As we can see in 'Frank O'Hara's Exhibition Record' (see page 157), O'Hara curated or played a significant role in organizing eighteen exhibitions, and assisted with many more, over the course of his eleven years working as a curator at MoMA. The overwhelming majority were staged outside the United States. These exhibitions can be, broadly speaking, categorized into three groups: single-artist retrospectives, such as those on Jackson Pollock, Robert Motherwell, Reuben Nakian and David Smith, reflections on the dominance of Abstract Expressionism as a curated style within the managerial decision-making at MoMA by the early 1960s; group shows, which includes *New Spanish Painting and Sculpture* (1960) and surveys of American artists differentiated by genre, medium or origin (such as watercolour or landscapes, and works of overseas artists from private American collections); and, with the greatest total audience reach, the organization of the United States representation at large-scale perennial exhibitions, including the *IV International Art Exhibition* at various host venues in Japan and the *IV Bienal do Museu de Arte Moderna* in São Paulo (both 1957), and the *I International Exhibition of Modern Art* in Buenos Aires (1960).

The second category entailed organizing displays of national art from American collections, which were then shown in that country, partly to demonstrate the United States' significant historical investment in foreign acquisitions as well as a show of ambassadorial goodwill and cultural respect. O'Hara's first project was administering the diplomatic offensive *Salute to France* (1955), a gala of exhibitions and concerts in Paris, the centrepiece of which was *De David à Toulouse-Lautrec: Chefs-d'œuvres des Collections Américaines* ('From David to Toulouse-Lautrec: Masterpieces from American Collections'). O'Hara's work on this exhibition is a focus of the next chapter. Another notable example of this curated mode was *Italian Art from American Collections* (1960), 'an American tribute to the major achievement of modern Italian painting and sculpture' that featured more than 190 works selected from over 80 American private and public collections.[61] James Thrall Soby hired O'Hara as a special assistant on this brief, advising on a range of pre-Futurist and Futurist works, as well as Metaphysical paintings and postwar abstractionists. An important moment for the International Program in its development of exhibitions partly for the purposes of diplomatic influence, *Italian Art from American Collections* was shown at the Galleria Nazionale d'Arte Moderna in Rome where it was the only major exhibition of modern Italian art during that summer's Olympic Games.

The category of single-artist shows, predominantly large-scale and inaugural retrospectives, began with the *Jackson Pollock 1912–1956* (1958–59) memorial show and became the principal mode of O'Hara's final three years at MoMA, during which time he curated *Franz Kline* (1963–64), *Robert Motherwell* (1965), [Reuben] *Nakian* (1966), and *David Smith 1906–1965* (1966). In the third category, O'Hara selected the official American representation for large-scale exhibitions including the *29th Venice Biennale* and *documenta 2*.[62] These latter two examples came at a time when a 'world language' of gestural abstraction felt both dominant and at a crisis as to its future direction, and are the case studies provided in Chapter Three. Using a range of archival material, I offer the first detailed examination of O'Hara's highly personal curatorial style and his significant contribution to American exhibition history.

III. Gestural Abstraction on Both Sides of the Atlantic

It is first worth outlining the background of the display of art in Europe in the late-1950s, and the political significance of *Art Informel* in particular. The European gallery-going public and localized art communities, for whom the circulation of art had proceeded in a staccato fashion during and in the immediate aftermath of the war, were interested in what Lytle Shaw called 'artistic gesture' amid the ongoing debates around abstraction and figuration, shifting ideological commitments, and the formal developments of modern art in increasingly globalized networks of exchange and circulation. Whatever it was called and wherever it was found, 'artistic gesture' was widely understood as an international and *internationalist* new style, often contrasted against 'parochial' realism, attached to locality and the politics of place.[63]

The term *Un art autre*, which translates from French as 'other art' or 'art of another kind', was first used by Michel Tapié in his 1952 treatise of the same title. Used synonymously with *Art Informel* (another Tapié construction) and *Tachisme* (from *tache*, meaning 'blot' or 'stain', coined by Charles Estienne), *Art autre* described the dominant style of lyrical abstraction that privileged improvizatory technique and the gestural application of paint. While Tapié focused on those artists who exhibited primarily in the Montparnasse district of Paris after the city's liberation in 1945, he was clear that it was an American as much as a European phenomenon, and even found global adherents from Venezuela and Japan. Briefly, these artists included those associated with the CoBrA movement in Copenhagen, Brussels, and Amsterdam, such as Asger Jorn and Karel Appel, as well as the German painter Wols, the existentialist artist *par excellence* for Jean-Paul Sartre, and the Barcelona-based Antoni Tàpies, as demonstrated by his involvement in O'Hara's *New Spanish Painting and Sculpture* exhibition. The critics positioned *Art autre* against the refined traditionalism of the École de Paris, the cold formalism of geometric abstraction or *art concret*, and the committed Socialist Realism of artists allied with the French Communist Party, like André Fougeron.[64] These international artists of *Art Informel*, for Tapié and others, were joined in a common endeavor to both push the formal boundaries of the art object and express the radical subjectivity of the artist.

Artistic gesture departed from the conventions of pictorial specificity (handed down from Analytical Cubism) and privileged instead a fiercely antigeometric, antinaturalistic and nonfigurative mode of expression, spontaneity of purpose, and the dynamic action of the brushstroke, often created in a kind of compositional performance. The German critic Werner Haftmann, who is an important figure in Chapter Three, identified the 'broad style' of painting as featuring 'gashes, thrusts, shattering and splattered tugs', and believed that, in part because of its non-representational subject, this form of gestural abstraction was a 'lingua franca' capable of uniting artists of various nationalities.[65] Perhaps more than any other ambassador for American art at the perennial international exhibition during this period, O'Hara helped shape the meaning of 'artistic gesture' in Europe. What is also true, however, is that O'Hara was early to recognize the limitations of this style and its precarious future at a time when a younger generation of Figurative Expressionist and Neo-Dada artists were emerging in the United States and Europe. This tension animates the American representation at the *29th Venice Biennale* and *documenta 2*, the focus of Chapter Three.

Two | The Bar Américain Continues to be French

We artists of the School of New York are a collection of co-existing separate pasts. So are the individuals who constitute the School of Paris. These two handfuls of individuals are closer to each other in their essential acts than either is to the herd of individuals who constitute his natural culture, French or American.[1]

ROBERT MOTHERWELL

I. In Search of a New Style

Of Frank O'Hara's liaisons with European culture, it was his love affair with France that lasted the longest and was the most fiercely felt.[2] No, a romantic affair isn't quite right: when O'Hara was asked about his 'relation to French poetry', he responded, revealingly, and to a ripple of laughter: 'Oh, French poetry is sort of like one's mother, I guess. As a matter of fact, much better.'[3] And like all complex mother–son relationships, this one was riven by a heady mix of deference and the desire to assert the child's independence. O'Hara's vexed, contradictory affections for the maternal France can be best understood in relation to an old Parisian washhouse at 13 Rue Ravignan, just below the Place du Tertre. Despite being, in the words of Annie Cohen-Solal, a 'rundown, three-story hovel, thirty feet high and ninety feet long, jerry-built from wooden planks and glass panes [. . .] a pitiful place, flea-ridden and horrible', the Bateau-Lavoir signified the gloried modernist age of Parisian bohemia.[4] As Barbara Guest recalls, when O'Hara finally visited Paris, on museum business, first in 1958 and then with her in 1960, he found himself conflicted over the legacy and enduring relevance of the École de Paris, symbolized by that hovel in the Grandes-Carrières quarter, for his own poetry and for the New York artists that he revered so much:

Frank and I happened to be in Paris at the same time in the summer of 1960. I was staying there with my family and had been very busy with the

Guide Bleu looking at every placard on every building I could find. And I had located the 'bateau lavoir' where Picasso and Max Jacob had first lived and where they had held all those studio parties with Apollinaire and Marie Laurencin. And across the street was a very good restaurant. I suggested that we have lunch there, our party included Grace Hartigan and her husband at the time, Robert Keene. We had a 'marvelous' lunch, much wine and talk and we all congratulated ourselves on being in Paris and moreover being in Paris at the same time – a continuation of the Cedar St. Bar, where we had formerly and consistently gathered. After lunch I suggested that we cross the street to the 'bateau lavoir,' a discovery of mine and one I thought would intrigue Frank. Not at all. He did go across the street, but he didn't bother to go into the building. 'Barbara,' he said, 'that was their history and it doesn't interest me. What does interest me is ours, and we're making it now.'[5]

O'Hara challenges the pedestal of Parisian modernism, while figuring his own coterie as the torchbearers of a new history.[6] Rod Mengham, whose essay reprints this anecdote and remains one of the most compelling on the subject of 'French Frank', notes an 'emerging tendency to attempt to negate French modernism and to put in its place an independent, autonomous American art that does not acknowledge its roots in, or its affiliations to, French modernism'.[7] There is a great deal of truth to this view. O'Hara's pithy, arrogant declaration on someone else's history is revealing in its forceful effort to distance the legacies of Parisian modernism from his own 'autonomous' clique. At the same time, this repudiation is clearly coloured by a belief that New York artists have surpassed some kind of place of origin in Paris, and therefore implicitly acknowledges its historical roots there. O'Hara's worldview was common currency back in New York. Fourteen years earlier, in the spring of 1946, Clement Greenberg and John Bernard Myers, later the co-founder of the Tibor de Nagy Gallery, met for a drink at the Vanderbilt Hotel in the *riche* Murray Hill neighbourhood of Manhattan. 'Paris has been limping along as the world center of art since 1936', Greenberg snarled. 'But what will replace the School of Paris?' Myers asked. 'The place where money is', Greenberg replied. 'New York.'[8] Greenberg wrote these ideas down two years later in an essay, 'The Decline of Cubism', in which he argued that 'the main premises of Western art have at last migrated to the United States, along with the center of gravity of industrial production and political power.'[9] Louis Menand notes that Greenberg was only half-right: 'New York did become the financial center of the art world, but art itself became international.'[10] But on whose terms did art become international? It is within and against these attitudes that O'Hara made his claim about the Bateau-Lavoir over a decade later, but we should not take this view at face value. In another interview, with Edward Lucie-Smith, he talks about the kind of poet he would like to be:

I would *rather* be the sort of poet who would do, you know, the great thing of, you know the story about Max Jacob, leaning out his window when Picasso is passing by the Bateau-Lavoir and Picasso calls up and says, 'Max, come out.' And he says, 'I won't.' He says, 'Why won't you?' And he says, 'Because I'm in search of a new style.' And Picasso walks down the hill and, as Max Jacob pulls his head back, says, 'There is no style.' That is the sort of thing that is, you know, like living and interesting.[11]

So the true intensity as an artist, for O'Hara, lies in what he believes to be immediate and part of the 'living situation' of art-making. Blue plaque tourism is different to the flash of revelation between two friends in the hurry of creativity who do not, and indeed cannot, imagine themselves as a historical subject. But the inheritances of Parisian modernism weighed upon him particularly hard as a curator. How would he stage exhibitions of American art that would prove a hit with French audiences? Can the answer be found in reverence to those mythologized stories of life in the shabby studios of the Bateau-Lavoir, or in Greenberg's shock tactics?

For MoMA, O'Hara exhibited modern art not only in the celebrated halls of the Musée d'Art Moderne de la Ville de Paris, which was then directed by another poet, the stern former Resistance fighter Jean Cassou, but in regional galleries far from Saint-Germain-des-Prés, such as the Musées des Beaux-Arts in Laon and Antoine Lecuyer in St. Quentin. O'Hara quickly became an important spokesperson for American art in France as he represented the International Program as curator or assistant on several important exhibitions. These included a diplomatic offensive that presented French 'masterpieces' from American collections to the Parisian public, a travelling exhibition of recent watercolours predominantly by gestural painters, and a posthumous evaluation of Jackson Pollock's career at a time when certain quarters of the École de Paris were touting him as one of the leading transatlantic artists working in an *Art autre* mode. These exhibitions took place between 1955 and 1959, which was, by all accounts, a trying time for the already strained Franc-American relationship. The period in question included some of the most hostile years of the Cold War and, therefore, also the busiest in terms of cultural exchange and collaboration. During this period, critics on both sides retreated to reductive, essentialized clichés of the other to mask their own anxieties as the *impudent, adolescent* New York School was seen to replace the *demure, fading* École de Paris as the dominant producer of advanced art. While O'Hara traded in some of those national stereotypes – of an effeminate and decadent France, and of an American avant-garde that may have had its roots in Paris but was now aggressively posturing as autonomous – his own sense of the fundamentally hybrid or cosmopolitan character of late modernist painting positioned him as an important critic within various, perhaps surprising, networks of affinity. O'Hara's important French exhibitions became contested markers of what Rebecca Walkowitz has characterized as 'vernacular cosmopolitanism', or a 'popular tradition that values the risks of social deviance and the resources of consumer culture and urban mobility', and in Europe has included such practices as 'flanerie, dance hall entertainment, department store shopping, and cultural exhibitions'.[12] It is this popular, vernacular tradition of cosmopolitanism, of which the art exhibition was an exemplar mode, that ended up illuminating much about this disputed moment in the cultural Cold War.

II. Different Forms of Internationalism

In 1955, O'Hara re-joined MoMA as a temporary exhibitions assistant after finishing his graduate studies at Ann Arbor.[13] (O'Hara would be hired in a more permanent position, the still dubiously bureaucratic and clerical title of 'administrative assistant', in April of the same year.) In the history of Cold War cultural diplomacy, 1955 was also the year that the 'Gaulois fought the Cowboy', as Serge Guilbaut memorably put it, and when there existed a 'clear correlation between the view held by the French that the United States had a mediocre culture and the related belief that American international relations were immature and crass', which were matched by the American view of a decadent French culture in irredeemable decline.[14] The view that American culture was inferior to the French, and that the United States was now an imperialist power or a 'super-European monster', was put forward by influential public intellectuals like Jean-Paul Sartre, as in his fictive 'Dear John letter', 'Les animax maladies de la rage' (1953) which, according to John Ireland, 'drew on more traditional French values and culture (its title is a parody of a famous La Fontaine fable), even as it sought to speak for a spectrum of European values (Sartre often invokes again the collective subject pronoun: "we") in its angry and sorrowful dismissal of a country that could perpetrate the barbarity and judicial travesty of the Rosenberg execution.'[15] The Americans needed to answer back. If American culture was to win the mind of someone like Sartre, never mind his heart, then there would need to be a smarter, more nuanced and intellectual, and less imperial, programme of cultural diplomacy.

On 12 May 1955, George F. Kennan, formerly the Ambassador to the Soviet Union and Director of the State Department Policy Planning Committee, delivered a lecture entitled 'International Exchange in the Arts' at MoMA. In many ways, this was surprising. Kennan had composed two documents – the Long Telegram, written in Moscow in February 1946 and 'The Sources of Soviet Conduct', better known as the infamous X Article and published in *Foreign Affairs* in July 1947 – that set out the strategic, geopolitical, and indeed moral case for President Truman's 'containment' policy during the Cold War. Kennan became known as one of the Wise Men, mostly graduates of Yale and mostly wealthy former bankers, who were, for

Louis Menand, 'the pragmatic and largely nonpartisan internationalists who played a major role in in the running of American foreign policy in the first two thirds of the twentieth century'.[16] Offering his credentials not as a man of refined modern tastes but as a statesman of *realpolitik*, Kennan reflected on his diplomatic discussions with international elites on both sides of the Iron Curtain, and concluded that their impression was that 'we are a nation of vulgar, materialistic *nouveaux riches,* lacking in manners and sensitivity'.[17] In Western Europe in particular, Kennan felt that the United States was identified 'with things and impulses of the modern age which they hate in themselves – such things as modern technology, standardization and mass culture'.[18] If one were to take Kennan's 1955 speech and place it alongside O'Hara's 1956 Ford Foundation proposal text, redact the titles and ask which was which, at the level of either their intended purpose or even rhetorical style, the reader would struggle. In essence, both Kennan's speech and O'Hara's proposal assert that the main body of European intellectuals believed that the culture of the United States was grounded in empty materialist values and was parochial by comparison to their own, and that only a strategic promotion of the new advanced American art could rectify this. For Kennan, Barr, and O'Hara, there was no time like the present.

We know that O'Hara personally attended the Kennan speech, although we cannot be sure what he made of it. What we can be certain of is that some sense of geopolitical cultural diplomacy had begun to govern curatorial decision-making at MoMA by 1957. Kennan recognized the power of what he characterized as the 'symbolic value in international life', something that had been toxified by 'an appalling number of clichés' and national stereotypes. Instead, Kennan concluded, in a full advocation of a realist foreign policy in the sphere of modern art, the peoples of the United States in general, and the curators of MoMA in particular, must be able to 'find an unfailing bridge between nations, even in the darkest moments of political bitterness and chauvinism and exclusiveness'.[19] MoMA dutifully followed this command to promote 'cultural values, universal in their meaning and their appeal' and spent most of the year, indeed the next five years, committed to this purpose.[20]

In 1955 the Soviet Union spent more on cultural programmes (mostly ballet, a big hit for Parisians) in France, than the United States on its entire overseas operations combined.[21] Whereas the Soviets had invested some $2 billion on cultural propaganda in the preceding two years, the Americans had only spent $2.5 million.[22] 'It was not until 1955', Nancy Jachec writes, 'marked by the numerical growth and the ideological disenfranchisement of the nonaligned left in France and Italy, that curatorial practices would become decidedly internationalist.'[23] Kennan's identification of the power of national cliché within the over-determined Cold War rivalry of the United States and France is significant and has a long, ugly, and reductive history.[24] Around the same time as Kennan's talk, in spring 1955, this attitude was developed further when Greenberg published '"American-Type" Painting' in *Partisan*

Review, two years after declaring Paris exhausted and defeated – 'la cause était entendue' – in *Arts Digest*.[25] In that earlier essay, Greenberg responded to the provocation 'Is the French Avant-Garde overrated?' by declaring 'Do I mean that the new American abstract art is superior on the whole to the French? I do.'[26] In Greenberg's view, the internal disagreements, and conflicts about ideology (the future of the Left) and form (the future of modernist painting) remained, but the École de Paris had no new answers to the anxieties that came now. Those were met by a younger generation in America. Greenberg doubles-down on this argument by gesturing to the 'proximity and attention' of the 'young abstract-expressionist painters' – a reference not only to the intimacy afforded by artistic community, support networks and productive competition but also, significantly, to the art market – that provided 'self-confidence and a sense of being in the center of art'.[27] In an intriguing construction, Greenberg goes on to say: 'in New York they could measure themselves against Europe with more benefit to themselves than they could ever have done as expatriates in Paris'.[28] In Guilbaut's words, both Paris and New York sought to 'fit the other into a non-threatening stereotype: ... America was violent, brutal, and free, while France was over-cultured, suave to the point of decadence, and riddled with inner contradictions. One was rough, the other was slick.'[29] On the surface at least, it might look as though O'Hara agreed with the broad premise of this codification of national cliché into an entire style, and even channels some of the more violent pastiche common to Greenberg's comparative assessment.

Five years later, O'Hara wrote in 'Art Chronicle I': 'Where else is the big, brave art happening? Certainly not in Paris, where artisanship has claimed and cured even the most demented intentions to the point where Helen Frankenthaler's recent show, or a single fugitive Kline, or something from the Spanish School (Tapiés or Canogar or Saura), is a sock in the eye along the rue de Seine. [. . .] A lot of interesting things are happening right here [in New York] which make Paris and Rome seem quite dull by comparison.'[30] The accounts of both Greenberg and O'Hara resemble the critic sat ringside in a heavyweight title bout, even if O'Hara is clearly writing partly in jest. In defending the 'big, brave art' of gestural abstraction against the pejorative 'artisanship' of a Paris obsessed by finish, O'Hara traded in clichés of a vigorous, competitive American art (allied with the Spanish artists, who are also able to land the knockout punch) that emasculates Paris (and Rome). But another statement by O'Hara might say more about the inferiority complexes that plagued the art scene back home. In the essay 'American Art and Non-American Art', printed in the 1959 Winter-Spring issue of *It Is* as one of 'Six Opinions on Abstract Art in Other Countries', O'Hara looked to define American art in relation to France. He felt he had to. O'Hara echoed this effort to trace the desire on the part of the American artists to shake off their 'provincial' label:

> If any of what I am saying is true, if there really is such a thing as American painting, I think it can only be because for the first time in our history an

art is appearing which is aware of the rest of the world in a non-imitative way. And the more naked we get, the more clearly we will be seen to ourselves. Why should we be ashamed? The French aren't ashamed of being French.[31]

Up until this moment, as O'Hara notes, the '*avant-garde* was not only a French word but an École de Paris monopoly'.[32] Rather than expressing American arrogance pure and simple, O'Hara was speaking to the historical insecurity on the part of the American gestural painters, who longed to emerge from the long shadow of Regionalism that had dominated art school training before another world war. In short, they no longer wanted to be cast as a bunch of fiddling rustics. Of course, this position does not depart too far from the main premises of '"American-Type" Painting'. Greenberg makes clear that he does not 'make allowances for American art' that he does not make for 'any other kind' and argues instead that what the American artists had 'in common from the first was an ambition – or rather the will to it – to break out of provinciality'.[33]

In an essay entitled 'Die Weltliteratur' (2007), the Czech–French novelist Milan Kundera distinguishes two types of provincialism, which he defines as 'the inability (or the refusal) to see one's own culture in *the large context*'.[34] That inability or unwillingness manifests itself in one of two ways: 'large-nation provincialism' and 'small-nation provincialism'. According to Kundera, the 'large-nation' strand refuses much of the universalism inherent in the idea of a world culture and is most clearly identifiable when a country has such an arrogant sense of its own status and influence that it ignores the art and literature of other peoples, which it regards as peripheral. For Kundera, the case of France serves as the pre-eminent example (although by the twentieth century he argues that French culture is already in decline, and beyond Marcel Proust and Albert Camus its major literary achievements were 'very little').[35] Small-nation provincialism, of which the culture of the United States in the immediate aftermath of the Second World War would surely be counted as an example, has the opposite problem: anxious that its art and its culture is inferior on the world stage, it only speaks to, and believes that art only belongs to, the native audience. For O'Hara, those definitions were starting to shift. For the most part, this was not because of American art's transition from a 'small-nation' to a 'large-nation' provincial: it would be another decade for that. Instead, he wondered why critics and curators needed such competitive distinctions between national 'schools', even if he stopped short of the one-world universalism that marked the curatorial attitude of exhibitions like *documenta 2*.

In short, again from 'American Art and Non-American Art': 'So far as I can see lately, what we mean by American art is, with a few exceptions such as Giacometti, Wols and Riopelle, simply *avant-garde* art. It is still alive, it is part of our lives (not nationally – personally), it can be experienced without necessarily being understood completely, it can move us and remain a mystery.'[36] It is no coincidence that O'Hara chose as his exemplar anomalies foreign-born artists who had settled in Paris – Giacometti, Wols, Riopelle – and who were all examples of what Pierre Descargues celebrated as the 'Individualist *Internationale*' for the new École de Paris.[37] Natalie Adamson has argued that it was in Paris that modernism assumed its 'universal' associations through the exilic imagination, and defines the 'Individualist *Internationale*' as such:

> 'In the recuperation of cosmopolitanism as a positive value, the foreign-born École de Paris artist became a citizen of the world, whose hybrid ethnic origins enriched the national culture and repudiated its parochial, sectarian and conformist tendencies. The city of Paris, where such artists lived and worked, is therefore presented as a site of redemptive creativity that transcends regional or national values and promises to maintain the particularities of each individual in balance with an over-arching "universal" human culture.'[38]

O'Hara defended the 'Individualist *Internationale*' in strong and forceful tones, and noted that during and even since the Fall of France, there existed an 'intense Francophilism among all liberal intellectuals [in New York]'; indeed, he celebrates those émigré artists and writers who had made the city their home.[39] These were the 'brightest lights of the École de Paris' and it was 'no accident' that they were themselves 'expatriates who had little or no means of expressing their social potency beyond their own work'.[40] For O'Hara, the painters of the École de Paris were the very 'emblems of art and also emblems of experience' and it was their 'insouciant survival in the face of disaster, partly through character, partly through belief in art' that became one of the 'great legends' in modernist history.[41] In the artistic imagination, both in Paris and amplified elsewhere, these 'refugees represented everything valuable in modern civilisation that was being threatened by physical extermination'.[42] But by the mid-fifties, the model of the 'Individualist *Internationale*', of a centre of art made up of foreign-born or expatriate artists, such as Willem de Kooning, Arshile Gorky and Mark Rothko had already become enmeshed in the minds of O'Hara's wider circle as having taken root in New York.[43] In aligning aesthetic and political commitment in these ways, a move he characterizes as rather European, O'Hara refers to the societal and ethnographic underpinnings of a movement, refashioned with an identity that 'belonged' not to local or national sources, but to a more localized version of community and one founded on a belief in modern art, more so than shared national borders or even language, as the common denominator.

This attitude was dominant in Parisian curatorial circles and was central to the assertion of the city as a renewed site as artistic power. René Huyghe, a curator at the Louvre, put it like this: 'At the same time the École française becomes the École de Paris: the cosmopolitanism of the metropolis recreates an ambience of uprootedness that favours, for opposite reasons, abstract art.'[44] Jean Cassou, the leftist poet and intellectual who became the inaugural Director of the Musée d'Art Moderne de la Ville de Paris, the most prestigious official venue for the display of modern art at the time, also shared this view. Cassou, like Descargues, believed in the essentially cosmopolitan character of the École de Paris. Pierre Restany said of Cassou that while he was 'very respected . . . he was not a man of the visual arts' and rather 'an intellectual' whose 'reactions to new art were negative'.[45] Cassou moderated the more nationalist ambitions of those around him at the Musée, those like Bernard Dorival who, for Restany, 'had a real artistic formation and culture' but who was 'fixated with the French tradition' and 'always tried to promote and help people who had French values'.[46] Nevertheless, Cassou worked in partnership with the Americans.[47] He consequently viewed, as Gay McDonald writes, 'mid-century American art in similar terms as that of the École de Paris at the turn of the century: the result of healthy, cross-cultural exchanges'.[48] With that said, Cassou reassured the French public by presenting 'masterpieces' from the museum's own collection at the same time as adopting an attitude that believed the potential threat posed by American art to the École de Paris could be neutralized by outwardly demonstrating a personal preference for cultural exchange, while privately setting boundaries that hoped to preserve Paris' long-held prerogatives as the gravitational centre of modern art.

In many ways, O'Hara saw Cassou as something of a kindred spirit. In the 1965 interview, Edward Lucie-Smith asked O'Hara about his extensive collaborative projects with artists and his close friendships with fellow poets, and whether they were 'unusual in a museum official' in the United States because, according to Lucie-Smith, in Europe they tended to be thought of 'as codifiers of art, a final court of appeals, but not as the participators'.[49] O'Hara was nonplussed, as he was often in this interview, and looked to Paris for a model: 'Well, it's a little more complicated than that because after all Jean Cassou is a poet, isn't he? And in America it's very hard to codify your interest in a sort of emotional way which leads you perhaps to understand a little bit better than the general public at the time the work is appearing. And then you're either right or wrong later.'[50] For O'Hara, Cassou personified the kind of curation he wanted to practice: an extension of creative production, interdisciplinary in approach, and broadly accepting of the transnational character of modern art. So how did O'Hara and his American colleagues seek to make their case to a curator like Cassou? First, they tried to be as courteous as they possibly could.

III. Salutes to France

As a festival of events, MoMA's travelling exhibition *Salute to France* was a transparent and unapologetic effort in cultural diplomacy to woo the French gallery-going audiences – largely with flattery. According to the official planning report, *Salute to France* served a two-fold purpose: 'to honor the cultural heritage and achievements of France' in *From David to Toulouse-Lautrec*, a *longue durée* of French painting from American collections, while *Fifty Years of Art from the United States* looked to 'display American cultural achievements to the French people, who, like many Europeans, tend to be blinded by American material accomplishments to American achievements in the arts'.[51] These attitudes, as Kennan made clear, were commonplace – and corrosive to the effort of refashioning the cultural image of the United States abroad. *Salute to France* was defined by an effort to demarcate common ground and to stress shared and long-held cultural affinities, strung somewhat tenuously together by the connoisseurly adventurism of American art collectors in the nineteenth century.[52] In short, it was an effort to show deference to French culture despite, or perhaps because of, the contemporary and widely-held attitude among American art critics that 'French painting between the wars and after the Second World War', as Arthur Danto put it, '[exemplified] so protracted a decline that [ultimately] the final three-quarters of the twentieth century could be written without scarcely a mention of France'.[53] Whether the United States and France had exchanged places in Kundera's theory of provincialism was an open question.

As we can see from promotional photographs of the exhibition posters (bearing the sub-heading '*Hommage Culturel Américain*'), which flooded the trendy central thoroughfares of the rue de Seine and Saint-Germain-des-Prés, and even right under the nose of the Eiffel Tower, Parisians could hardly have avoided the compliment (see Figure 2.1). *Salute to France* opened to great fanfare and was a programme of cultural exchange that included orchestral concerts, ballet, and theatre in Paris, as well an exhibition schedule heralded by the major *Fifty Years of American Art*, the largest exhibition of American art shown abroad to date.[54] It drew the highest attendance of any non-French contemporary art exhibition since the Second World War, with a footfall of 14,530 paying visitors plus several thousand by invitation. The majority of works on show were by American modernists, especially those who had already gained significant stature abroad, and of 108 canvases 44, or just under half of the paintings in the exhibition, were by figures within that category. It was also a relatively early moment for the display of MoMA's wider collection of Abstract Expressionist painting in a major French gallery, and 28 paintings by Gorky, de Kooning, Kline, Motherwell, Rothko, and Clyfford Still were displayed, together with younger artists closer to O'Hara, like Guston and Hartigan, as well as Theodore Stamos and Mark Tobey. The entire programme did not just include painting and sculpture, but prints, architecture, typographical and industrial design, films and photography. The events were organized by the International Program, in concert with the United States Information Agency (USIA), at the request of Jacques Jaujard of the Ministère de l'Éducation nationale, Paris.

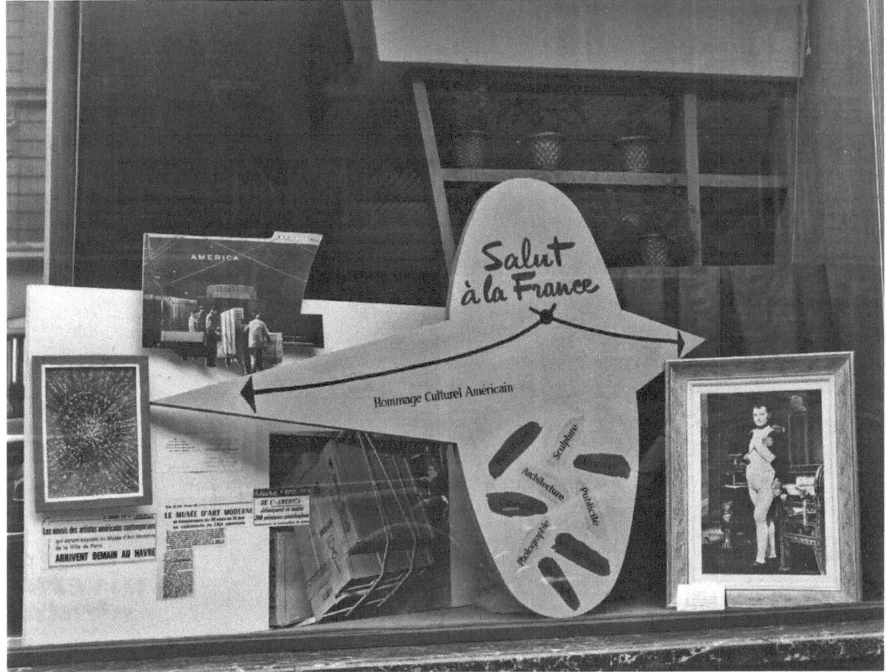

FIGURE 2.1 Transportation, Loading and Unloading in conjunction with the exhibition 'De David à Toulouse-Lautrec', prepared in association with a series of interdisciplinary cultural events *Salute to France*. Musée de l'Orangerie, Paris, France; organized by the International Program of The Museum of Modern Art, New York, 20 April 1955 through 3 July 1955.

O'Hara and McCray coordinated with a transatlantic network that also included the entrepreneurial Darthea Speyer, a childhood friend of Alfred Barr. Since 1950, Speyer had been cultural attaché in Paris to the United States Embassy under the aegis of the USIA. A charismatic figure, Speyer was instrumental in securing funding for exhibitions of American art in Paris, sometimes through private benefactors but often from the French government through the Association Française d'Action Artistique (AFAA). The USIA was broadly supportive of cultural exchange initiatives if they received non-governmental assistance although, according to Speyer, the Embassy received 'crazy' telegrams from Washington that advised against too intimate a working relationship with the International Program: 'Don't have anything to do with them; they're communists.'[55] It is a view that, if true, indicates the ongoing scale of misunderstanding of the international situation, or a disagreement about tactics, on the part of some government decision-makers as late as 1955. *Salute to France* marked the high point in a diplomatic offensive on the part of the United States in France.

Some of O'Hara's responsibilities on *Fifty Years of American Art* were limited to administrative duties as he represented McCray back in New York. Some of that work, however, was firmly in the remit of a cultural diplomat as he brokered White House meetings to drum up the case for why the enthusiasms of American collectors for nineteenth-century French oil paintings could curry diplomatic favour in the Élysée Palace. Instead, O'Hara worked closely on an accompanying display of French nineteenth-century paintings – *belle peinture française* – and an unapologetic appeal to the country's 'large-nation' provincialist sensibilities. *From David to Toulouse-Lautrec* was unlike *Fifty Years of American Art*, which had been drawn from a single museum, and included 62 cases that comprised 59

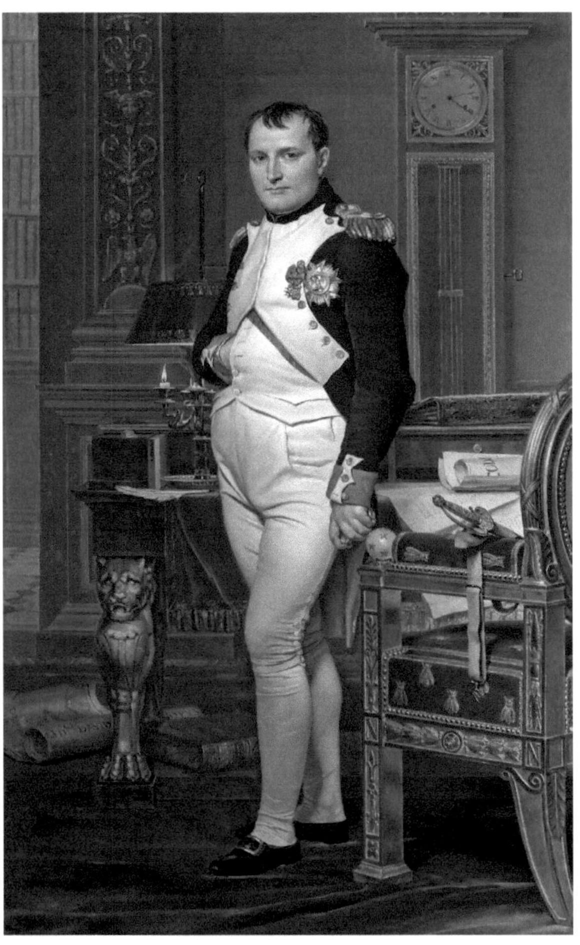

FIGURE 2.2 Jacques-Louis David, *The Emperor Napoleon in His Study at the Tuileries*, 1812.

paintings and 39 drawings from 40 museums and private collections. The show included several blockbuster French works, not least *The Emperor Napoleon in His Study at the Tuileries* by David (1812), which had been bought by the Samuel H. Kress Foundation in 1954 (see Figure 2.2). Together with Grace Davis, it was O'Hara's task to collate reception material in periodicals, newspapers, and magazines, and to make an institutional record which, although consistent with what was expected of all International Program exhibitions, was far larger in scope. One newspaper cutting he felt was important to keep was a humorous cartoon sketch of these Old Masters returning home from the New World, published by *Les Nouvelles littéraires* and entitled 'Le retour des oncles d'Amérique' ('The return of the American uncles'). This imagined scene became an important representation for MoMA to grapple with the reception and success of the exhibition. In the picture, a boat, powered by American industrial steam, billows smoke up above the Seine and into the face of Henri de Toulouse-Lautrec, while Honoré Daumier tips his hat dramatically, Gustave Courbet stands aloft, and Vincent van Gogh peeks out meekly from the hull. The mock-heroic scene is more than just a send-up of the artists' famed personalities; the cartoon brilliantly captures both the performative arrival of the homecoming facilitated only by American power, but also the creeping insecurities felt about French artistic prestige adrift between this nostalgic past and the more ambiguous present.

Where necessary, O'Hara also translated in his passable French, as we can see from the many reams of press documents with his handwriting in the margins held in the MoMA Archive. For example, in a letter to William Burden, then President of MoMA's Board of Trustees, the Ambassador to France, C. Douglas Dillon, referenced a telegram he had received from the President of the French Republic, M. René Coty, in which he affirmed that he and his 'compatriots [were] deeply touched by the affection and good will which has inspired and marked the series of manifestations of Salute to France'.[56] Coty, who was broadly in favour of European integration, but who held reservations about the expanded military involvement of the United States in the continent, offered his 'thanks to American individuals and groups who so generously participated in this initiative and its splendid success'.[57] By the time of the telegram, O'Hara was already in the inner sanctum of curators at MoMA, and was carbon copied into this correspondence with the Embassy directly, together with McCray and d'Harnoncourt. In the top right of the letter he showed his recognition of the importance of this diplomatic endorsement: 'as many copies [to be made of the letter] as possible Paris F'OH'.[58] Coty's message was reprinted in the opening comments of the official report that O'Hara produced.

In terms of cultural diplomacy, *From David to Toulouse-Lautrec* was viewed by the International Program as a triumph, as demonstrated by the press reaction which was 'impressive from every point of view':

An analysis of these articles [reviewing *From David to Toulouse-Lautrec*] seems to confirm the comments made by the Paris correspondent of the *New York Times* (July 3): 'It was the show of French artists' owned by Americans that captured most of the praise in the entire program'; and the *New Yorker*'s Genêt (Janet Flanner) in her 'Letter from Paris' (July 16): 'Our overwhelming success in saluting the French was ... our return of their own American-owned masterpiece Impressionist paintings for Parisian contemplation in the Musée de l'Orangerie, where the greatest crowds the museum has known since the war assembled in admiration and pleasure. This was the ideal *Salut Franco-Américaine*.' It is highly significant to note that in the midst of this flood of favorable publicity, the Communist daily *Humanité* gave no coverage whatsoever to the exhibition; while the Communist weekly, *Lettres Françaises,* published a highly laudatory review without any mention of the auspices under which the exhibition was held nor reference to the fact that the works of art were lent from American collections. . . . It had been anticipated that some of the extreme right- or left-wing press might make this an occasion to accuse America of having taken advantage of her wealth to rob France of her artistic patrimony; this sour note, however, was never once sounded.[59]

O'Hara produced a pragmatic report that, while outwardly detailed in its own account, missed some of the quietly critical pieces that drew attention to 'sour notes' sounded by those critics (mostly on the Left), who saw the festival in its entirety as a display that spoke back to the status of the United States as a political, economic, and – dare they say – cultural superpower. For example, the focus on American material achievements beyond its own artistic advances was acerbically criticized through irony, as in one review by Descargues in *Les Lettres françaises*: 'An extensive section has been given over to saucepans, lemon-squeezers, can openers, and plastic chairs . . . Only a Cadillac, a jet plane, and a H-bomb are lacking but will undoubtedly be included another time.'[60] This reflects the fact that when *Fifty Years of American Art* was then circulated to Frankfurt, Barcelona, Zurich, Vienna, The Hague, and London as *Modern Art in the United States*, it did not include this section on design. The anxieties around cultural Americanization were not unique to the Left, and the right-wing paper *Témoignage chrétien*, wrote of 'the avant-garde of an offensive of economic colonization against which we feel the duty to struggle here'.[61] But O'Hara's account was, for the most part, accurate. In *Preuves,* the Paris-based monthly publication of the Congress for Cultural Freedom, which has since been identified as a clandestine mouthpiece for the CIA, Michel Seuphor described the Abstract Expressionists as dealing with 'purely human preoccupations of an inward order . . . that bear great resemblance to those of generations of Paris painters'.[62] Seupher's premise chimed with the semantics of an international language of gestural painting that sought to represent not external reality but internal anxieties. Robert Motherwell, for example, in a lecture that also provides this chapter's epigraph, had earlier argued that the 'whole universe – external and internal – constitutes potential objects' and that it is the task of abstract painting, like the works that would be shown in *Cinquante ans d'art aux États-Unis*, to excel 'in choosing a new class of objects' that has 'enriched human experience'.[63] This was a formal 'enhancement': 'neither French nor American', Motherwell concluded, 'but international'.[64] O'Hara played a supporting role on *Salute to France*, but the following year he would take on his own curatorial project in France which allowed him space to set out his enthusiasms for contemporary American painting.

IV. Intimacies of the Occasional: Watercolour, Poetry, Colonialism

While in Paris for the *Salute to France* exhibition, McCray discussed with Speyer the possibility of another travelling exhibition of American art. This would travel to cities outside of Paris and focus on watercolour.[65] What an unfashionable prospect in 1955, Speyer thought. But as early as January 1956 McCray had persuaded Dorothy Miller to select the works, and to set about 'assembling an exhibition of around 70 watercolors by the younger generation of American painters for showing in Paris and other French cities during the year beginning July 1, 1956'.[66] Miller, who had been gradually researching the subject for a possible exhibition, knew she would have to bring O'Hara into the fold. It is possible that Miller believed O'Hara had more first-hand insights into the ways in which watercolour had been taken up by advanced abstract artists in New York than any other curator in the city. Miller asked O'Hara to write the catalogue essay. *Recent American Watercolors* was the start of a creative curatorial partnership between Miller and O'Hara that would be consolidated in *The New American Painting* two years later, when O'Hara subbed for Miller on her major travelling exhibition borne out of her *Americans* exhibition series.[67] Despite Waldo Rasmussen's vocal reservations about the timeliness of an American watercolour show in France, echoing Speyer and citing a government-sponsored show that toured only very recently with the Meltzer Gallery, O'Hara made the case that the advanced developments in gestural abstract painting brought a new framework within which to contextualize the perceived traditionalism of the watercolour technique and, for a moment, gave the latter a radical inflection.[68] Rather than a nostalgic turn to a style of painting that appeared to be moribund or amateurish (famously the medium of such Sunday painters as Winston Churchill), advanced artists working in oil had turned to watercolour because it felt consistent with the compositional strategies that had come to codify gestural abstraction. These included fierce and quick-tempered brushstrokes, smudged pigment to create blurred-edged forms, and drawing attention to the medium specificity of the exposed surface. In his catalogue essay, O'Hara stressed correlations were more of individual style and compositional approach than of a universal form:

> those qualities which have distinguished watercolor in the past – qualities of brevity, wit, freshness, the intimacy of the occasional – have of late become preoccupations of works in oil, particularly among the artists in the United States often referred to by critics as 'action painters,' 'abstract expressionists,' or 'American-type painters.' And in turn the contemporary American artist tends to bring a serious compositional intention to the watercolor and a formal intensity which may seem far from the casual graces and felicitous 'renderings' that we admire in certain watercolors of the past. Above all, he does not turn to the watercolor in a spirit of relaxation.[69]

Those qualities – brevity, wit, freshness, the intimacy of the occasional – are obviously the qualities of O'Hara's own poetics, as he makes a case for action over decoration at a time when these values had become clichéd through their attachment to an American present and a French past. It might seem unclear, at least at the outset, if any real distinction can be established between what is meant by 'qualities of brevity' and the 'intimacy of the occasional', characteristics that O'Hara recognizes in the most advanced art of his age, against the 'casual graces' of a former one. But the essay charts the course of the watercolour in modern American art and acknowledges that the '19th-century vogue for charming watercolors', which might be read through its association with amateurism, meant that 'few American artists seemed to realise how full an expression watercolor provided'.[70]

In O'Hara's view, it was natural that the Abstract Expressionists would recognize the medium's potential given its correspondence to the kinds of experiments in oil that was in vogue at the time. According to O'Hara's prose chronology, this process began with John Marin but was now taken forward by a younger generation that included Nell Blaine and Joan Mitchell.[71] The argument for Abstract Expressionism as the 'artist's inspirational act of painting [becoming] the work of art' and the 'immediacy of a rehearsal of the act of painting' emphasizes the importance of biography and the body of the artist during making.[72] These characterizations were, of course, common parlance in the critical discourse of the time. O'Hara's position reproduces a claim made by Harold Rosenberg that 'a painting that is an act is inseparable from the biography of the artist'.[73] On the subject of biography, the case of Mitchell is particularly compelling. As he prepared research for *Recent American Watercolors*, O'Hara oversaw the collection of artist biographies from their representing galleries. These were then gently revised and included in the catalogue materials.

Mitchell, who participated in the show with three works, all untitled works on paper and all dated 1956, had recently moved to a plush apartment at 77 rue Daguerre, where O'Hara would visit her in 1958 (Figure 2.3). It was in France that Mitchell painted 'semi-abstractly from nature', as O'Hara put it in her artist biography.[74] By 1956, Mitchell was experimenting with a painterly style that achieved an architectonic balance between structural density, often fern green or ultramarine, and expanses of off-white that appear to centrifugally slope off to the corners of the canvas. This created a wash of negative light that animates the massive off-centre form, heaving as it does, and represents what Mitchell called 'remembered landscapes' – tributaries of water or the build-up of vegetation against the expanse of clear lagoons or blue sky.[75] By the mid-1950s, too, her titles increasingly drew on literary and poetic reference, such as *Hemlock* (1956), a reference to a line in Wallace Stevens' poem 'Domination of Black' that is in turn an homage to John Keats. Mitchell's painting *To the Harbormaster*, dedicated to O'Hara and named after one of his major poems, was featured at *documenta 2*, which I will discuss in the next chapter. Mitchell held a particularly contested position within the nationhood debates between the United States and France.[76] In an April 1965 article for *Art News*, Ashbery wrote that his friend Mitchell was 'not an expatriate, but an apatride' – or, roughly translated, 'stateless'.[77] While 'expatriate' has strong implications of a flight from a native culture and an implicit sense of eventual return ('ex'), 'apatride' holds within it all the messy hybridity of the intensified yet precarious mobility of subjects across weakening geopolitical borders ('a'). In an essay published the following year, Ashbery made it clear that this predicament was not unique to Mitchell: 'it is difficult for anybody to remain

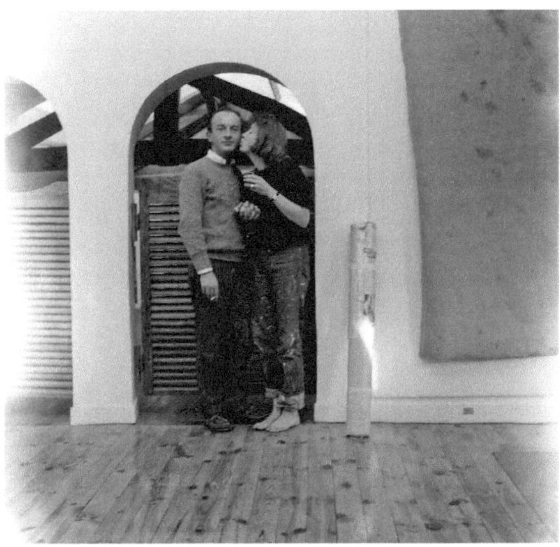

FIGURE 2.3 Frank O'Hara and Joan Mitchell in her rue Frémicourt studio, Paris, ca. 1961.

undiscovered any more, and with today's communications and transportation, nobody is an expatriate'.[78] Globalization meant that where an artist chose to make their art became less important, which in turn resulted in a more ambivalent commitment to where one lived.

These themes of transatlantic similitude and difference were dramatized in O'Hara's poem, 'Far from the Porte des Lilas and the Rue Pergolèse' which, like 'Adieu to Norman, Bon Jour to Joan and Jean-Paul', initially appears to be another occasional poem on the comings-and-goings of a transatlantic elite operating on the Paris–New York axis. It is similarly addressed to Mitchell, only this time saying 'goodby [sic]' as he leaves her in September 1958, a self-consciously bohemian artist – 'surrounded by paintings' – as though that is as much a statement of one's preferred lifestyle or mark of gendered identity as wearing 'lipstick' (CP, 311). In this way, as in the *Recent American Watercolors* catalogue essay which narrates the 'artist's inspirational act of painting [becoming] the work of art' and the 'immediacy of a rehearsal of the act of painting', this poem coalesces art and life that is threatened by the speech commands – 'of it! / with it! / out' (CP, 311) – and obstinately demand what happens next, which seems to be another question: what happens to American painting after Abstract Expressionism? Any confident or firm conviction in the realities of cultural difference between the United States and France is provocatively foreclosed without explanation or nuance: the other continent (America) is the 'same as this one' (Europe), as though both are beset by American imperialism or the worst parts of vernacular cosmopolitanism (CP, 311). The poem never closes its opening parenthesis and so its whole expressive movement feels like an aside; but in breaking this 'original syntax', reflects Lytle Shaw, 'the second stanza simply lists a series of "dangers" that, in 1958, threaten to overcode any attempt to value the gestural act as an instance of freedom.'[79] These are dangers of resemblance mostly, of looking or seeming like something else; nationhood becomes hybridized and less secure in itself, and therefore confronts those seeking to police inside and out. It is this context that frames the authority figures of the 'cops' racially profiling Algerians, who are positioned as unthreatening and at play.[80] This scene re-emerges in the late poem 'For Bill Berkson (On Again Looking into *Saturday Night*)', in which O'Hara links the 'balls' of play and leisure with the homophonic French word for bullet, 'balles', and asks whether it was their ruthless colonial project in Algeria that made the 'French important after all' (CP, 438).

If O'Hara's travels to Paris had made him sensitive to the accusation of cultural imperialism on the part of the United States, he could not ignore the status of French colonialism at a time when the Algerian Question was centre stage. In 'Far from the Porte des Lilas and the Rue Pergolèse', we might also think about the dangers remaining for Boris Pasternak (and the 'Pasternakesque'), for that year he would be awarded the Nobel Prize for Literature only to be denied it by the Soviet Union, much to O'Hara's well-publicized consternation.[81] All of this serves to remind us that the common measure of *postwar* (be that as a historical juncture on or around 1945 or, more pertinently for our study, as an art historical term for the transitional moment for modernist painting's endgame) was anything but, and it was instead true that during this time, colonial France fought the longest wars of the twentieth century. As such, and following the recent scholarship of Hannah Feldman, it might be better to call this period 'art *during*-war'.[82]

There is little doubt that *Recent American Watercolors* lacked the ambition and scale that had attended *Salute to France*, and it is this distinction which makes them apposite comparisons for my study. This is, of course, initially biographical and concerns the development of O'Hara's career: *Salute to France* was a major diplomatic event that was endorsed by the Presidents of both the French Republic and the United States, whereas *Recent American Watercolors* did not show in Paris after all, but rather toured regional museums in Laon, St. Quentin, Reims, Clermont-Ferrand, and Nice. Throughout the organizational correspondence, both representatives of MoMA and the USIA spoke of the 'provincial' quality of the exhibition. Speyer maintained that Paris was the centre and efforts to broadcast modernism to the regions would yield only diminished returns for the institutional objectives of MoMA. 'Often the critic for a provincial paper is not cognisant of modern art', Speyer wrote without irony: 'He is frequently more conservative in his taste. The show was well received by students, writers, architects, musicians and the intellectual elite.'[83] In O'Hara's conclusion to his catalogue essay for *Recent American Watercolors*, he changes tack. Moving away from a stress on the compositional similarities between gestural abstraction and watercolour as practiced by American artists, O'Hara positions both under the influence of French painting:

> 'Of even greater relevance is the influence of the impressionists and the cubists. Their discoveries and accomplishments are felt by most of the younger American artists as a constant source of inspiration in their individual explorations and an aesthetic permission to carry these explorations as far as their abilities and artistic purposes require.'[84]

If, in Guest's Bateau-Lavoir anecdote, O'Hara was disinterested in the history of French art and its relevance to a new generation of American painters, then he did not show it in his curatorial writings. The precedent of the Cubists and the Impressionists, for O'Hara, was what made gestural abstraction possible. Looking backwards, this attitude might seem naïve. It is easy to see that by 1958 and *The New American Painting* exhibition, the New York artists in general, and Jackson Pollock in particular, had solved some of the problems in painting set down by the French modernists. Abstraction seemed like the future, as the Parisians were about to find out.

V. Jackson Pollock Between Abstraction and Figuration

France was often depicted as the origin story for Abstract Expressionism, but this view should also be seen within the context of contemporary institutional collecting practices.[85] In '"American-Type" Painting', Greenberg's fixation with a linear formalism that began in France – principally with the 'all-over' painterliness of the late Monet and its 'unity and power', and his doctrine of modernism that grew ever more self-aware of the truth that they were working on a flat canvas, easel or otherwise – modelled a long historical narrative of abstraction on a teleological and pyramidal trajectory that would, by the end of the 1940s, reach its end-point with Pollock.[86] 'They all started from French painting, got their fundamental sense of style from it', wrote Greenberg, 'and still maintain some sort of continuity with it.'[87] Integral to this narrative, though, regardless of origins, was the story of French decline.[88] For Greenberg, too, the Paris at the time of High Cubism that had been irrepressible in a more enlightened age was now exhausted and therefore exposed. The extent to which O'Hara subscribed to the view on French decline and the 'continuity' of the influence of the Cubists is debatable, the evidence for which is scattered in the fragments of his art criticism we have on the subject, whether from the *Recent American Watercolors* catalogue or his review writing for *Art News,* as in 'Art Chronicle'.

However, his view on the development of modern art departs from Greenberg, who argued for a teleological trajectory that necessarily moved from figuration to abstraction. O'Hara's attitude to curation can be seen in a 1956 piece of note-paper kept in his personal folders at the MoMA Archives, which may be preparation for an exhibition, or – just for fun – may be the doodles of a curator contemplating the problems of aesthetic continuity or doubting the inexorable movement towards abstraction in American art. Headed 'Changes in Style', O'Hara lists a series of artists with abbreviated designations in parentheses, privileging individual versatility and conveying a sense of the momentum of art that was digressionary rather than linear:

> Blaine (ab + fig)
> Ossorio (sur + ab)
> Vicente (allover + neo p)
> Pearlstein (ab + fig)
> Reinhardt (lyr + geo)
> Grillo (neo + ab)
> Rothko (symb + ab)
> Guston (fig + ab)
> Hartigan (ab + fig)
> Ferrer? (3: ab, fig, ab)[89]

This seemingly casual and even throwaway scrap of paper reveals much about O'Hara's approach to art history, which recognizes even in its rudimentary form of one plus another a philosophy in which (Mark) Rothko is influenced as much by symbolism as abstraction; identifies in (Ad) Reinhardt both the lyrical and geometric, values conventionally conceived of only dialectically; and in (Rafael) Ferrer not the inexorable journey from figuration to abstraction, but abstraction to figuration and back again.

As Jeff Dolven has noted, this latter attribution suggests 'that O'Hara's abbreviations take the painter's modes in the order of their influence on his practice, and that he returns to where he started', which makes a wider point that abstraction 'is as likely to lead to figuration as the reverse, or elsewhere'.[90] This is an important distinction, and one that might on the surface appear incongruous to one of Barr's intellectual missions for MoMA from its establishment onwards, which stressed the influence of Cubism as a historiographical origin. As has been well-discussed, on the dust jacket for the catalogue of his 1936 exhibition *Cubism and Abstract Art*, an American defence of what a year later Adolf Hitler exhibited and derided as 'degenerate art', Barr devised a now very familiar directional flow-chart for the development of modernism in the visual arts. An original print of the flow-chart adorns the entrance to their Archives as the gateway to its past.[91] While some critics, like the *New York Times'* critic Holland Cotter, have characterized Barr's flow-chart as 'a snugly tailored origin myth for modern art . . . mapped out in a began-and-begat chart of labels and directional arrows . . . [and embodying] the operational logic of a computer board', more recent scholars have stressed how Barr saw modern art in a more elastic, and not teleological or rigidly genealogical, sense.[92] O'Hara never spoke publicly about Barr's flow-chart, but he did write poems that spoke to a view of Barr's modernism as multi-directional and digressive, as opposed to definitively authoritative, in his poetry. In 'Digression on *Number 1, 1948*', for instance, O'Hara loops through MoMA on his 'lunch hour', meandering past what feels like a random sequence of highlights from the collection – Miró, 'the sea by Léger', 'complicated Metzingers', a 'rude awakening by Brauner', all Parisian figures of the 'Individualist *Internationale*', and 'a little table by Picasso, pink' (CP, 260) – towards the main event: Pollock's *No. 1*. Characterized by distraction, absorption, and the resonant clarities afforded only by the jolts of afterthought, the poem oscillates between extremes which put pressure on the coherence of different states of being – it is 'warm for winter, cold for fall' (CP, 260). O'Hara would include Pollock's *No. 1* in his 1958/59 memorial retrospective on the artist. This exhibition was assembled from the same selection used at the São Paulo Bienal in 1957. *Jackson Pollock 1912–1956* circulated to Rome, Basel, Amsterdam, Hamburg, Berlin, London and finally completed its tour in Paris in 1959.

In a late-in-the-day letter deputizing for McCray in November 1958, O'Hara wrote to Lee Krasner to persuade her of the obvious merits of agreeing to an extension to her considerable loan list for *Jackson Pollock 1912–1956* for a French opening, after the retrospective had been due to close at the Whitechapel Art Gallery, London, that December.[93] Because of the 'extraordinary reception which Pollock's work has been given in each of the previously exhibiting cities', which by then had included Rome, Basel, Amsterdam, Hamburg and Berlin, 'M. Jean Cassou has made a most urgent request that the Pollock exhibition be shown at the Musée National d'Art Moderne, Paris, in January, 1959.'[94] As O'Hara goes on to explain, 'an earlier showing scheduled for Paris had to be cancelled because of delays in the reconstruction of the galleries in the Musée d'Art Moderne de la Ville de Paris assigned to special exhibitions' and, in light of this change in capacity, 'M. Cassou is therefore doubly anxious to obtain the exhibition for a January showing'.[95] In forcing Krasner's arm, O'Hara was not telling the whole truth. Cassou had mixed feelings about the promotion of American art after he became the founding director of Paris' official venue for the display of modern art. It is worth noting that those 'delays in the reconstruction of the galleries' to which O'Hara refers had likewise caused the temporary cancellation of *The New American Painting*, although this may have provided a convenient premise with which to persuade Krasner. In fact, Cassou had earlier intended to stage a large survey from the Musée's

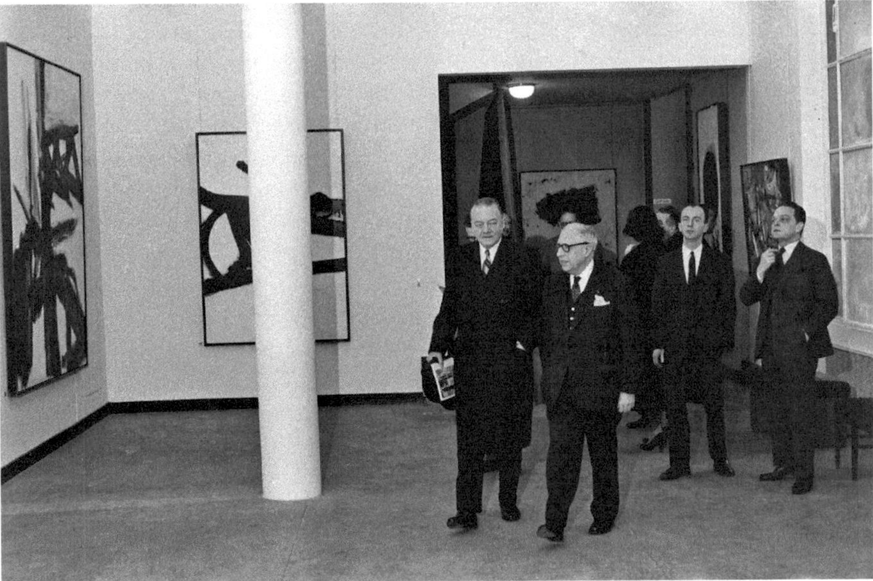

FIGURE 2.4 Second from left, Jean Cassou, far right, Porter McCray, second from right, Frank O'Hara, at the exhibition *The New American Painting*. 16 January 1959 through 15 February 1959, Musée National d'Art Moderne, Paris, France; organized by the International Program of The Museum of Modern Art, New York.

own collection for this time in the recently refurbished galleries (Figure 2.4). Ultimately, though, he acquiesced, and agreed to both *The New American Painting* and *Jackson Pollock, 1912–1956* after, in the words of curator Jeremy Lewison, 'political and diplomatic pressure was brought to bear on him'.[96] It seems likely that O'Hara knew well those reservations, and soon after his correspondence with Krasner was entreated by Speyer to move quickly and confirm the exhibition by the end of November in order to allow Cassou – who was 'anxious for news' – more time to plan catalogue publicity and administrative details.[97] While Cassou eventually agreed to show both exhibitions at the same time, he and his staff were not overly supportive of them. This can be seen most clearly in his personal introduction to the Pollock catalogue, in which he disdainfully observed that 'we are too often inclined to see in these productions only a movement analogous to certain of our own movements . . . in particular those called *taschistes*'.[98] This might be another pitch for the status of the Paris-based artist and an extension of the 'Individualist *Internationale*', but it also betrayed his own lukewarm attitude towards Pollock's work.

In Paris, the loudest praise for the artist was made by his early promoter Tapié, who had been the first to show Pollock's work in the city. The March 1951 manifesto exhibition *Véhémences confrontées* opened at the Galerie Nina Dausset, in which Tapié hung Pollock and De Kooning alongside other artists he categorized as *Art Informel* or *Art autre*, in what seems now like a roll-call of the *brut* gesturalism and *matière* violence within the anti-traditional and abstract wing of the invigorated École de Paris: Hartung, Mathieu, Giuseppe Capogrossi, Wols, and Riopelle. Seeking to link American Abstract Expressionism formally and philosophically with recent developments in western Europe, the exhibition's promotional material claimed that 'for the first time in France, an encounter between the extreme trends of non-figurative American, Italian and Parisian painting' was on show.[99]

In the catalogue, Tapié insisted on the importance of 'authentic artists' of 'exceptional individuality' who had incorporated styles consistent with the 'violence of the gesture'.[100] While the exhibition was an important event that shook the languid, academic Parisian art-world from its rest, and offered a defence of *Art autre* against both geometric abstraction and the stable traditions of colour harmony and balance that had been the convincing cultural discourse of Paris for centuries, Tapié was a largely incoherent theorist.[101] In an essay for the exhibition catalogue of his '*Jackson Pollock avec nous*' show, the artist's first solo exhibition in Paris, Tapié confirmed Pollock's place on the frontline of his avant-garde: 'that proposes to us not the security of a finished work, but the exciting vertigo, the vertiginous anguish, even, of a gesture of which there is no question of seeing its limits', and confirmed the US as the 'crossroads' of the deepest artistic currents in both the East and the West.[102] Conscious of Pollock's appeal for certain quarters of European audiences, in his own catalogue essay eight years later, O'Hara reprinted a statement made by Pollock that is unambiguously internationalist:

> The idea of an isolated American painting, so popular in this country during the 1930s, seems absurd to me just as the idea of creating a purely American mathematics or physics would seem absurd . . . And in another sense, the problem doesn't exist at all: or, if it did, would solve itself: An American is an American and his painting would naturally be qualified by that fact, whether he wills it or not. But the basic problems of contemporary painting are independent of any one country.[103]

O'Hara was still a year away from completing his monograph on Pollock, the first on the artist, and once again opted for Sam Hunter's introduction, which remained a curious choice. Hunter's introduction followed the long-history account of O'Hara's selection. In it, Hunter reflects that, in retrospect, 'it now seems anomalous that [Thomas Hart] Benton should have exercised a formative influence on the rebellious young Westerner', given his parochial subject matter, 'for Benton's paintings were closely identified with a particular American locale and with a violent repudiation of advanced European art forms'.[104] That influence was particularly pronounced in the case of Picasso and the Cubists, which mirrors the developmental history outlined in the *Recent American Watercolors* catalogue: those forces 'gave Pollock his first intimations of the radical nature of modern painting'.[105] Hunter then argues that it was Pollock's revivification of these styles and the 'intensity of his conviction' that contributed 'to his remarkable international reputation'.[106] But these internationalist appeals were balanced in conclusion with what European audiences often saw in Pollock: his raw Americana, the cowboy thrashing household paint, which was expressed as 'his unapologetic materialism' that was 'refreshing and unregenerately American' in quality, a 'distinctly native' mixture of realism and respect for materials.[107] In the same way that the Pollock representation at *documenta 2* was a clear attempt by O'Hara to show the full extent of the artist's career, so too was the posthumous memorial retrospective – and most of the works remained. The exhibition presented around 60 works, ranging from the early painting *The Flame* (1937) to *Untitled (Scent)* (1955), Pollock's final canvas, both of which hum with the vibrancy of an all-over composition and fiery colour palette.

The practicalities that brought *Jackson Pollock 1912–1956* and *The New American Painting* to Paris could be understood, at least in part, as a collaboration between the New York School poets, an extension of the forms of collaboration pursued by O'Hara, Ashbery, and Schuyler for instance, in their 1952 film *Presenting Jane*. On 19 December 1958, O'Hara wrote to Ashbery in Paris:

> Holiday greetings to you and Pierre and listen, there is a possibility that I'll be winging my way St. Germain-ward in the near future to unpack and install The New American Painting and Jackson Pollock in the Musée d'Art Moderne! What do you think of that? I can't seem to get anything definite out of Porter but he is going too and it would have to be quite soon

since the show will open on January 13th. Now don't tell me you'll be in Rome then! how often do I get to Paris after all, and besides Paris without you would be like a performance of Manon without a soprano. . . . Anyhow, I'll let you know when I'm arriving when I know if this all goes through. Nobody else is able to go so I imagine it will. And with my French it should be a cinch. Wouldn't you like to come down to the sequestered halls of the Musée and help out with the distribution of the Gottliebs?[108]

One week later, two days before flying to France, a rather more frantic O'Hara had his answer from McCray and entreated Ashbery, who was then staying on the Via del Consolato in Rome, via telegram: 'ARRIVE PARIS MORNING JANUARY FIRST PLEASE CABLE WHETHER YOU PLAN RETURN AND COULD HELP ME ON SHOWS BEST OHARA.'[109] Ashbery obliged, and became a trusted assistant to O'Hara on the ground, and supported with the install and with the organization of the celebratory cocktail party (more on this in a moment), as well as supporting as a translator for negotiations with French officials. Later, in February 1959, when *The New American Painting* needed to be disassembled, packed and shipped for the London opening at the Tate Gallery, Schuyler – who seemed to be managing O'Hara's correspondence while he was away – asked Ashbery to 'work for us one more day' and supervise the de-installation together with Gabrielle Vienne, Cassou's assistant.[110] O'Hara and Vienne had worked together very closely as they helped to prepare the work for display, including overseeing the handlers directly in the gallery-space. Ashbery, too, was then well-trusted by MoMA, and Schuyler indicated this by noting how his help would be invaluable given the tight time constraints: 'The cable is very important, because the time allowed for taking down the show, shipping it to London and installing it has been cut to the minimum.'[111] Ashbery also collated the clippings for McCray and noted that 'so far the shows have gotten more good reviews than bad ones, and everybody seems quite interested.'[112] More accurately, the critical reception of the Pollock exhibition was decidedly mixed and split mostly along ideological lines. Broadly speaking, the pro-Communist papers asked, 'why Pollock deserved a one-man show . . . unless on account of his turbulent reputation and recent death'.[113] Other critics, like Dorival, took a more nationalist approach, casting doubt on the appeals of gestural painting to a kind of international language:

This artistic activity is resolutely turned first toward abstraction and then toward originality, of a kind where one of the points made by the exhibition is that abstract art, far from being an international jargon where particularities of national genius are abolished, is also rooted in the countries which produce it as is figurative painting, and is also as rigorously modelled to the likeness of the country and rich in information about the country's essential nature.[114]

This approach is revealing insofar as one of the central claims made by Tapié is categorically refuted. *Informel* abstraction is not any more international (internationalist, or internationalizing) because of its retreat from external reality. For Dorival, the objects and things comprising the world and therefore the nation have their own national peculiarities (although Dorival does not define what these may be). Restany, in the provocatively titled essay 'U.S. Go Home and Come Back Later' reflected that:

> This Yankee rendezvous was not useless. It gave proof to those who didn't know, or didn't want to know, that from now on a spiritual climate exists on the other side of the Atlantic that is capable of bringing some original solutions to the essential necessities of modern art. So go back home, Americans, and come back to us when you have something new to astonish us with: for instance, a second Pollock.[115]

The Americans did not find a second Pollock. But what did happen over the next half-decade, up to and including the *coup de grace* of Robert Rauschenberg's victory at Venice in 1964, when his works were shipped over in US Army crates, was the carefully choreographed expression of an artistic 'spiritual climate'. Perhaps just as importantly as his collation of press releases, Ashbery helped O'Hara navigate the Parisian art-world, fractured as it was, and the two friends organized a cocktail party in honour of the exhibition, hosted by Julius Fleischmann Jr., philanthropist and founder of World Art, Inc., at La Closerie des Lilas on the Boulevard Montparnasse.[116] The invite list was a who's who of the Parisian avant-garde – Appel, Jean Arp, Balthus, Breton, Marc Chagall, Max Ernst, Fautrier, Hartung, Eugène Ionesco, André Malraux, Man Ray, Mathieu, Joan Miró, Pierre Soulages, Jacques Villon – as well as the younger artists with whom the two poets were close personally: Shirley Jaffe, Mitchell, Riopelle. O'Hara even tried to 'invite Brigitte Bardot' but McCray 'just couldn't be led that far out'; many of these invitations were accepted, which Ashbery and O'Hara found 'quite amusing for some reason or another'.[117] However, one such artist luminary, Jean Dubuffet, sent his regrets to McCray that he was unable to attend the cocktail party.

O'Hara's 1959 poem 'Naphtha' might serve to illustrate French references even when he is in New York and opens with a homage to Dubuffet and imagines him doing military service in the Eiffel Tower, leading the poet to exclaim 'how wonderful the 20th Century / can be' (CP, 337).[118] The poem moves from Dubuffet at work in *the* Parisian metropolitan symbol to two lines that stutter and read like caveats or afterthoughts: Dubuffet's position is 'as a meteorologist', as in not active military service, and is dated as '1922', and therefore not during wartime. Instead, and in contradistinction to Greenberg who championed the astounding force of American art as self-evidently wilder or less refined, rougher and more brutal, O'Hara calls on those instead oppressed by American power. These are the outsiders akin to

Dubuffet's *Art Brut* (the phrase he coined in 1945 to refer to self-taught artists 'unscathed by artistic culture') – the Native American labourer, the black musician during segregation, and O'Hara himself, the 'queer sissy' who can only perform accepted codes of masculinity (CP, 338). The poem shifts in an architectonic manoeuvre, remaining high-up, from Paris back to New York, and to the 'gaited Iroquois on the girders / fierce and unflinching-footed', a reference to the Native American labourers who helped construct the city's skyscrapers. The building of a century, the American Century, elsewhere invoked as 'the 20th Century', transitioning into 'our century' and ultimately 'my century', is necessarily complicit in a colonial project that maintained racial inequalities (CP, 337–338). O'Hara continued by stressing a 'debt' owed to the Iroquois and to jazz pianist Duke Ellington, who played 'in the buildings when they are built', an oblique reference to the segregated cafes and bars (CP, 337). The figures in 'Naphtha' are all outsiders from totalizing national histories.

But more than being linked to the 1959 Paris visit and O'Hara's brief correspondence with Dubuffet, 'Naphtha' emerges contemporaneously with the French artist featuring prominently in MoMA's *New Images of Man*, curated by Peter Selz, who would stage a solo show of Dubuffet at the museum in 1962. This all creates the atmosphere of bridging the distances between Paris and New York, France and the United States, in a way that Rona Cran has argued emphasizes the 'complex anxieties and responsibilities felt by many New York artists about living and working in the new capital of the art world, while the former capital deteriorated within the wider context of a politically and culturally weakened Europe'.[119] In the mid-to-late fifties, in the exhibition hall and the poetry collection, to think about Paris was also to think about the United States, and about a sense of order and continuity, of what came before and what might come next, which is linked in the despondent and non-generative act of *to 'fuck'* with questions of cultural relativism:

> [. . .] It is impossible
> to be American if you're not French first it is
> impossible to fuck without thinking of *oeufs sur*
> *le plat* or being welcomed to Paris at night
> after a long boring train ride [. . .][120]

Perhaps unavoidably, France was once more an origin story.

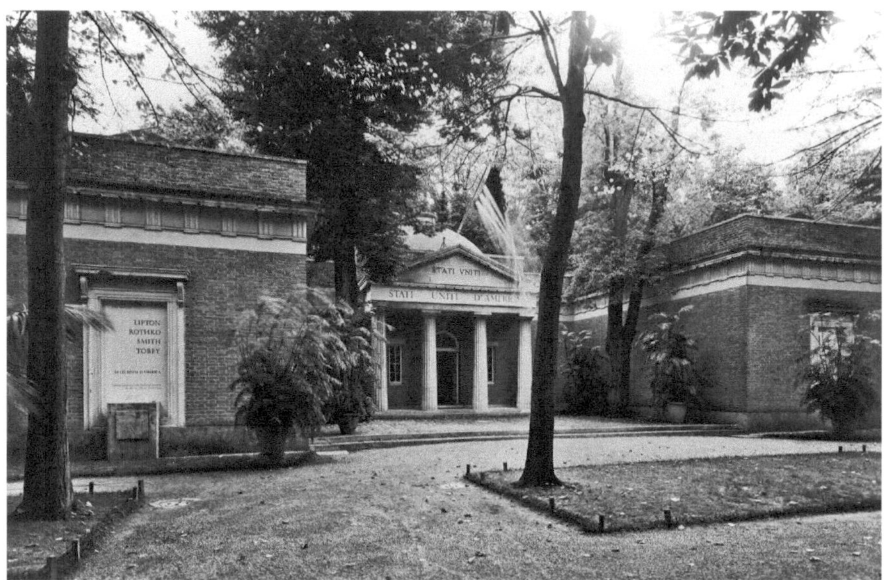

FIGURE 3.1 Exterior of the American Pavilion at the *29th Venice Biennale*. Venice, 1958.

Three | In Favor of One's Time

Frank O'Hara's first responsibility working on the perennial international exhibition calendar was to select work for the American representation at the São Paulo Bienal in 1957. Featuring the first major posthumous retrospective of Jackson Pollock's *oeuvre*, in which his work was entered *hors concours*, the Bienal was in many ways a testing-ground for *Jackson Pollock, 1912–1956*, O'Hara's major memorial display. The São Paulo selections, 34 in total, would remain almost identical to those that travelled to the seven European host institutions over the next two years, which I discussed in the previous chapter. The Bienal also enabled O'Hara to mediate back and forth between abstract and figurative media, and between the promotion of established gestural painters, in particular Franz Kline, and the 'younger painters' Hartigan and Rivers who, as he wrote in the catalogue introduction, 'have formed their styles partly in reaction to abstract-expressionist tendencies, partly in a re-evaluation of the plastic validity of figurative elements'.[1] Hartigan was represented by four paintings, as was Rivers. One of her paintings, which also travelled in *The New American Painting* exhibition in which Hartigan was the only woman artist, the second youngest after Sam Francis, and the only member of O'Hara's inner circle represented, was *Essex Market* (1956). Named after the food market at the intersection of Essex Street and Delancey Street, the painting appears to integrate fragments and morsels of urban life – an awning, flower-stands, commuters – which Hartigan sought to reassemble in her paintings as all 'that which is vulgar and vital in American modern life and [represented] the possibilities of its transcendence into the beautiful'.[2] Whereas Kline, Philip Guston and James Brooks (who were each represented by five canvases) determinedly pursued 'their discoveries in the act of painting', which is to say in the highly subjective process of producing the work largely independent of an external referent, Hartigan and Rivers featured 'recognizable images as points of compositional emphasis and clarification'.[3]

Among the four paintings by Rivers that O'Hara chose for the São Paulo Bienal, *Washington Crossing the Delaware* (1953) had recently been the subject of O'Hara's 1955 ekphrastic poem 'On Seeing Larry Rivers' *Washington Crossing the Delaware* at The Museum of Modern Art', in which he caustically announces that 'our hero has come back to us' in a 'beautiful history' (CP, 233). For O'Hara, *Washington Crossing the Delaware* served as an example of the way that Rivers used 'varying degrees of semi-realistic detail as a strong compositional element in his delineation of space' even, or especially, as that spatial plane is busied and hurried by a build-up that sees the central figure of Washington out of scale with the rest of the scene, or in ambivalent relation to it.[4] Suzanne Ferguson has suggested that this resembles a 'cinquecento nativity' in which the 'background itself is multiple, not single', and that Rivers' 'blatant foregrounding of multiple, contradictory conventions consequently ... [replaces] one myth with another: that of the post-modern Washington'.[5] In this way, it is difficult to settle on whether this reappraisal of a pervasive patriotic myth was *critical* of its perverse status as national genesis, or else performed a *reinterpretation* of that national legend in its own time. The point is that both interpretations emerged; Rivers even later claimed that as the producer of *Washington Crossing the Delaware*, he had the dubious commendation as a 'patriot ... in the eyes of Senator Joe McCarthy'.[6] O'Hara's inclusion of the painting in a national representation at a biennale does raise intriguing questions in relation to the status of American art – and American political power – in 1957. Was O'Hara reaffirming, inadvertently or consciously, this prevalent American patriot myth through the national pavilion at an international exhibition, or else anticipating the camp hijacking of cultural Americanization that would become the dominant Pop mode in the 1960s? The answer is probably both. We will see how O'Hara championed the Neo-Dada and Combine works of Jasper Johns and Robert Rauschenberg simultaneously at the perennial international exhibition, but also how he promoted a certain kind of self-aware American sensibility in order to affirm many of the internationalist claims he was making about American art in 1958/59, in this chapter.

O'Hara also curated a display of sculpture, which included works by Seymour Lipton, David Hare, and Ibram Lassaw. While the international press reception was modest, Lipton was awarded the 'top purchase prize' of the Acquisition Prize for Sculpture, and 'distinguished award' of 100,000 cruzeiros offered by the Jockey Club of São Paulo.[7] If his selections for São Paulo tested the waters for the global reception of American gestural abstraction, then O'Hara's co-curation of the American representation at the *29th Venice Biennale* the following year was the ideal venue to articulate his idiosyncratic approach to this art form, which was still only emergent in the eyes of the world.

I. *29th Venice Biennale*, 1958

On the back of Lipton's victory in São Paulo, the only award given to any of the living American artists, McCray asked O'Hara to work on an even bigger brief and to help curate the American Pavilion at the *29th Venice Biennale* in 1958, with Lipton's recent success surely in mind (Figure 3.1). Described by O'Hara in an unpublished press release as 'the oldest and most extensive periodic exposition of contemporary art in the world', the Venice Biennale was then – and remains – 'the most important exhibition in the international field of cultural exchange for living artists'.[8] Four solo shows (two painters, two sculptors) represented American art in its national pavilion at the *29th Venice Biennale*, the largest since its inauguration in 1895, requiring temporary exhibition spaces to be erected from plywood to support the permanent pavilions and the increase in the number of participants.[9] Sam Hunter, with whom O'Hara often competed for curatorial oversight (until his sudden and somewhat unexplained departure from MoMA later in the year) was responsible for sections on Mark Rothko and David Smith; O'Hara for Lipton, once more, and Mark Tobey.

While there is some truth to Gooch's view that O'Hara felt Hunter's assignments to be 'more major', demonstrated by the fact that he would soon begin research on a touring Smith retrospective, O'Hara had been an international supporter of Lipton, as shown in São Paulo.[10] In the catalogue essay, O'Hara celebrated Lipton's work, which he described as 'an abstract search for the significance of a life experience which was not to be exclusively that of humans', referring to the angular yet biomorphic shapes of the sculptures.[11] O'Hara's narration of the careers of both Lipton and Tobey stressed their development not in the philosophically universal aspirations of abstraction, but first in the socially committed period of the Great Depression and the widespread focus on realist and materialist subjects. On Lipton, O'Hara said: his 'early interest in primitive sculpture, Gothic bestiaries, the painting of Hieronymus Bosch, and German Expressionism, led toward his work of the late 1930s, representational figures carved of wood which made a fierce social commentary'.[12] Similarly, in his catalogue essay on Tobey, O'Hara problematized the strict boundaries that had been policed in the abstraction–realism debate and positioned Tobey between the two extremes:

> After his return to Seattle in 1938, he painted pictures allied in content to the Social Realism of the Depression period, figurative compositions of laborers and mournful elegies of the impoverished and suffering. Many of these works continued and developed his use of 'white writing' in a non-abstract context.[13]

It is worth noting, though, that – like Lipton's Germanic obsessions – Tobey's formative period was coloured by strong international influences, in which he travelled 'in Europe, the Near East and the Orient, and began a long period of intense formal experimentations'.[14] O'Hara balanced the status of two important abstract artists within a longer history, one that was produced by a thorough-going political engagement during the Great Depression, while at the same time eschewing much of the provincialism of that decade by exerting proud engagements with the art of Europe and Asia.

Between its inaugural event leading the national representation in 1954 and 1958, MoMA displayed modern art in its abstract and realist tendencies, as well as between an assertion of national independence and internationalist *Art Informel*.[15] Before 1958, this was most visible when d'Harnoncourt, as the 27th Commissioner in 1954, directed McCray to support Soby and Andrew Carnduff Ritchie in their curation of Willem de Kooning and Ben Shahn at that year's Venice Biennale. For Frances K. Pohl, while De Kooning was one of the major figures of Abstract Expressionism, then seen as the most advanced artistic style in the United States, Shahn's inclusion posed 'certain problems' because of his 'active involvement in various forms of social protest and his belief in the primacy of socially-relevant content in art' that placed him outside of the avant-garde traditions of his time.[16] This moment demonstrates the figurative and even overtly left-wing credentials of some artists that MoMA exhibited at the Biennale during this period dominated by international abstraction. It was a curatorial decision that was motivated, at least in part, by the conviction that displaying an artist like Shahn demonstrates the political pluralism and diversity of formal developments unlike the allegedly uniform art that was produced under the Soviet Union. It is worth remembering that it was on this Biennale that Barr solidified a curatorial position that demonstrated 'our tolerance of self-criticism and diversity of social attitudes'.

Two years later in 1956, MoMA delegated the sponsorship of the American Pavilion to the Art Institute of Chicago. This illustrates how MoMA did not hold an iron grip on representation but sought a range of curatorial perspectives from outside, and so Eva Cockroft was wrong to state that afterwards MoMA 'took sole responsibility for the exhibitions from 1954 to 1962'.[17] In fact, MoMA explicitly wanted to 'emphasize' that it had no 'intention of monopolizing the selection for future years' and that it would 'offer the choice of exhibitions from time to time to other museums in different parts of the country' in order to ensure that 'each American showing [had] a distinct character and flavor of its own'.[18]

When O'Hara selected works by Tobey in 1958, he had an advantage in that the artist's Venetian recognition had been steadily building since *Broadway* (1935–6), his dreamlike figurative tempera, was shown at the *24th Venice Biennale* in 1948. More recently, Tobey had been featured with four canvases (by comparison to the other artists' having one or two) in the thematic exhibition *American Artists Paint the City* when Katherine Kuh, curator at the Art Institute of Chicago and selector of the American Pavilion in 1956, positioned the artist as best-placed to represent 'all the shining lights of America' with a coherent focus on urban representations that made abstraction newly accessible.[19] Kuh had helped promote Tobey in Chicago through his dealer Marian Willard and knew his work well. Despite the fact that the American artists failed to win major prizes at the 1956 event – a disappointment that Kuh attributed to the lack of a one-person show that jurors could focus on above all else – *American Artists Paint the City* was largely well-received by Italian critics, such as Lionello Venturi who, in his catalogue text for Kuh's show, announced that 'American art has truly come of age'.[20] In a MoMA field report from Venice, widely circulated through the Associated Press, Daniel Catton Rich, the commissioner of the Biennale's international jury, proudly announced: 'Europe is imitating our paintings for the first time.'[21]

O'Hara's curation at the *29th Venice Biennale* came at a critical time. Circumstances had changed, even since 1956. 'The year 1958 is generally acknowledged as a watershed in the history of the fine arts exhibition of the Venice Biennale in the postwar period', argued Nancy Jachec, the most authoritative writer on this subject.[22] *Art Informel* had become something of a global phenomenon, and the possibilities afforded to its various strands around the world, from 'India to Egypt, from Israel to Venezuela' according to the French critic Françoise Choay, were extensive and probably a little overly-determined.[23] Choay believed this 'planetary esperanto' or 'universal pseudomorphosis' was merely 'empty of meaning' and instrumentalized like any other commodity in the 'exportation of ideas, fashion and technology'.[24] Silvano Giannelli, in a similarly sceptical tone, wrote in his review of the *29th Venice Biennale*: 'The fact is that, according to the theory of pictorial and plastic documents offered to us by Western nations, one would have been led to believe that at least the whole non-Soviet world has really become, in art, one great country.'[25] If Giannelli was right, and the retreat from figurative representation in painting by the end of the fifties was covertly backed up by the Western cultural establishment and packaged to 'universalize' those countries as a happy family against Soviet art, culture, and society, then the Olympiad palazzos of the Venice Biennale was probably the right place to do it.

But some critics saw the globalism of *Art Informel* not as an artificial construct but as a great virtue capable even of uniting the disparate cultural destinies of nations. Giovanni Ponti, a centrist Christian Democrat Senator, fierce proponent of Europeanist cultural integration, and affectionately the 'doge' of the postwar Biennale, was special commissioner of the long-standing perennial exhibition after being reinstated for a second term in 1957, lasting until 1960, during a period of almost exclusive dedication to *Art Informel*. He saw gestural abstraction as a fundamentally western European enterprise, which was recently developed by their American cousins. Likewise, the classical critic Gian Alberto Dell'Acqua, the new General Secretary of the Biennale, was also a representative for the Council of Europe which pursued an 'Idea of Europe' campaign that sought to 'strengthen cultural relations across the continent' and 'to make Europe a single cultural identity'.[26] In his official introduction, Dell'Acqua called attention to the 'language of the *informel*' which now 'characterises contemporary taste', believing it to be a style and approach consistent with the internationalist appeals that prefigured the 'Idea of Europe' ideology.[27] The international art exhibition was uniquely suited to the promotion of these ideas of the 'lingua franca' of gesture painting, of which the Venice Biennale was the most absolute example, and was characterized 'in the ten years after the end of World War II' by Lawrence Alloway as 'clear evidence of a new, solid, cosmopolitan art world'.[28]

Critics have argued that the *29th Venice Biennale* represented a high-point in the Americanization of what MoMA recognized as the 'oldest and most famous recurrent exhibition in Europe'.[29] 'The presentation of abstract expressionism in Venice', argues Claire Brandon, 'secured its international status and attempted to mark this brand of abstraction as a distinctly American enterprise.'[30] This was only partly true, as McCray and O'Hara struck a balance between stressing the new advances in American art while arguing that those advances were coexistent with the global appeals of gestural abstraction. Indeed, as archival records show, the expression of those supposedly noble aspirations were the very means through which McCray and O'Hara helped ensure American success. In the press release, McCray states that each 'of these artists has been a pioneer, concerned with finding his own personal means of expression. Though all use some idiom of abstraction, they are all deeply concerned with content; their new techniques and formal innovations have been evolved in order to clothe timeless, universal symbols in a language appropriate to our day.'[31] Note how McCray moves from the American vernacular of the pioneer, the modern outlier beset by freedom and angst, crafting an individuated art on their own terms, to the 'timeless, universal' language of this moment – an international moment seemingly all converging on shared material properties associated with *Art Informel*. O'Hara argued for a similar interpretation in his single-artist study by claiming that Tobey's *Written Over the Plains* (1950) was a 'recreation of the specific experience of travel as well as a Whitmanesque invocation'.[32] O'Hara links Tobey with Whitman and necessarily imbues the former's work not only with the beautified, typically American image of the pioneer on the plain, but also with a queer American cosmopolitanism.[33] In this way, O'Hara was furthering but subtly revising the work of previous MoMA curators of Tobey who, in their catalogues and in their travelling displays, have called on the artist to stand for a kind of Whitmanian assertion of the global position of the United States in the world.[34] In his interview and essay 'Franz Kline Talking', O'Hara writes that the:

> painters of this movement, so totally different from each other in aspect, so totally without the look of a school, have given us as Americans an art which for the first time in our history we can love and emulate, aspire to and understand, without provincial digression or prejudice. The Europeanization of our sensibilities has at last been exorcized as if by magic, an event of some violence which Henry James would have hailed as eagerly as Walt Whitman and which allows us as a nation to exist internationally.[35]

This declaration paraphrases the anti-provincial argument in defence of Abstract Expressionism made by O'Hara in 'American Art and Non-American Art', in which he argued that for 'the first time in [American] history an art is appearing which is aware of the rest of the world in a non-imitative way'.[36] His evocation of the 'fatal antipodes', James and Whitman, calls to mind Philip Rahv, literary critic and co-founder of *Partisan Review*, whose essay 'Paleface and Redskin' similarly positioned the two nineteenth-century writers as opposing forces within the determination of the place of American art and literature in the world.[37] Rahv argued that these two writers were the 'purest examples of this disassociation', which was figured as the 'disassociation between energy and sensibility, between conduct and theories of conduct, between life conceived as an opportunity and life conceived as a discipline', and O'Hara argues that Kline and those artists of gestural abstraction around him had reconciled these two competing impulses.[38]

Of course, in describing each artist as a pioneer, McCray was also referencing the largest of Lipton's sculptures, which bore that title, a work that itself straddled abstraction and figuration – and for O'Hara a 'monumental' sculpture that demonstrated the 'lyrical duality of [Lipton's] work' and 'his ability to render articulate the aesthetic relationship of concave forms enclosing space, convex form shielding space'.[39] But if for Lipton the language of the pioneer was predicated more on the 'adventure' and 'struggle' of the universalized 'human hero', and not the myth of the free pioneer on the American plain, then Tobey was presented as even more explicitly an international artist with appeals to the subjectivity of his practice.[40] In the artist's statement that O'Hara had reprinted for the catalogue, Tobey waxed lyrical: 'Our ground today is not so much the national or regional ground as it is the understanding of this single earth. The earth has been round for some time now, but not in man's relations to man nor in the understanding of the arts of each as part of that roundness. As usual we have occupied ourselves too much with the outer, the objective, at the expense of the inner world wherein the true roundness lies.'[41] For the Bahá'í artist Tobey, in line with the central premises of *Art Informel* as articulated by Tapié, the modern artist expresses their cosmopolitan values through a retreat into the 'inner world' of their psyche when creating art. Philosophically speaking, this artist no longer seeks to represent the world of external referents, attached as they are to the particularities of place and therefore nation, but to create from the place where 'true roundness lies' beyond the 'national or regional ground'. In other words, Tobey understood abstraction as an inherently cosmopolitan and humanistic expression because of its turn towards representing radical subjectivity, away from material realities. Some Italian critics were convinced by this framing of Tobey's internationalist credentials. Lionello Venturi, one of the most influential voices in support of abstraction, spoke of a 'renewal' in the arts, but that the 'high level of international abstract art production' at the 1958

Biennale 'does not allow us to dwell on everyone who deserves such a characterisation'.[42] For Venturi, however, Tobey was a highlight: 'a creator of an ideal weave of beauty and of colours' who could even compete with Pollock.[43]

While O'Hara was primarily responsible for the selection of Tobey's work and catalogue, Venice in the fifties was a place to buy and sell as much as to comment on brushstroke and clay, and he also played the role of informal dealer. Until it became politically unfeasible after changes in 1968 following student riots, the Biennale was an art fair replete with sales offices taking commissions. O'Hara negotiated between Tobey's dealer, the Willard Gallery in New York, and Ettore Dian Ferrari, Director of the Biennale Sales Office. He helped sell at least four paintings by Tobey off the wall of the American Pavilion – *Fete* (1944); *Ravine* (1957), a customary gift to the Ca 'Pesaro Galleria Internazionale d'Art Moderna in Venice; *Towards the Whites* (1957), shipped to the Museo Civico di Torino; and *Circus Transformed* (1957), which was purchased on behalf of the Galleria Nazionale d'Arte Moderna in Rome by the Ministry of Public Education for 1.94 million lire.[44] Generally speaking, the press were less ebullient in their praise than Venturi and the national art institutions. Mario Monteverdi joked: 'the great Mark Tobey, but are we kidding?'[45] Indeed, many of the Italian critics – especially those on the Left – doubted the wisdom of any promoter who used public money to assure a national museum that 'enormous spiritual emotion' had been aroused by an artist whose work resembled 'the wool ball ruffled by the cat'.[46] Brutally, Monteverdi argued that even one lire 'would be too much'.[47] Maintaining the view that Tobey was an intellectual lightweight, the painter and art critic Leonardo Borgese wrote that Tobey's work was obsessed by 'the cravings of supreme philosophies, a big boy who wastes his time and enjoys filling canvases with small signs and then he explains them too seriously'.[48] But if Monteverdi and Borgese were persuasive in their acerbic takedown of some of the widely circulated and fairly woolly philosophical statements made by Tobey on his international style of art, they did not sway the Biennale's organizing committee from its Atlanticist predilections. Tobey became the first American to win the Golden Lion, or the International Prize for Painting, since (another Japanophile) James McNeill Whistler in the first Biennale in 1895. It was the greatest success of his career.

In addition to the national pavilion, the International Program accepted an invitation to send works by three young American artists to be shown together in the Italian-owned Central Pavilion with emerging artists from France, West Germany, Great Britain, Spain, and Italy. O'Hara ultimately chose the painters Jasper Johns and Joan Mitchell, and the sculptor Richard Stankiewicz, but the internal debate on this selection exposed some of the generational differences between curatorial staff at MoMA on how best to present American art at the international exhibition. On the evening of 1 May 1958, O'Hara met with Barr and Dorothy Miller to discuss the selection. Who should supplement the single-artist exhibitions on Smith, Rothko, Tobey and Lipton? O'Hara made the case for the inclusions of Mitchell, Stankiewicz and Johns. The latter especially was a source of contention, and several substitutes were also discussed because the conservator Jean Volkmer 'was very dubious' as to the condition of Johns' paintings in encaustic, before O'Hara overruled and assured the conservation team that they could 'travel with safety'.[49] However, Barr had 'some misgivings' around what he derided as 'the "international style"' – the modes of gestural abstraction discussed in this chapter – and feared that Mitchell in particular was vulnerable to 'not being distinct enough from possible entries from other countries'.[50] This exchange exposed the differences in curatorial strategy between an older generation, epitomized here by Barr, and younger curators like O'Hara, who recognized the benefits of pushing a more cohesive, internationalist approach. The Biennale begged it, O'Hara argued. By acknowledging that the fruits of positioning American artists as part of 'the "international style"' and not separate or set against it were great, O'Hara also spoke to a new shift in the dynamics of international painting. Being on the side of overly determined categories of national schools of art – something the Americans had heretofore been so desperate to establish – may backfire if they were so vigorously policed in an exhibition of this kind, despite the temptation to do so in the national pavilion format.

In a reflective memorandum to McCray, O'Hara continued, half in jest and half in earnest, by noting that Barr 'seemed to favor [Jan] Müller as a substitute for Johns rather than [Joe] Steffanelli or [Norman] Bluhm, who also, he felt, represent the "international style." However, the style in question is really "American type" painting and its adoption by artists of other nationalities should not be a disqualifying factor, I think personally, any more than Müller's Germanicism.'[51] In this quip, O'Hara betrays much about his own sense of purpose at MoMA in relation to the curation of a national pavilion in the late 1950s. By curiously identifying the origins of gesture painting as 'American type', an allusion to Greenberg's 1955 essay, it is unclear whether O'Hara gave the title as the art critic's proper designation or whether it should be seen as consistent with the ironic assertion on 'Müller's Germanicism'. The joke here, of course, is that the late Hamburg-born New Yorker Müller, who had died at only 36 earlier than January, would be German if they displayed him as German or not. O'Hara was becoming suspicious, and now lightly mocking, of all these national rivalries. Ashbery was particularly taken by Müller, and praised his 'dream landscapes' in an *Art News* obituary as embodying a kind of 'magical painterliness'.[52] With his block humanoid outlines and often drab palette, Müller resembled Shahn far more rather than any of the gesture painters. It is perhaps in the fact of his realist tendencies that Barr wanted to show Müller, and to maintain his own personally favoured policy of formal pluralism in selection practices at the Biennale from 1954 onwards, as opposed to a disdain of gestural abstraction as such. But O'Hara was nothing if not a man who knew his moment, positioning curatorial choices forward 'in favor of one's time', as he put it in a 1959 poem, and he knew that Müller's works, brilliant as Figurative Expressionist landscapes as they were, would be seen as regressive alongside a display of specifically younger artists in Venice. Mitchell was represented by *October Island* (1956) and *Ladybug* (1957), a work that belies its careful construction with a tonal atmosphere of spontaneous accumulation of gestural brushstrokes. Short and arm-length lashes of paint in marigold, mauve, dark berry, and brown vie for space across the surface of the canvas, which is made up not of negative space from the canvas but blankets of white paint. *Ladybug* was one of Mitchell's transitional paintings: between her lives in New York and Paris, between the linear colour of the mid-1950s urban landscapes to the 'hive' forms of *Mud Time* (1960) and *Calvi* (1963–65), and between her status as a junior figure in the spit-and-sawdust New York scene to one of Abstract Expressionism's most impressive ambassadors internationally.

The Central Pavilion was an opportunity to look forward, with artists from other countries. This meant looking beyond the long shadow of the 1930s, that dire decade for the American economy and a vibrant one for its contribution to realism. But it also meant looking beyond gestural abstraction. Once it became the 'official' style of Venice, it declined. From the perspective of some Europeans looking at Americans looking at Europeans, Pop was the future. Johns, who was then only 28 and whose inclusion was seen as even more of a risk than Mitchell, was represented by three encaustics: *Flag* (1954), *Green Target* (1955), and *Grey Alphabets* (1956). In choosing Johns and Mitchell, O'Hara was making an observation on the future of gesture painting in 1958 that recognized in these two artists qualities that extended them beyond merely New York representatives of Barr's so-called 'international style'. Jachec has argued that 'in an exhibition dominated by gesture painting, and which presented artistic developments on both sides of the Atlantic as equivalent, the American painting entries of Jasper Johns and Joan Mitchell were somewhat out of step'.[53] Nevertheless, both the choices of Mitchell and Johns were framed by the curator Franco Russoli as pragmatic in quality.[54] They were evidence of the American artist's presence in the new 'common international climate', a new kind of artist who could speak the 'linguistic "koine"' in the 'international art scene', but did not have to apologize for being American.[55] This is intriguing and shows the difference in critical opinion between Barr and Russoli as to the definition and significance of any coherent 'international style' of gesture painting at the Biennale. But if Jachec is right that the showing of Johns and Mitchell 'suggests a willingness on the part of the Italian organisers to include the US in a shared cultural project that had yet to be embraced, or fully understood, by their American counterparts', then O'Hara's curatorial pragmatism in anticipating the immediate future of painting in 1958 was a shrewd move.[56] In a highly revealing report reflecting on the achievements of the International Program in 1958, McCray stressed the success of the American representation at the *29th Venice Biennale*, which had, in his mind, 'concentrated attention on recent developments in American art, especially those advanced tendencies which have influenced contemporary European artists, but which have never been shown in Europe on an extensive scale. Acceptance by the European public and press of the originality and vitality of new movements in American art has established a precedent which will henceforth be reflected in almost all other areas of the world. We have won an important battle for the position of American art.'[57]

With its language of victories and triumphs on a global stage, McCray's statement can feel tired and overly familiar to readers today. It is statements like these that add fuel to the revisionist's fire – Eva Cockroft's claim, referencing a 1941 Central Press wire story during the Second World War, that MoMA was now 'the latest and strangest recruit in Uncle Sam's defense line up' feels more than just a passing coincidence.[58] But McCray's confidence also clouds some of the complexities and ambiguities about the status of American art by the late 1950s. Semantics aside, O'Hara's first major foray into the international exhibition was a measured success, and he proved his abilities as a trusted collaborator to McCray when the two men installed the American presentation in August 1958. While he did not visit Kassel himself for the *documenta* festival a year later in 1959, the intensification of the formal and ideological debates on the existence and tentative future of a 'lingua franca' of gestural abstraction had reached fever pitch. Widely acknowledged as a turning point for the history of American art in Germany, *documenta 2* was O'Hara's opportunity to make his mark as an indispensable figure in the International Program.[59]

II. *documenta 2*, 1959

But one can also not overlook the fact that modern art has already become a powerful world-wide means of drawing peoples together. In the past decade it has actually done so and it has been able to overcome all the hindering differences of speech, location, history, racial feeling and folklore. Its forms of expression and its depiction of experiences have, for the first time since its inception, given a positive reality to the romantic idea of a world culture. From Europe over both the Americas, over Africa and Asia as far as the Far East, it has awakened an inner accord and has invested this accord with a speech-form that makes possible direct communication [. . .][60]

In his catalogue introduction to the international exhibition *documenta 2* in 1959, Werner Haftmann, perhaps the most vociferous champion of modern art in postwar West Germany, argued that a 'world language' of abstraction had become a reality. Haftmann focused on the *Art Informel* painters who had emerged in the early 1940s, and who demonstrated that abstraction need not be represented geometrically, but could lyrically express the artist's 'personal mode of existence' (*Daseinsweise*).[61] As discussed, this strand of abstraction was perceived as inherently international, and Haftmann describes its movement like the imperialistic spread of a new style, moving from France to be absorbed by 'the Japanese [Kumi] Sugai, the Chilean [Roberto] Matta, the Cuban [Wilfredo] Lam and the American [Jackson] Pollock'.[62] As in Franco Russoli's sentiments at Venice the year before, these formal correspondences cast thinly-veiled signals to Cold War-era political unions, pan-European and transatlantic, that first provided the backdrop to the formation of the *documenta* exhibition series, established by Haftmann and Arnold Bode, Professor at the School of the Visual Arts in Kassel, in 1955. Crucially, *documenta* was formed after West Germany's admission to the Western European Union (WEU), which was the predecessor to the European Union and established by the Modified Treaty of Brussels, and the North Atlantic Treaty Organization (NATO) in 1954 and 1955, respectively. Originally a quadriennale series of modern art exhibitions, in its infancy *documenta* focused almost solely on abstraction. It had the dual purpose of reconciling German society with a globalized art market and artists banned as 'degenerate' under Nazism, together with showcasing non-communist modernism as formally opposed to East German Socialist Realism. Only two months before Haftmann's speech, the First Secretary of the German Communist Party, Walter Ulbricht, emphasized 'socialist national culture' and its artistic surrogate Socialist Realism as the only official sanctioned style of the German Democratic Republic, of which he was the *de facto* leader.[63] (The absolute rejection of abstract art under the Zhdanov Doctrine in the USSR and its ongoing influence on Soviet satellite states made Dondero's McCarthyite pronouncements on modern art as a communist plot, as late as 1952, seem all the more absurd.) In contradistinction to Ulbricht, Haftmann argued that 'the belief in authority, the will to power, and contemporary forms of political totalitarianism oppose the freedom of the individual' and that abstract art was a consequence of its freedom from restrictions, representational and ideological.[64] As such, the *documenta* project was intended to signal the cultural awakenings of a Europeanist and democratic society, underpinned by liberal capitalism, and was therefore a conscious 'intervention into the polemics of the Cold War', as Charlotte Klonk and Heather Elizabeth Mathews have explained.[65] In Cold War West Germany, art and politics needed an uplift; one was used for the other. Or, as the celebrated art critic Will Grohmann put it a year earlier, in 1958, in a review of *The New American Painting* in Berlin: 'Something happens, and that something is unsettling and at the same time contains the seeds of the future.'[66]

On the opening of *documenta 1* (1955), Bode made this triangulation of art, geography, and politics explicit: 'It is worth promoting – and important to promote – the idea of a common European form of art as part of the Europe movement. Kassel is the German city that is predestined for an exhibition like this. Kassel is close to the East German border, was largely destroyed, and has been very actively reconstructed. It is an exemplary deed to manifest the idea of Europe in an art exhibition thirty kilometers from the East German border.'[67] Bode may have broadly intended that this proximity to the border be a fraternal gesture of rebuilding and friendship, but it reads like the construction of an aesthetic front-line. The success of *documenta 1* led to a second incarnation, but this time the historical scope was shortened to include only 'art since 1945' ('Kunst nach 1945' became the subtitle of *documenta 2*), while expanding its geographical scope to include artworks from the United States. With that said, the overwhelming majority of paintings were more recent. Some 6 per cent of the works exhibited were from first five-year period after 1945; 8 per cent from the second five-year period; and 84 per cent from the third, between 1955 and 1959, of which the vast majority were produced in the year immediately preceding the exhibition itself. 'That is: well over half', offered Wolfgang Christlieb of the Munich-based *Die Abendzeitung*, 'or up to 80% of the exhibition was painted for the exhibition'.[68] Of the 700 paintings included, 685 were non-figurative. For Knud W. Jensen, writing in the exhibition catalogue on the occasion of the *documenta* showing travelling to his Louisiana Museum in Denmark (which had only opened in 1958), this demonstrated the 'victory of non-representational art', which was 'so absolute that it was now just about using freedom, the disappearance of norms, and the unlimited power of expressionism'.[69] Further, the decision to concentrate on painters over the age of 36 necessarily lent the European representation a more conservative and perhaps less contemporary inflection; 'it might have been different', mused Alloway, 'if the age-limit had been lowered by about eight years' and 'admitted American-influenced painters' because, in his view, 'the American avant-garde has been, during the period under review, the main pace-setter for abstract art'.[70]

The collection was ultimately divided into three: painting was shown in the Museum Fridericianum, a domineering neoclassical-fronted former local parliament building; an array of miscellaneous graphic arts and works on paper took up the relatively small Bellevue Schloss; and the blasted shell of the rococo palace, the Orangerie, destroyed during the war and newly opened as an exhibition space, provided the backdrop to sculpture. Bode's staging principle of 'art and ruins' intended to highlight the radicalism of modern sculpture, as shown by Alexander Calder's *Hectopus* (1955), which commanded a central position against the ruins. On the transformational moment when he first visited *documenta 2*, Jensen wrote that the 'bombed-out baroque palaces with their empty window recesses and blackened walls were an effective frame' for the new conditions in which modern art was created under the shadow of history and ongoing division or, as he put it, the 'society of wars, nuclear build-up, mass production and human standardization'.[71] For many who attended, the exhibition heralded the utopian idealism of a new internationalism in art, prefigured by the ambition for European unification and continental rebuilding.

'Dramatic banners outside each of the three buildings and visible from the central square of the city', noted McCray, 'identified each section – red for paintings, blue for sculpture and yellow for graphic works.'[72] A lavishly illustrated three-volume catalogue was also issued, accompanied by a smaller, paper-bound edition. In a move integral to Haftmann's political sense, to 'de-nationalize' was to disregard referential subject matter, and it was at the festival's second incarnation that the language of internationalism reached a new height. Ditching the curatorial blueprint of its Venetian model used in 1955, but consistent with the majority of mid-century biennials and the large-scale perennial exhibition format, Haftmann and Bode opted to display artworks not by nationality, but formally: 'Since it is [. . .] the wish and desire of the committee of *documenta* not to accentuate the various countries in their characteristics, but to call special attention to the multiplicity of international directions in art since World War II, the paintings and sculptures will not be arranged according to nationalities.'[73]

This change in approach was reflected in the list of artists represented, which was now neutral and alphabetical, with national affiliation only given by place of birth and residence. The vexed scheme of displaying art along the borders of political geography was replaced by an emphatic privileging of shared aesthetic correlations. In *The Bulletin*, an English-language magazine of the Press and Information Office of the German Federal Government, on the same day as an article celebrating the arrival of the US Secretary of State Christian Herter to West Berlin under the article caption 'Berlin's confidence in the Western powers', a feature re-printed the *documenta* organizers' expressed purpose. 'The endeavor', read the declaration, 'is to present personalities in the sphere of art, irrespective of their mother tongue', and for Kassel to be 'a centre of attraction for the great fellowship of the friends of modern art'.[74] Abstraction in general, and the work of those artists exhibiting gestural tendencies in particular, was promoted to scaffold the case for a shared cultural history among the Western bloc nations.

And yet this second *documenta*, for all its loud efforts to 'de-nationalize' through the space and dimension of display, fell victim to an ironic logistical oversight. For reasons that most likely pertain to the fact that they were unable to 'assume all the [financial] charges involved in the organization of an exhibition of that size and importance', Bode and Haftmann, otherwise curator-directors for the entire programme, entrusted the independent American representation to the International Program.[75] The choice of artworks 'was made by the members of the Working Committee', remarked Haftmann in his introduction, and only 'in the case of the American Section, did we, for practical reasons, transfer this responsibility to Mr. Porter McCray of The Museum of Modern Art'.[76] This decision changed the entire complexion of the exhibition. In exchange for financing costs associated with assembling and preparing the selection in the United States and collating material for the American section of the catalogue, McCray would be given a 'free hand' so long as a wish-list of artists was included and the tone and approach was consistent with the 'general pattern' of Haftmann's introduction.[77] 'While various organizations in the European countries represented are also cooperating,' reported a self-congratulatory McCray in a project proposal for internal circulation in November 1958, 'the International Program is the only organization that has been accorded the honour of being invited to choose the artists as well as the work included in its national section.'[78] The Executive Committee of *documenta* 2 set aside for the United States some 250 to 300 metres of running wall space, and for a Pollock retrospective up to 60 metres. With that said, the organizers barely acknowledged that they received assistance through various means from other collaborators that fulfilled a similar purpose, such as the British Council, Association Française d'Action Artistique (AFAA) and the Musée des Beaux Arts of Brussels. McCray warned that 'they [*documenta*] do not want to make an exception in our [The Museum of Modern Art's] case'.[79] Regardless, and not for the first time, internationally minded Europeans abandoned the initiative as the International Program solidified its campaign to display American art abroad. While McCray was identified as the organizer of the American representation in the press, described as a 'native specialist' in a critical article by Herta Wescher, it was O'Hara who conducted research and made most preparatory decisions.[80] In a letter to his junior colleague, McCray described the American section as consisting only of 'your selections'.[81]

O'Hara settled on twenty-seven painters, including sixteen canvases by Pollock, who had died just three years previously and remained the artist most likely to attract attention. In alphabetical order, the full list of represented painters were: William Baziotes, Norman Bluhm, James Brooks, Giorgio Cavallon, Willem de Kooning, Sam Francis, Helen Frankenthaler, Michael Goldberg, Adolph Gottlieb, Arshile Gorky, Philip Guston, Grace Hartigan, Hans Hofmann, Franz Kline, Conrad Marca-Relli, Joan Mitchell, Robert Motherwell, Barnett Newman, Pollock, Richard Pousette-Dart, Robert Rauschenberg, Mark Rothko, Theodoros Stamos, Clyfford Still, Mark Tobey, Bradley Walker Tomlin and Jack Tworkov. There would also be seven sculptors.[82] Of those twenty-seven, seventeen had been sent as part of the previous year's seventeen-strong *The New American Painting* exhibition that toured western Europe alongside *Jackson Pollock 1912–1956*, which O'Hara had curated. This time around, O'Hara was 'not particularly anxious' to present the most familiar works of Pollock's career, many of which had travelled for that purpose.[83] There remained however, as in the memorial retrospective, an emphasis on the full span of Pollock's career and not just the high point of his 1947–1950 period when he perfected the 'drip' method. Restany argued that outside of this critical acme, Pollock's output was 'nothing very much' and the fact that the presentation was 'rigorously balanced in point of time' only 'serve[d] to underline the briefness of Pollock's maturity which extend[ed] over a period of barely seven years' (significantly, Restany expands the period to 1946–1953).[84] According to John Anthony Thwaites, one young abstract painter moaned: 'Pollock was wretchedly chosen. Everyone agreed on that.'[85] Elsewhere, a pre-eminent German art teacher was disappointed: 'I expected a great deal. But apart from the big canvas [*No. 32 (1950)*] he seemed to me repetitive and lacking in sensibility.'[86] These remarks demonstrate that, only the year after O'Hara's Pollock retrospective was shown at the Festival of Berlin, there was still the perception that gestural abstraction, or at least its American strain, had not fully arrived – or that it was somehow over-determinedly curated.

But for other critics, precedents were already emerging to see Pollock as a harbinger, in Will Grohmann's words, of 'the reality not of yesterday but of tomorrow', as he put in a review of *The New American Painting* at the Hochschule für Bildende Künste in Berlin the previous spring. Like O'Hara on Tobey, Grohmann saw Pollock as a 'Walt Whitman redivivus' whose 'exuberance of the American continent, the sea, the forests, a vision of this undiscovered world as it was there three hundred years ago, before the pioneers arrived'.[87] A reader today will see the problems with the widespread language of the pioneer on the plains, and rightly scrutinize the idea of the Americas as hitherto 'undiscovered'. But this extended metaphor held widespread currency in West Germany at the time when the idea of nation building was at the forefront of the minds of art critics and statesmen alike. A collective mentality that viewed the world of the late fifties as always on one side of a historical 'Year Zero' – be that the founding of the United States, before and after National Socialism, the advances of modernist painting – filled the pages of critical journals. Regional and national newspaper critics also wrote in these terms, with Albert Schulze Vellinghausen for the *Frankfurter Allgemeine Zeitung* writing that the 'Pollock room [was] a true demonstration of an "oeuvre" which has set a new date for our time, so that we only speak of "before" and "after" Pollock'.[88] The stress on a historicized teleology common to many of Pollock's critics – that the artist had brought about painting's end-times – was absent in O'Hara's writing on him. But O'Hara did place emphasis on chronology when it was useful to open the thematic scope of Pollock's career, as he did in the retrospective selection. This meant that questions of Pollock's formal invention in his mature phase were situated and contextualized in sometimes surprising ways, as O'Hara wrote in his 1959 monograph: 'the crisis of figurative as opposed to nonfigurative art pursued him throughout his life'.[89] In the conclusion of this essay, O'Hara wrote: 'Giving up all that he had conquered in the previous period [1947–50], Pollock reconfronted himself with the crisis of figuration and achieved remarkable things.'[90] O'Hara was one of the very few critics, if not the only major one at the time, who strongly defended the 'before' and 'after' the 'drip' period, and neither does he view the work of the 1950s as evidence that Pollock was in decline, an accusation that many critics, including Greenberg, levelled at him. (Greenberg was wildly hostile to O'Hara's criticism, and singled out his 1959 Pollock monograph as the worst possible version of art writing as 'pseudo-poetry'.[91]) But a memorandum from O'Hara to McCray, written as they were organizing the Pollock presentation, shows an altogether more historicized approach to the artist's career, one that recognizes gradual development over singular revolution and, importantly, argues for an art without 'decoration':

> As you know, I feel that he was a master of several styles, successively discarded, and that it's especially important to show this fullness in an international exhibition where the strength and extent of his achievement is not known, especially so that the most popular period of '47–'50 does not seem like a technical invention or a lucky find of method. Representing the last period, as well as the early works, well creates or at least leads to the means by which the over-all paintings can be experienced and understood without turning to 'decoration' reasoning. I think.[92]

These observations form part of O'Hara's narrative arc about Pollock that would be succinctly expressed at the close of 'Art Chronicle', in which he maintained that 'Pollock had several' more techniques than just those for which he was 'best known' – which was, in his words, 'all about the look'.[93] He defended Pollock's practice, even or especially as he experimented against the codified 'look' that entailed him to be both within and outside what might be characterized as the painting performance of the mature phase that audiences and critics had come to expect.[94] Such an approach also allowed O'Hara to speak in support of Pollock's formal innovations beyond the 'drip' period, as he did in an acerbic exchange with an unnamed British art critic when he selected Pollock's *Out of the Web* (1949) for his memorial retrospective at the Whitechapel Gallery in 1958. In a letter to the editor of *ARTS* after a particularly scathing review, O'Hara defended the work: he 'did not wish to argue about the quality' of the painting, although he did admit he believed it to be 'superb', but to correct the reviewer by explaining how the parts of the canvas were not covered up before the paint was poured, thus giving the effect of 'canvas-colored abstract insets'.[95] Instead, given that Pollock had made the painting on masonite, the areas of naked masonite 'which are revealed as forms in the surface' were cut out, and 'the difference between an arbitrary placement or coverings over certain areas before the surface was even painted and the *decision* to create specific forms by cutting them "out of the web" of paint is quite important'.[96] Thoughtful compositional understandings of how artists made their work like this demonstrate a curator dealing in more than 'pseudo-poetry', and O'Hara regularly stressed the techniques and experimentation in the compositional process. As he did so, he built relationships with lenders and estates through his very public and often unconditional support for artists.

When considering the autonomous selection of artworks for an international exhibition of this kind, especially as we seek to identify the political conditions that determine what kind of messaging that selection is intended to send, the catalogue and its essays are usually an important part of the investigation. In the case of the Pollock representation at *documenta 2*, however, the *documenta* organizing committee reprinted an older essay by Sam Hunter despite the fact that, according to McCray, O'Hara 'had selected both the European Pollock exhibitions and had written more beautifully and more recently on the subject'.[97] Little had changed from the exhibition at the Festival of Berlin the year before, held at the Hochschule für Bildende Künste which Grohmann reviewed with such gusto. As such, this *documenta* became a memorial to four recently deceased American and European modernists. Pollock, whom Haftmann described as 'a dancing Dervish with a dripping paint can performing the desperate choreography of his life', was one of four artists whose 'intensity . . . of nature cost them their lives' over the preceding decade and who were granted their 'own place' in memorial selections.[98] The others were: Willi Baumeister (1889–1955), Nicolas de Staël (1914–1955), and Wols (1913–1951). Pollock, however, was the only late painter given a room of his own. Bode chose *No. 32*, which he positioned against the short side of the room and against which he gesticulated and introduced the paintings, in what became widely circulated promotional photographs of the selection. In order to link American Abstract Expressionism to European gesture painting, the German artist Ernst Wilhelm Nay's equally large *Freiburger Bild* (1956) was positioned in a parallel way in the other main hall.

The shipment from New York proved controversial for several reasons. The decision to allow only the Americans the liberty to curate their own representation had inevitably raised eyebrows among many West German critics, artists and dealers. Some critics, like Albert Schulze Vellinghausen, regretted that various difficulties prevented 'this "world communication in speech"' to be a 'complete demonstration', chief among them 'the ambiguity of the American section, which was undertaken by official authorities *over there*' and 'could not be "moderated" *here*'.[99] So much for 'a powerful world-wide means of drawing peoples together'. Others bemoaned what the American selection signified, which was the narrowing of aesthetic discourse and formal possibilities: 'The debate nowadays is no longer between figurative and abstract art as it was twenty or even fifteen years ago,' rued Guy Habasque, 'but between various modes of abstract expressionism.'[100] In Thwaites' exhibition profile in the November 1959 issue of *ARTS*, the consternation in Kassel spilled over into unapologetic national resentment:

> "'*documenta*'? An American assault on Europe! They dictated their own contribution: chose it, sent it, paid for it. The pictures as big as possible. And look how weakly the Europeans are picked. Don't you see an intention in that? But the whole thing's a failure. They've only got one painter, Mark Tobey. He continues the pictorial thought of Klee; and after all, pictorial thinking is the thing. Why do you think they had to

hang Tobey away from the others? Because he would have shown them up. They're nothing but Freudian-complex illustrators, 'all of them'!"

The speaker? A fanatic, a Communist or a jealous Parisian? Not at all. One of the few art dealers in present Germany who works in something of the grand old style.'[101] This position smacks of anti-American bias, and obvious resentment against perceived American cultural imperialism, and raises important logistical and symbolic questions that return us to the asymmetrical internationalization of postwar art.

For an exhibition expressly orientated towards showcasing a 'world language' of gestural abstraction, it exposes latent inconsistencies that O'Hara and McCray were at liberty to choose as many works as they did. The size and scale felt symbolic, too. Indeed, many of the artworks, the Pollocks especially, some of which measured over 2.6 × 4.5 metres, were so enormous that they required the largest and most prestigious space in the Fridericianum for display. 'The American artists are not, of course, separated from the past', complained Alloway, 'but their intention seems to be to occupy the present as bulkily, as absolutely, as possible.'[102] Floor plans and room allocations had to be altered and rearranged hectically, and many involved were exasperated by the feeling that the American artworks had arrived rather late. Two halls had to be entirely vacated for the International Program's contribution and, with cruel irony, they afforded the only arrangement maintaining the national logic Haftmann and Bode desperately sought to avoid.

From Moscow, McCray reported this advantageous set of circumstances to O'Hara with a definite tinge of competitive conquest:

You should be quite proud of your selections which make the American selection overwhelmingly dominate the show. They have given Pollock the only single large gallery to himself and it is quite handsome. Their effort to integrate the Americans with the Europeans did not work for with every effort our artists knocked Hell out of the others. This worked to our disadvantage in the end, for they had to isolate the Americans for which they had not provided sufficiently continuous wall space. As a result, our people were frequently shown so that upon entering a large area one is confronted by some 8 or 10 paintings all in a series of planes in busy juxtaposition. The Newmans and Stills are hung in a second tier very high and are on the eye level from a series of intricate bridges that run through the second floor.[103]

We might treat McCray's statement as rather flippant, even chauvinistic, and as a private riposte to the public anti-American criticism inevitably expressed after the perceived privileges accorded to the Americans. But despite being 'extraordinary . . . in size', even 'colossal' in its scope, McCray's reservations regarding 'busy juxtapositions' in the display were well-founded.[104] On arrival, with the paintings already on the walls, McCray identified some sixteen works omitted from display, including Robert Rauschenberg's *Bed* (1955) and Joan Mitchell's *To the Harbormaster* (1957), both of which I will return to in a moment. 'All in all about paintings must be hung', McCray quipped.[105] One of Kline's paintings, most likely *Myceanae* (1958), was hung horizontally, which meant the white paint drippings appeared as though they ran towards the top of the canvas. Barnett Newman's *Cathedra* (1951) was badly damaged in transit, as was Sam Francis' *Deep Orange on Black* (1955) which had been shipped folded and had created severe cracks in the surface. (The fact that *Cathedra* was badly damaged in transit only added to the comedy of errors that attended its unfortunate display: a popular work, it was nevertheless dismissed by audiences and critics alike as a misplaced table-tennis table.) Delays to the arrival of the publicity papers, which did not arrive until the day before the press review, and the biographies (which arrived later still) meant that for the opening days the International Program relied on press cuttings and photographic material from the Amerika-Haus across the road from the Fridericianum. Despite these issues, the general perception of American dominance of the exhibition was palpable. The handsome young art dealer Rudolf Zwirner, who was then only twenty-six but had just opened his first gallery in Essen and was commissioned as General Secretary to *documenta* 2, reflected on the confrontational, juxtaposing, and American-led atmosphere in 1959:

> The second *documenta* . . . was intended as an apotheosis of international Art Informel; it ended up as its funeral. Unavoidable comparisons between paintings by Pierre Soulages and Franz Kline, or between the Tachists and Pollock, revealed differences not only of principle but quality . . . The confrontation was total, and so was the effect. . . . École de Paris prices and paintings tumbled off their pedestals, and the pro-American euphoria mounted slowly but surely, until the 1970s.[106]

There was a lot to base the euphoria – or resentment – on. As Bode's handlers and the American delegation moved the works into the Fridericianum, this conviction was quite transparent in the overpopulation, even surplus of gestural abstraction from New York, and caused economies of space that meant wooden mezzanine sections had to break up and organize the rooms. Three archival photographs taken of the same room and from the same wall but from different (although partially overlapping) perspectives demonstrate this point well. In the first, seen from a central position on one wall of a room dedicated to postwar American painting, we are immediately struck by the claustrophobic positioning of the extensive modular panels that permit only two visitors to comfortably pass and view the paintings displayed on this narrow viewing corridor (Figure 3.2). Note the difference in how space was used here compared to the Pollock room. The reviewer for *Süddeutsche Zeitung* lamented simply: 'The picture gallery is crowded.'[107]

On the reverse of the archive photograph, O'Hara scribbled the identities of the paintings, from left to right: Tomlin's *Number 10* (1952–53), Kline's *Painting Number 2* (1954) on the far facing wall; and two works by De Kooning, *Street Corner Incident* (1955), lent by Barney Rossett, and *Suburb in Havana* (1958), seen through either side of a dividing panel on the right. Two canvases by Theodoros Stamos, somewhat obscured, can be identified in the left foreground. The exhibition was described as a 'Labyrinth der modernen Kunst' (Labyrinth of modern art) by a contemporary newsreel held by Das Bundesarchiv (UFA Wochenshau, July 1959), which recorded a lengthy succession of diplomatic officials arriving into Kassel, followed by a parade of fashionable West German attendees.[108] Haftmann made the 'labyrinth' a staging principle for *documenta 2* as a whole, as Harald Kimpel and Karin Stengel note in their essay on the exhibition: 'While the exhibition

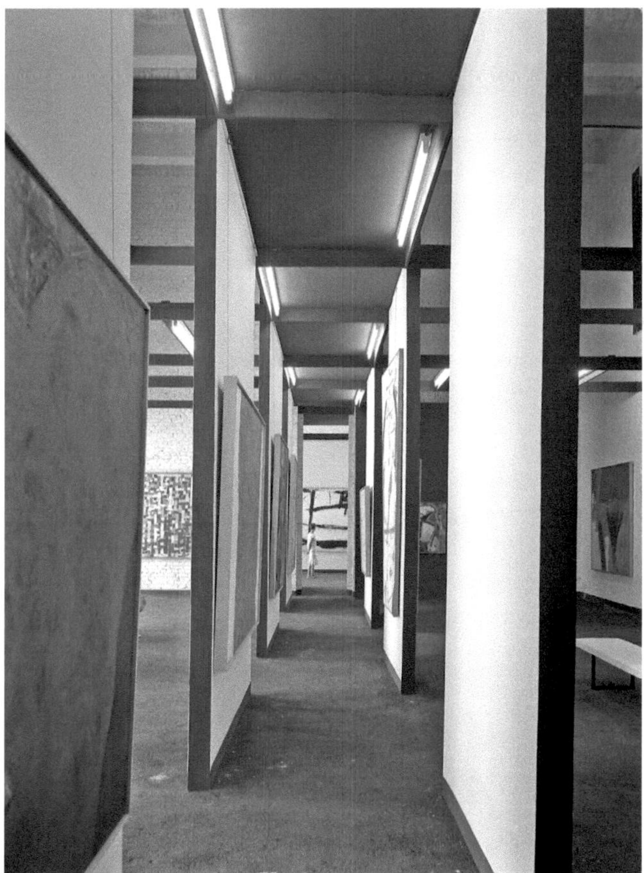

FIGURE 3.2 Exhibition view of *documenta 2* (1959).

presented itself as a directory through the labyrinth of contemporary art, it appeared as a labyrinth itself, where a minotaur waited around every corner.'[109]

In the second archive photograph, we see the upper tier that McCray criticized at the top left of the image, as well as the space divided by the intercalation of the walls, and the suggestion of a secondary viewing gallery at the top right if not the stairway itself, which allowed for different viewpoints – both in perspective and transversely (Figure 3.3). And finally, we see more clearly Bode's interior structure – what McCray described as a 'vast shell . . . transformed into a Mies van der Rohe architectural maze' – that operated throughout the Fridericianum in order to present as many pictures as possible (Figure 3.4).[110] The black beams construct a grid-like structure that support the temporary vertical panels, extended from the floor to almost the ceiling with paintings affixed in the lower half on

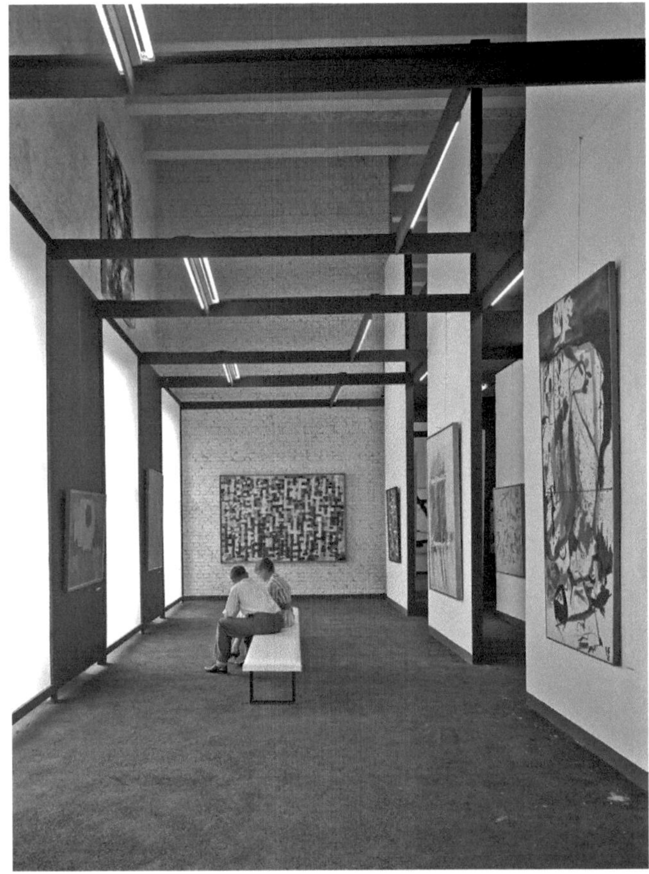

FIGURE 3.3 Exhibition view of *documenta 2* (1959).

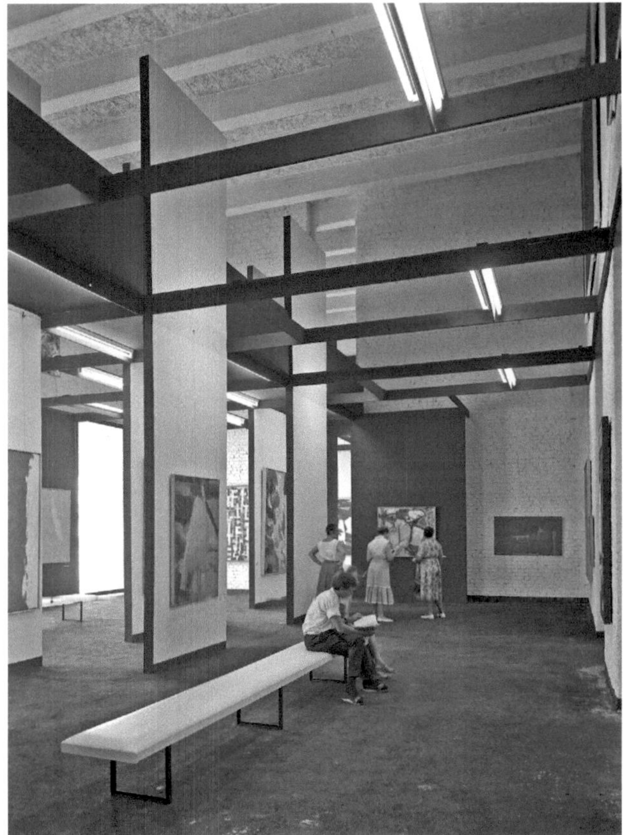

FIGURE 3.4 Exhibition view of *documenta 2* (1959).

shantung in shades of grey, black, white and red. Strip LED lighting was positioned diametrically in some areas of the gallery-space. As we note from this image, the open space (around two metres) above the beams allowed natural light, from a large exterior window on the left background, to pass through so the room was not reliant on artificial illumination alone. In this scene, three paintings by De Kooning, *Detour* (1958), more clearly *Street Corner Incident* (with attendees observing), and *Painting* [hereafter by its informal title, *Summer Couch*] (c. 1943), which was mounted on the permanent brick wall, and one by William Baziotes, *Morning* (1959), rather claustrophobically announced the predetermined nature of the American representation. At this time, O'Hara had De Kooning's *Summer Couch* in his possession but, unlike the other four private collectors who lent work by the artist, chose to remain anonymous on the wall text and catalogue. (We know it was O'Hara's De Kooning, though, because he had scribbled his surname in parentheses with red pen beside the entry on the Museum checklist.) Fairfield and Ann Porter had given the painting to O'Hara after a visit to their 'labyrinthine sprawl of a house in Southampton' during the early 1950s (Fairfield abruptly retrieved the painting around eight years later when he was short of money).[111] 'It was out of the blue,' O'Hara recalled on the gift, 'completely unexpected.'[112] Joe LeSueur described *Summer Couch* as 'semi-abstract and influenced by [Arshile] Gorky' and having 'brilliantly contrasting colors, predominantly bright orange and bright green, along with blue, pink, yellow, light purple, and umber'.[113] Edith Schloss remembered how everyone 'in those days borrowed paintings from each other or exchanged them', some being lent on ambiguous provisos and others commandeered for this purpose or that, which was all part of the spirit of friendship at the time.[114] Sometime after he had 'lent' De Kooning's *Summer Couch* to O'Hara, Porter, 'the most generous of men', as Schloss put it, 'discovered the green painting on Frank's wall in Manhattan. "By the way, Frank, bring it back", he said. "It's really quite interesting." Frank was hurt. "But you gave it to me!" There ensued one of the first art world quarrels.'[115] O'Hara managed to hold on to *Summer Couch* in his University Place apartment – where, over the course of recordings for 'Franz Kline Talking', Franz Kline exclaimed: 'That's Bill's, isn't it? Terrific! You can always tell a De Kooning' – as well as above his desk at MoMA.[116] A work that returned De Kooning to a version of figuration after a period painting in a late Cubist style, *Summer Couch* was reworked over a more complex composition underneath, and depicts either a puckered mattress or a reclining body with jagged edges, or a representation somewhere between the two.[117] It also inspired O'Hara's poem 'Radio' (1955), in which he aspires towards his 'beautiful de Kooning', a symbol of leisure and freedom, that along with operas by Sergei Prokofiev is what the poet surely deserved after he trudged 'fatiguingly / from desk to desk in the museum' (CP, 234). The poet, at work, asked 'Am I not / shut in too' (CP, 234) and it is an irony that as *Summer Couch* was transported from O'Hara's office to the walls of the Fridericianum, its interpretation as a canvas that privileged abundance over restraint was then 'shut in' by the architectures of display.

But O'Hara's leadership of the selection process this time around led to bolder choices, in 1959, than De Kooning: perhaps most notably, Robert Rauschenberg. This was still five years before Rauschenberg caused a storm in western Europe, capped by his victory at the *32nd Venice Biennale* in 1964, and Rauschenberg and Johns were little known in Europe, especially compared to the Abstract Expressionists. O'Hara decided to ship three of his Combines, works that attached found objects to a traditional canvas support: *Bed* (1958), *Thaw* (1958) and *Kickback* (1959).

The latter two paintings were displayed in the exhibition's parcourse. Given that *Kickback* featured a necktie and a pair of trousers as part of its overall assemblage, enthusiastic visitors to the exhibition deemed it acceptable to add their own collaged items, which had to be removed on a daily basis by bemused security staff. *Bed*, today one of Rauschenberg's most famous works, was deemed too provocative with its suggestion of scatological, ejaculatory or hematological drips of paint. Or, as Adrienne Rich put it, the 'kindly quilt' that became an 'unsleepable site of anarchy' in which the 'horizontal' bed is now 'vertical' and covered with 'inarticulate liquids spent from a spectral pillow'.[118] Rauschenberg's *Bed* was quietly relegated to a secretary's office, although it was reprinted in the catalogue, alongside *Thaw* and *Kickback*. *Bed* referenced several important stylistic movements that were then associated with American modernism: Rauschenberg mixes the 'drip' method of Pollock, and the material recordings of fluid distribution, with the recuperation of the Dadaist readymade that would develop a mainstream alternative to Abstract Expressionist hyper-masculinity and earnestness by the end of the decade. Some German critics, many of whom were not won over by the exhibition's self-issued mandate to exhibit abstraction over figuration and realism, singled out Rauschenberg's Dada style as derivative of European precedents. Helmuth Kotschenreuther, a reviewer with *Erlangener Tageblatt*, bemoaned the abstract artists' lack of radicalism, apparently marketed for the demands of a German art market guided by American trends. For him, the Dada constructions of Alberto Burri and Rauschenberg had been 'sold out, promoted, premiered, and exhibited with deadly seriousness at *documenta*'.[119] Many collectors, however, were ahead of the critics and conversant with the movements of the art market in New York that had repercussions in West Germany, with Heinz Beck arguing that Abstract Expressionism did not 'represent a radical breakthrough such as the one pop art came to initiate'.[120]

O'Hara wrote 'For Bob Rauschenberg' in May 1959, while he was putting together the finishing touches to the *documenta* selection. In this poem, after deliberations on music ('so easily drowned in Liszt') to prose ('I despise my love for Pasternak') and poetry ('the heavenly aspirations of / Spenser and Keats and Ginsberg'), O'Hara moves to Rauschenberg's intimate collagist aesthetic and to, in the artist's words, 'the gap between . . . art and life':

> what
> can heaven mean up, down, or <u>sidewise</u>
> who knows what is happening to him,
> what has happened and is here, a
> paper rubbed against the heart
> and still too moist to be framed.
>   (CP, 322)[121]

With its register of emotional latency taking on a materiality of incomplete exposure, which is vulnerable to a biographical reading, O'Hara appears to anticipate the curatorial processes that beset the Combine's (abandoned) exhibition at *documenta 2*. The ambiguous line 'still too moist to be framed' implies that *Bed* reproduces an excess of emotion and intimacy that resists

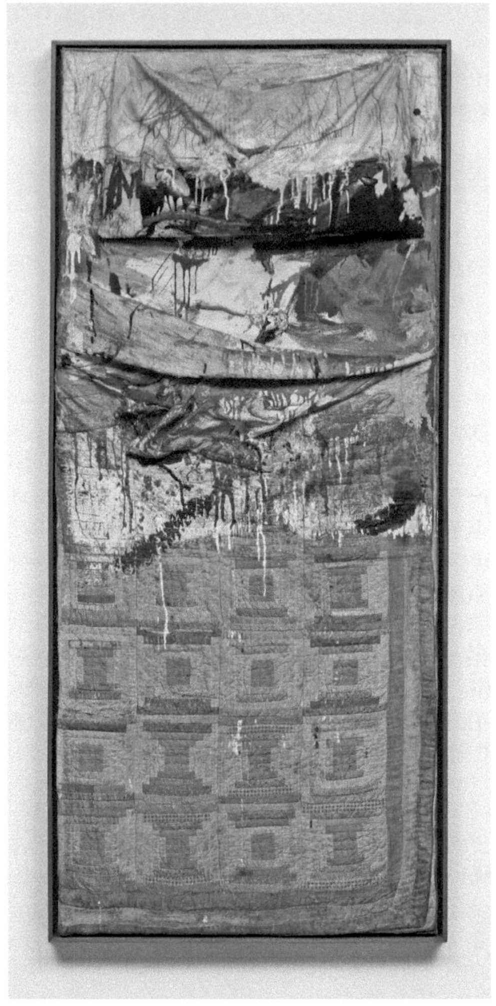

FIGURE 3.5 Robert Rauschenberg, *Bed*, 1955. Combine: oil and graphite on pillow, quilt, and sheet, mounted on wood support. 75 1/4 × 31 1/2 × 8 inches (191.1 × 80 × 20.3 cm). The Museum of Modern Art, New York. Gift of Leo Castelli in honour of Alfred H. Barr, Jr.

the conventions of gallery display. In drawing attention to the emotional vulnerability of the work, O'Hara also highlights Europe's apparent unreadiness for Rauschenberg's art. The spatial organization of *Bed*, 'up, down, or sidewise' is given as less interpretatively important than the meaning generated by defamiliarizing the contours of our intimate lives to feel them differently. *Bed* privileges experiential honesty (to 'what has happened') and presence (to 'here') over the more codifiable observations of material form. 'I think a picture is more like the real world', Rauschenberg once noted, 'when it's made out of the real world.'[122] *Bed* remains a difficult work to interpret, not least because its power is inextricable from the simple truth that we are looking at a familiar object, even if it has been transformed from likeness.

O'Hara's poem, retrospectively understood through the lens of the artwork's controversy in Kassel, might serve as the most total example of his philosophy of the 'living situation'. Rick Barot addresses these difficulties in his essay dedicated to the Combine: 'Is the painting a playful folly? Is it an accusation? Is it a political comment? Is it a story? Is it a joke? Whether the slashes of paint should be read as impudent gestures against the domestic sublime of the Eisenhower years, or a pitying suggestion of a specific household's travail, the explosive paintwork is movingly ambiguous. The bright affront of it, and its sad anomie, seem pointedly American.'[123] If the 'pointedly American' quality of *Bed* anticipates the Pop recuperation of domestic objects, in part to critique the high seriousness of gestural abstraction, then the work may have appeared somewhat incongruous in the halls of the Fridericianum in 1959. Europeans' perceptions of American art were changing. Pierre Restany was all too sensitive to this: 'We have an immediate example in Rauschenberg (who is 34 years old). Rauschenberg, with his extraordinary mountains, frankly discloses his Dadaist derivation. The only "young" one among the great, his unconventional and unorthodox works display a fine intransigence, coupled with a very sure instinct for the possibilities of the specific plastic materials he employs . . .'[124]

Haftmann and Bode's expansive definition of a present that looked backwards from 1959 to the regenerative possibilities of 1945, combined with their attendant desire to solidify the coherence of an international language of gestural abstraction, feels like the last calls to a future that would not respond. Rauschenberg represented the efforts of contemporary art in the 1960s to free itself from the historical category of modern art and, in so doing, the break in the link for such internationalizing beliefs in a global art. Nevertheless, in representing so clearly the historical approach to gestural abstraction as a 'lingua franca', *documenta 2* was an important point in exhibition history, in which O'Hara played a significant and, as the driving force of the American representation, singular role.

O'Hara's selection process had been beset by accusations of preferment at home as abroad. When O'Hara was deciding on which work should be shipped to Kassel, the abstract artist Friedel Dzubas felt he had been overlooked. A German Jew, Dzubas was born in Berlin and had fled Nazism in 1939, when he settled in New York and shared a studio with Helen Frankenthaler.[125] The opportunity to be shown in West Germany with his American contemporaries naturally excited Dzubas, both because the exhibition offered the express purpose of showing refugee artists who had fled Germany – *documenta* was imagined, perhaps above all else, as a historical corrective to Adolf Ziegler's *Degenerate Art Exhibition* in Munich in 1937 – and because of its emphasis on representing disparate examples of pan-continental styles of abstraction. Once he had heard that Ernst Goldschmidt, who sat on the *documenta* organizing committee, was interested in showing him, Dzubas approached his dealer, Leo Castelli, and suggested that they discuss the matter with McCray or O'Hara (whom, Dzubas mentioned, he ran into 'at least once a week and [was] friendly with').[126] Castelli's advice, however, was that would be the 'wrong policy' and that MoMA 'usually responds negatively [when dealers] push anything or anybody'.[127] But there was another issue. Dzubas was frustrated when he learnt that Rauschenberg and Norman Bluhm had been chosen, two artists in Castelli's stable. When Dzubas confronted Castelli, Dzubas was told that he was not as close personally to O'Hara as these two artists. 'This, of course, leaves me again with the bitter taste of the seeming importance of who is a good friend at a crucial moment', Dzubas wrote regretfully to Goldschmidt, 'rather than what the free objective worth of one's work may be.'[128] Integral to Dzubas' criticism was that O'Hara had not visited 'the most prominent galleries' and had certainly not 'made any contact or specific request' to see his work with Castelli, and 'therefore could objectively not possibly have known what he had decided against'.[129] Dzubas' grievance exposes some of the central problems of the American representation at *documenta* 2, as well as O'Hara's personal brand of curatorship.

The narrative that presaged *documenta* 2 relied on a certain kind of 'objective' thinking: that there was a determinable universalism to the kinds of artistic production of the period that was borne out of non-objective modes of representation. This highly individuated subjectivity that was then manifest in variants of gestural abstraction, or so this view goes, could be readily identified, and grouped together. Works of this kind – Haftmann's gashes, thrusts and tugs – became manifestly identifiable, especially in the works produced within the year of the exhibition. Egon Vietta, who participated in a lively discussion on the merits and future of abstraction in the pages of the *Frankfurter Allgemeine Zeitung* during and after *documenta* 2, acknowledged that the 'spontaneous, deliberate development' of *Art Informel* will pass onto a new style, perhaps Pop Art, but that he 'resolutely refuse[d] to allow the current lack of an objective (*gegenständlichen*) genius who could measure up to [Jean-Paul] Riopelle, Wols, or [Hans] Hartung, Baumeister or many promising young artists to be blamed on the non-objective artists'.[130]

But in this way, it must be remembered that exhibitions are always put together by people (conditioned by their own subjectivities), just as artworks are always made by people (likewise conditioned by their own subjectivities). The format of an exhibition might be rationalized by the genre or medium of work on display, and certainly by the constraints of architecture, but the dilemma (and quite possibly, even the impossibility) of determining the 'objective' quality of an artwork remains. O'Hara may not have chosen Dzubas' work because he did not believe it represented the 'pattern' of *documenta 2* (or indeed that it represented it *too* much); or because he personally did not think it as good as the works that were chosen; or, as Dzubas feared, because he did not visit Castelli's gallery to take a proper inventory of the new styles in New York galleries at all. Dzubas' criticism holds even as we acknowledge O'Hara's curatorial process, in which he would oftentimes bypass the middle management of dealers and gallerists to visit the artist's studio directly. 'I have just been to Franz [Kline]'s studio', O'Hara scribbled in a memorandum as he made the selections, 'and, while he is working a lot, there is nothing completely finished that would allow one to decide that it was preferable to *Delaware Gap* [1958], that terrific painting which was just shown in the Janis *8 Americans* show.'[131] O'Hara leant on Sidney Janis to reserve or, failing that, to sell the painting with a loan to *documenta* as a condition of sale, despite there being other possibilities. Why? O'Hara believed that the painting was '*superb*'.[132] As a curator and art critic, O'Hara 'neither views art from an elevated vantage point', writes John Yau, 'nor presents himself as an omniscient narrator or puppet master who defines art according to a narrative he himself has created'.[133] O'Hara never sought 'objectivity' in art. For him, that too distracted from the 'living situation' of the art and the exhibition.

There may also have been other, and no less personal, reasons for O'Hara's selections. As mentioned previously, one of the sixteen artworks that was shipped to Kassel but not originally displayed on McCray's arrival was Joan Mitchell's *To the Harbormaster* (1957), named after O'Hara's 1954 lyric and on loan from Eleanor Ward. How could O'Hara resist the temptation to choose this painting? How could he have chosen it 'objectively', even if he tried? The canvas stayed in the custody of the International Program for several years after it was lent to *documenta 2* and was hung for a time in McCray's office.[134] 'To the Harbormaster' is in many ways a love letter to Rivers, as the poet, beset 'by the waves' is unable to master his 'Polish rudder' (Rivers had Polish–Russian heritage) and ultimately 'unable / to understand the forms of my vanity' (CP, 217). *To the Harbormaster* is one of Mitchell's greatest achievements because of its balance between fiercely controlled brushstrokes in crimson and ultramarine (what Judith E. Bernstock called the 'cacophonous frenzy of short, crisscrossing strokes of intense colour') and its lyrical flow of intertangled aleatory drips.[135] Mitchell's painterly response, a polychromatic racket that pulses with short, staccato strokes that pull out and into the centre, is itself an expression of what in the poem O'Hara identifies as 'tying up' and 'then deciding to depart' (CP, 217). It is also important because of the way that Mitchell was now experimenting with much bigger canvases, the agitation of the painting intensified by full-stretched, arm-long sweeps at the top of the canvas that apply pressure to the turmoil below. Bernstock called this 'the excitement and the anxiety of constant departures'.[136] O'Hara may not have made it to *documenta 2*, but 'the excitement and the anxiety of constant departures' would be a persistent feature of his life as a curator for MoMA, just as it was in his career as a poet.

Four | Blue Territory

It was the last Friday in May, 1957. As sunlight darted across the turquoise ceiling fresco of Grand Central Station, stretching out over celestial dots and astrological signs, Frank O'Hara arrived to meet Helen Frankenthaler. Up until this weekend, the curator and artist were friendly but not intimate, acquaintances but not compatriots. Their circles overlapped like the intersection of a Venn diagram: O'Hara was only a year into his assistant curatorship at MoMA, and his circle centred on the ragged crowd of downtown bohemians, while Frankenthaler's was the scene of uptown cocktail parties, the world in which she grew up. 'My life', Frankenthaler said later in an interview, 'is square and bourgeois.' She thought of herself as a 'controlling [person], . . . afraid of big risks' who never climbed mountains or got on the back of a motorcycle, or went on safaris: 'My safaris are all on the studio floor. That's where I take my danger.'[1] More on risks shortly. While Frankenthaler was the romantic partner of Clement Greenberg from 1950 to 1955, her sojourns to Long Island were most often to visit Jackson Pollock and Lee Krasner at their cottage in Springs, or upstate to Bolton Landing to see David Smith and his second wife Jean Freas. O'Hara's set were a touch younger than Greenberg's, included Nell Blaine and Jane Freilicher, and centred around Fairfield Porter's palatial white house on South Main Street in Southampton. By the summer of 1957, though, social constellations were shifting. Frankenthaler was now single, and Greenberg's snide comments about O'Hara's camp friends quietly receded into the distance. She was going to spend the weekend at Grace Hartigan's Creek cottage; O'Hara had persuaded Larry Rivers to lend him the use of an attic in his old farmhouse for much of the summer. 'The topics ranged from art (their struggles) to life (where they were going)', noted Mary Gabriel, 'to the drunken ridiculous', as the cast of friends swam all day, swilled chilled vermouths in the early evening, dined at Alfonso Ossorio's, and drank late at Barney Rossett's.[2]

Everyone on the trip to the Creeks felt as though they were in transition, or on the edge, perhaps, of something significant. O'Hara was working on *The New American Painting* and *Jackson Pollock 1912–1956* exhibitions, both major undertakings, and working on a new series of poems for Rossett's Grove Press. Frankenthaler's career was heading in only one direction:

famously, a few months earlier, she had posed for Gordon Parks, the most famous black photographer in the United States and the most sought-after lensman of *Life* magazine, in her plush West End Avenue apartment and studio. In the photographs, Frankenthaler coyly angles her chin downward and tries on a fierce and sultry stare. Wearing a salmon button-down shirt tied at the waist and a white pencil skirt, surrounded by the pastel shades of her recent paintings, Frankenthaler embodied the article's headline, published on 13 May: 'Woman Artists in Ascendance.' In his biography of Frankenthaler, Alexander Nemerov wrote that 'her direct gaze suggest[ed] a pride and power of ownership, a sense that she is the resident mermaid of this aqua-exotica, the maker of all the wall-to-wall shades of blue that translate so well to the magazine's bright pages'.[3] This survey piece also featured sections on Hartigan, Blaine, Joan Mitchell and Jane Wilson. On her frustrations about women-only exhibitions and gendered categories that would not be asked of their male counterparts, Elaine de Kooning said that 'to be put in any category not defined by one's work is to be falsified'.[4] But if the article itself engaged in a sleight of hand – seemingly promoting these women artists as *ascending* while essentializing them as women and cutting them off from their male counterparts who, by this logic, might be said to have *ascended* – Parks sought to neutralize this approach by surrounding his subjects with their canvases. Over Frankenthaler's shoulder is *Mountains and Sea* (1952), often seen as her most radical and certainly most celebrated work, not least because it is the first painting in which she pioneered her 'soak-stain' technique, which involved turpentine-thinned oil paint poured from coffee cans onto unprimed raw duck canvas, which laid horizontally on the floor, usually with no predetermined sense of orientation.

Inspired by a travelling holiday on Cape Breton, a rugged and irregularly shaped island on the Atlantic Coast of Nova Scotia, in which Frankenthaler painted landscapes with folding easel equipment, *Mountains and Sea* is certainly an abstraction but one that feels true to the landscape. It is a painting about the memories of a place as opposed to a rendering of the place itself, which was nevertheless contemporaneously described by critic Sam Feinstein as a 'lyric, washy, . . . composite of fluid spontaneities'.[5] Frankenthaler dated *Mountains and Sea* – '10/26/52' – because, many presume, she wanted to record the moment of revelation in which she developed the soak-stain technique. It is easy to see how O'Hara, the restless episodicist, who wrote occasional poems on the birthdays of friends and famous composers, or on the days when a friend travelled from one city to another, would have admired this gesture.[6] 'Episodicists feel and see little connection between the different parts of their life, have a more fragmentary sense of self', Julian Barnes wrote on Lucian Freud, 'and think that one thing happens, and then another thing happens.'[7] I can imagine that O'Hara liked to think that Frankenthaler's marking that day in October had little to do with keeping the date for posterity, as though a pre-emptive defence against the misogynistic claims on technical and stylistic precedence by male artists. Instead, by recording the date on the canvas, Frankenthaler acknowledged the fact that life moves forward, passing scene by scene.

The painting that takes up most of the space in Parks' photograph, however, is not *Mountains and Sea* but another abstract canvas, perhaps another landscape study, *Blue Territory* (1955), which would also give its name to a 1971 Mitchell work (one of her 'Fields' paintings), as well as a difficult, abstract and brittle poem by O'Hara.[8] Bizarrely, even though the painting was already finished and previously exhibited, Anne Wagner notes how it 'was demoted: sent back to the floor of its maker's studio, [where] it lay there passively, its once wild expanse doing domestic service as a rug', all to 'document this new and unfamiliar quantity, the young and photogenic female painter'.[9] The painting thus becomes a kind of prop, but a prop that is not only exigent as a visual framing device for Frankenthaler's body but also to remind the viewer that hers is a life lived in the company of art. There is no distinction between the world that she inhabits and the world of her abstractions. Art and life are one. *Blue Territory* itself is an aqueous comportment of turquoise curves and jagged lines of blood orange, off-white, and teal, some lined like carriages that seem to have been made by a firm and not a coarse instrument across space, as though Frankenthaler had taken the back end of the paintbrush to delicately create zones of thinned out tracks in the sheer expanse of flooded plains beyond. When imagining the painting as a territory unto itself, as a space in which action is recorded and gesture traces the extent of the artist's reach, we imagine Frankenthaler on the outer perimeter of the canvas, kneeling and reaching into the centre. 'When I say gesture, my gesture, I mean what my mark is', Frankenthaler asserted, effectively conjoining the verb of making a 'gesture' with the noun of the 'mark', as though the paint is the past tense residue of her movement across space.[10] It is this that she defines as a kind of personal 'style', which O'Hara found so compelling when preparing the 1960 Jewish Museum retrospective of her work. *Blue Territory* constituted 'a shift' in Frankenthaler's way of working from the mid-fifties.[11] In an interview with Barbara Rose, Frankenthaler describes feeling 'lonelier because [she] was lonelier' during the period of her making the work, and this painting 'certainly is different from a lot of the pictures' she had produced in the first half of the decade.[12]

O'Hara wrote his 'Blue Territory' on 31 March 1957, two months before his train journey to Long Island with Frankenthaler. Originally written for the English modernist Mary Butts, whose experimental and spectral prose often depicted the coastal bluster of Dorset and Cornwall, 'Blue Territory' is a chaotic frenzy of a lyric poem that finds O'Hara, like Frankenthaler in Nova Scotia, in an overwhelming and unreal landscape by sand and water. It feels possible that he re-dedicated it to Frankenthaler after that weekend on Long Island. Perloff dismisses 'Blue Territory' as a less than successful 'translation' of painting into poem: 'if one knows this abstract painting, whose curvilinear shapes, vibrant colours, and shimmering surfaces carry minimal suggestions of an ocean landscape, O'Hara's rendition is interesting'.[13] A euphemism for errant or wacky, Perloff's 'interesting' offers a professorial raised eyebrow on the poem's quality, as though to say 'fine try, but this fails to satisfy the rubric of a successful ekphrastic poem'. The 8 April 1957 letter by O'Hara to Frankenthaler, from which Perloff quotes, includes a typed poem, and it is possible that O'Hara had seen the painting at the Whitney Museum of American Art, where it was then on view in the *Young America 1957* exhibition, which ran until 14 April.

At the outset, 'Blue Territory' sees the speaker amidst overwhelmingly abject 'bags of sand' as seagulls swoop and gulp along the shore (CP, 270). Eleanor Careless, in her extraordinary but unpublished exposition of O'Hara's creative friendship with Frankenthaler, writes on these lines: 'Immediately, O'Hara shifts the primary frame by which the picture is translated into poetry from description to raw materials – sand, movement, space. The float and overlap of the individual lines creates duration as well as depth and texture, foregrounding the physicality of the poetic line much as the action painters foregrounded the physical movement of painting.'[14] But it is difficult to say whether the poem should be read as ekphrastic, or descriptive, in any strict sense: it does not feel painterly like many of O'Hara's poems do. The tangential references to the hydrous composition of Frankenthaler's painting seem to help construct the atmosphere of arbitrary disarray, or else irreverent play – 'Here I am! / blue, blue / whoops!' (CP, 270). It is difficult to ignore the abject sexuality of the lines, from the account of drinking 'sweat and piss, yum yum' to the 'curling anemones of the thigh, art-nouveau kissings' (CP, 270–271). The laborious enjambment has a knack to jolt and halt the poem forwards from supple movement into paralysis: an entire line consists of 'up, de–' before the caesura, as brutally effective as the butcher's cleaver, reveals the word as 'desire' (CP, 270). In the end, though, it is unclear what O'Hara desires to do with the poem. Its wilful difficulty and performed surrealism feel at odds with the measured brilliance of Frankenthaler's painting. Perhaps a clue to understanding the poem can be found in his criticism on Frankenthaler's landscapes, from her first exhibition at the Tibor de Nagy gallery. Writing in 1954, O'Hara claims that Frankenthaler

> refuses to abandon her sensitivity to nature or any other force external to the act of painting. Although there is a vague feeling of landscape about many of her new pictures, she goes no further towards representation than her experience leads her . . . [o]n the other hand, she will not "make a picture" in the technical sense: she is the medium of her material, never polishing her insights into a rhetorical statement, but rather letting the truth stand forth plainly and for itself.[15]

'She is the medium of her material.' O'Hara argues here that while Frankenthaler's paintings might imply landscape, or any other kind of referent to a reality outside, which was implied not least by the virtue of her post-facto naming of her works *as* landscapes, this is incidental to their meaning. The meaning, then, is to be found in the fact that she has not set out to determine the subject matter of her paintings in advance: there is no rhetorical ploy, but the desire is to still register an effect on the viewer. (Nemerov has gestured to the fact that such an approach can be traced back to William Empson's *Seven Types of Ambiguity*, the title of a Frankenthaler painting in the 1960 exhibition, especially to the 'fifth type', a 'fortunate confusion, as when the author is discovering [his or her] idea in the act of writing'.)[16] By the time O'Hara curated Frankenthaler's first museum retrospective, at the Jewish Museum on the Upper East Side in late winter and early spring 1960, the 31-year-old artist had ascended. 'The show marked in every way a turning point for Helen,' writes Gabriel: 'displaying in the museum's three rooms how far the young woman who appeared on the scene fresh from Bennington had come and the revolution in painting she had created.'[17] For John Elderfield, 'the 1960 exhibition at the Jewish Museum, which was her first retrospective, really mobilized her to change and push ahead, and feel [like] she had done this now, what's she going to do next?'[18] O'Hara hung nineteen paintings by Frankenthaler from her enormously productive decade of the fifties. Judging from Rudy Burckhardt's installation photographs, some of O'Hara's hanging decisions require explanation. The dimensions of the panelled interior of the Châteauesque Felix M. Warburg House, on the corner of 92nd and 5th, which has been the site of New York's Jewish Museum since 1947, are tight. The cramped format of display helped to generate surprising correspondences between the works, and the sculptor-cum-critic Donald Judd celebrated, in *Arts Magazine*, how all the works 'contribute remarkably to one another'.[19]

A photograph of the opening night depicts Frankenthaler and O'Hara, each with a cocktail in hand, greeting guests in front of her canvas *Hotel Cro-Magnon* (Figure 4.1). O'Hara grins into the middle distance, unmoved between drags on a cigarette as Frankenthaler, dressed in a tailored blue suit and perfectly sculptured hair, looks like a Hollywood actress. For its part, *Hotel Cro-Magnon* was an apposite choice for the entrance to this show. Named after the ivy-fronted hotel in Les Eyzies, in the Dordogne region of southern France, and where Frankenthaler honeymooned with Robert Motherwell earlier in 1958, *Hotel Cro-Magnon* is a restless jut of a painting that O'Hara described as 'tragic in tone'.[20] Look at the way the calligraphic sweep of the central black line arcs off into loop-the-loops, like a loosed rope on a plush boat out on the Mediterranean, while the staggered stamps of red in the lower ground coil and plunge on the sandy base layer below. The pastel blue section of porous paint might resemble an empty sky befitting the Riviera beach where two lovers celebrate their new union. But the black cluster menacingly hangs above: we assume that, should we read the painting as a kind of landscape, that O'Hara believed to be heralding or forecasting some unnamed tragedy.

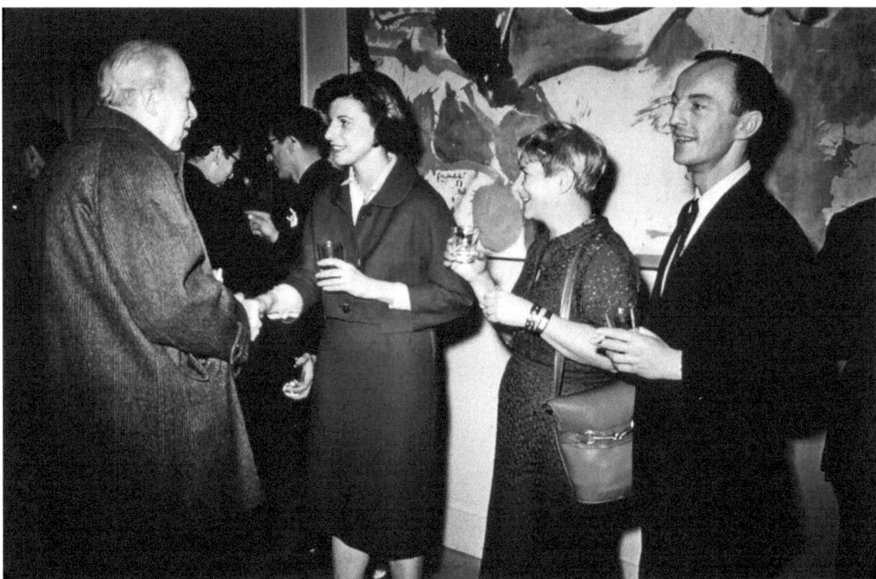

FIGURE 4.1 Helen Frankenthaler greets a visitor at the opening of her first one-person museum show, at the Jewish Museum, on 26 January 1960. Frank O'Hara stands to the right.

Hotel Cro-Magnon is one of several paintings that titularly refer to places, real and imagined, in the exhibition. *Eden* (1956) is a joyous floret in subdued colours, with two '100' markings that may well double as the vertical lines and obstinate oblongs in Motherwell's *Elegies* series. 'As astounding and sudden an invention in some respects as *Mountains and Sea* itself, it tells of an ideal and abstracted world of sensuous delight, cut off in the ironical form of its representation from any real landscape,' Elderfield wrote in 1989: '[h]oisted into its trees, the winning 100 scores of prelapsarian perfection are marvellously witty inventions that also carry extraordinary visual force.'[21] Another Biblical title, *Jacob's Ladder* (1957), or the Prophet's dream of direct access to heaven, opens like a butterfly in a snare. Allegedly inspired by Jusepe de Ribera's version of the Genesis story held at the Prado in Madrid, which Frankenthaler saw in 1953 and then again in 1954, the rough structure of the central rectangular section with loose lines arcing off to the right and four expressive circles on either side suggests at least some vague reference to a physicalized ladder. The rest of the painting is pure exhilaration, including the subject Frankenthaler described as the 'exuberant figure', a kind of Jacob lost in raptures.[22] In those sections where the flooding of pigment is the most raucous, Frankenthaler used an unmediated process, secreting thinned oil paint across the unprimed canvas. That the artworks titularly responded to the Jacob's Ladder story, as well as Mount Sinai, where Moses received the Ten Commandments, and Eden, seemed relevant, in view of Frankenthaler's first retrospective being hosted at the Jewish Museum.[23]

The 1960 Frankenthaler retrospective was O'Hara's only major exhibition not commissioned by the Museum of Modern Art and was his second single-artist retrospective after *Jackson Pollock 1912–1956*, which toured Europe. Writing in the catalogue, O'Hara even suggests that Frankenthaler represents the decade that has just ended: 'Her sensibility is to me very "fifties": her tradition, to use the phrase of Harold Rosenberg, is the "tradition of the new" to which she brings her own authoritative, and at times speculative, lyricism as a heightening presence in each occasion of risk and paint-adventure.'[24] Careless has explained how the semantics of 'risk' permeate O'Hara's writings on Frankenthaler. 'O'Hara locates Frankenthaler's risk-taking in her lack of compositional deliberation, that is, her tendency towards "mess" (letting it happen) rather than "measure" (deliberate making)', Careless writes: '"A complete mess", in O'Hara's adaption of the critical idiom of the fifties, is the pitfall of Surrealist tendencies that prioritise the expression of the unconscious over rational deliberation.'[25] O'Hara's small catalogue essay, frantically written in December 1959, is a lyrical text that bears the marks of having been rushed. Described by Nemerov as 'among the most perceptive of all writings about her art', the essay does not depart too far from conventional readings of Abstract Expressionism as operating somewhere between control and restraint.[26] 'One of the crucial decisions for the contemporary artist, representing a great conflict in temperament', O'Hara probes, 'is the very question of conscious composition, whether to "make the picture" or "let it happen"'.[27] Despite being retrospectively lauded by Nemerov, as well as Elderfield, Wagner and Carl Belz, who said that '[t]ypically, O'Hara used few words to express many insights, and he allowed plenty of room for expansion', O'Hara's essay is ambiguous and it is not clear even he always knows what he means.[28] O'Hara refuses to explain the significance of the paintings, or even offer much insight into their form and composition. Instead, he semantically calibrates them around 'risk':

The beauties of Helen Frankenthaler's work are various and dramatic. [. . .]. Frankenthaler is a daring painter. She is willing to risk the big gesture, to employ huge formats so that her essentially intimate revelations may be more fully explored and delineated . . . She is willing to declare erotic and sentimental preoccupations full-scale and with full conviction.[29]

As he did in the Tibor de Nagy review some six years earlier, which stressed Frankenthaler's 'artistic temper' and 'unimpeded self-assertion', O'Hara made looking at one of her canvases feel like an event, more a high-octane athletics race than the silent reverence of a museum, but her subject remained intimate and private, like the change of light on a mountaintop or the unannounced arrival of an old friend to one's apartment door.[30]

Some of O'Hara's more extravagant phrasing in the catalogue essay had an unintended effect. He compared Frankenthaler's 'erotic overtones' to two artists: Jean-Antoine Watteau and Francisco Goya. If Frankenthaler captured something of the 'sweetness' of the former in paintings like *Jacob's Ladder* (1957), O'Hara wrote, then her paintings also contain the 'irony' of the latter's earlier work.[31] Critics seized on the saccharine Watteau example. Barbara Butler, for *Art International*, praised the retrospective for delivering a 'particular vision' of a decade's body of work, but ultimately advanced a gendered reading which argued that the paintings themselves were 'fragile' and merely 'quietly beautiful' with their individual sensation 'more like that of watercolour than of oil painting'.[32] Ultimately, Butler turned O'Hara's words against Frankenthaler, reproducing out of context one of his lavish descriptions of her work as offering tinges of 'Watteau-like sweetness'.[33] Critics immediately picked up on what they believed to be the more 'personal' aspects of these paintings, which was only extenuated by how intimately they were hung. In a review piece for *The New Yorker*, Robert Coates commented that in paintings like *Mother Goose Melody* Frankenthaler 'verges on the coyly sentimental'.[34] O'Hara, who took the same approach but with a different conclusion, put it differently: '[o]n the sentimental side, the superb *Mother Goose Melody* ... [does] not fail to refer to emotional enthusiasms which are real and amusing and likeable'.[35] The most brutal criticism came from the pages of O'Hara's erstwhile employer, though, in Anne Seelye's devastating review for *Art News*:

> The goddess Ate, patroness of reckless blindness and mad impulse, may be responsible for the work of Helen Frankenthaler ... If so, the artist has allowed the goddess every liberty of gesture and intention in these canvases, which are not so much painted as stained. . . . One cannot be satisfied only to look for the sudden, surprising visual beauties; one is in the presence of an hysterical temperament, and must take account of that. There are women who wish that they had these qualities, and there are men who wish that they might fall in love, tragically, with that personality. The paintings are romantic, hypersensitive, sulky, and filled with surface tensions.[36]

In Homer's *The Iliad*, Zeus blames Ate for blinding him to Hera's trickery, and so the thunder god banishes her from Olympus by whirling her from the starry heaven to the tilled fields of men. Is Seelye not suggesting, then, that Frankenthaler's personal beauty and her ability to trick men made those around her blind to her deeds? Or that Frankenthaler deserves some kind of heavenly retribution for her womanly hubris, to be thrown back down to earth (figuratively speaking)? 'The sexual symbology of Miss Frankenthaler's work is subconsciously intentional,' continued Seelye, 'that is, she has tried to show it and not to show it at the same time.'[37] Seelye's brand of review was unfortunately commonplace at the time, and demonstrated a double standard over how women artists were criticized. As Sybil E. Gohari has explained, Frankenthaler 'was cast as an artistic link, a follower, not central to any art movement, a position which, ironically, enabled her fame, success, and inclusion in "the narrative of modernism"'.[38] Seelye's critique showed that even at a retrospective when 'a feeling of grand and irreproachable accomplishment is even more solemnly in the air', as Nemerov put it, and when 'even critics and skeptics might examine the art with a due appreciation that, after all, the artist has stayed with her convictions and pursued them with a seriousness worthy of respect', Frankenthaler's work was attacked.[39] Readers were incensed by Seelye's review. In a claim that itself might be construed as a sexist critique of a sexist critique, Constance Emmerich wrote that 'Seelye seems so concerned with qualities of sexuality and seduction that she appears to project her own hysterical anxieties into the content of the pictures'.[40] Everett Ellin, an art dealer and computer engineer who opened his own gallery on Sunset Boulevard in Los Angeles in 1960, continued the wave of indignant responses to the editorial staff at *Art News*:

> Your critic's speculations as to Helen Frankenthaler's Freudian orientation struck me as an unwarranted invasion of the artist's right to privacy and a line of inquiry of dubious taste or validity. I do not believe that an artist is fair game to psychoanalysis at the hands of reviewers simply because she has the courage to make highly personal statements in her work, which deserves to be evaluated on its own merits.[41]

B. H. Friedman wrote to the editor to argue that Seelye's review '[was] hysterical and dishonest: strong adjectives, but one which "A. S." applies, with less justice, to this work'.[42] It is easy to see how critics of the exhibition were marked by who Frankenthaler was, over and above the quality of her paintings. 'I'm willing to go out on a limb', continued Freidman, and 'bet' the critic did not like Frankenthaler 'for reasons completely outside of the work'.[43] Instead, Friedman believed that Frankenthaler's show 'was like reliving a part of the fifties that meant something'.[44] In the May 1960 issue, Frankenthaler herself wrote a letter to the editor ostensibly stating her disinterest in her friend Alfred Leslie's 'hyper-active career', as one reviewer put it, and the fact that readers should not care 'what he was doing while his paintings were on view' in April.[45] But she was really writing to express her grievance at the way her own exhibition was reviewed. 'Why must you gossip about the personality of the artist? Some of us are interested in painting.'[46] And finally, the literary critic and Victorianist, Sonya Rudikoff, who was one of Frankenthaler's best friends from Bennington, asked: 'Certainly the art world does not need more expressions of vendetta, self-indulgence and impotent fury, yet this tone becomes increasingly evident in your magazine. What is gained by it? Why all this divisiveness? Where is editorial responsibility?'[47]

But if O'Hara's unintended outcome in his essay was to unleash the sadly predictable and latent sexism that underpinned contemporary readings of

Frankenthaler's work through her personality, it was not because he did not think her personality was unimportant nor that the motivations and ambitions of artists was not relevant to their work. Quite the opposite. He knows that Frankenthaler's motivation to take risks in her studio (if not in her life, as she herself admits) is central to the power of the work; it *is* the work. But he struggles to know where to take that realization. 'She does not hesitate to deal with her subject with a frankness approaching sordidness,' O'Hara wrote on Frankenthaler's paintings at the Tibor de Nagy, another occasion which offered confusion and clarity in equal measure, 'for the power of their impact is that of natural violence evoked in a lofty and immaculate tone – the compacted sordidness of one of those "unspeakable" chapters in Henry James.'[48] The reference to James is intriguing: in his novels and often in our lives, we are more aware of the 'unspeakable' because it is not, or cannot be, said. What is happening off stage – often sex, but also death, or shame about money – is more frightening, as Mona Brigstock found out all too well in *The Spoils of Poynton*, because anything can happen off stage.[49] Was it that the paintings had a sexuality, a sordidness that critics, let alone Frankenthaler herself, were unable to express with a straight face? Is this O'Hara's point? Perhaps, but what does it have to do with the painting? O'Hara's art criticism is often celebrated for its charming mix of insouciance and as a refreshing embrace of culture both high and low, but in moments like these, spraying words 'through a fire hose' instead of an 'eyedropper', as Dan Chiasson said of O'Hara's anti-academic writing style in a profile for *The New Yorker*, O'Hara revels in the joy of getting wet, but the experience seldom makes the canvases easier to understand.[50] But O'Hara's exuberant art writing seems disinterested in making the paintings of his friends easier to understand. Instead, it is more committed to offering up experience as another kind of understanding abstraction.

O'Hara's Frankenthaler retrospective was important for several reasons. For Frankenthaler, it would be the most significant exhibition of her career, save only for E. A. Carmen Jr.'s retrospective at the Museum of Modern Art, Fort Worth, Texas, in 1989.[51] To have had a major body of work for a retrospective so young and, despite criticism from some quarters of the press, to have proceeded so soon after her winning the painting prize at the Première Biennale de Paris, at the Musée d'art moderne de la ville de Paris in the previous autumn, demonstrated that there was truth to the *Life* article on Frankenthaler's ascendancy. For O'Hara, it was equally significant. The Frankenthaler exhibition marked the start of a new model of monographic curation that would be his preferred format until his death. Shows on Motherwell, David Smith, Reuben Nakian and Franz Kline would all be staged in the sixties, and O'Hara's personal intimacy with the artists was foundational to their success but also drew the ire of critics. 'I feel ashamed that [the catalogue essay] took so long', O'Hara wrote to Frankenthaler to apologise for how long his essay took to finish, and explained that criticism of how enthusiastically he curated the Pollock show had distracted his attention, and left him 'very self-conscious and with absolutely no brio about my ideas about your work since I thought my admiration might just bring about the same situation'.[52] Even by 1960, and not without a small sense of paradox, O'Hara knew that he needed to tread lighter in his enthusiasms for painting as a curator than as a poet. The days when Abstract Expressionists needed the passionate support of curators and critics inside influential institutions to justify the movement to sceptical audiences were over. Opting to be enthusiastic in 1960, as opposed to calmly judicial and historically minded, surveying the movement from a distance given its ascendancy, might well have seemed gauche to some. But O'Hara did tread this line: on one side of the street, he was the unapologetic champion of the work of his closest friends, writing about them with the energetic verve that characterized how they made their paintings; on the other side of the street, he was the inside man working in the museum institution, the curator who needed to remain impartial to the personality of the artist. 'He became quite engagé in the cogs and all the manoeuvring and manipulation and excitement of Museum matters,' Frankenthaler said later in an interview: 'He was as involved with the Museum as he was with his friendships.'[53] That's the point: O'Hara knew he needed to play the game in order to fulfil his ambitions to place friendship at the heart of his exhibitions, and to keep joy in the experience of art at the heart of friendship. Whether that made the paintings more enjoyable for those who went to his shows is an open question.

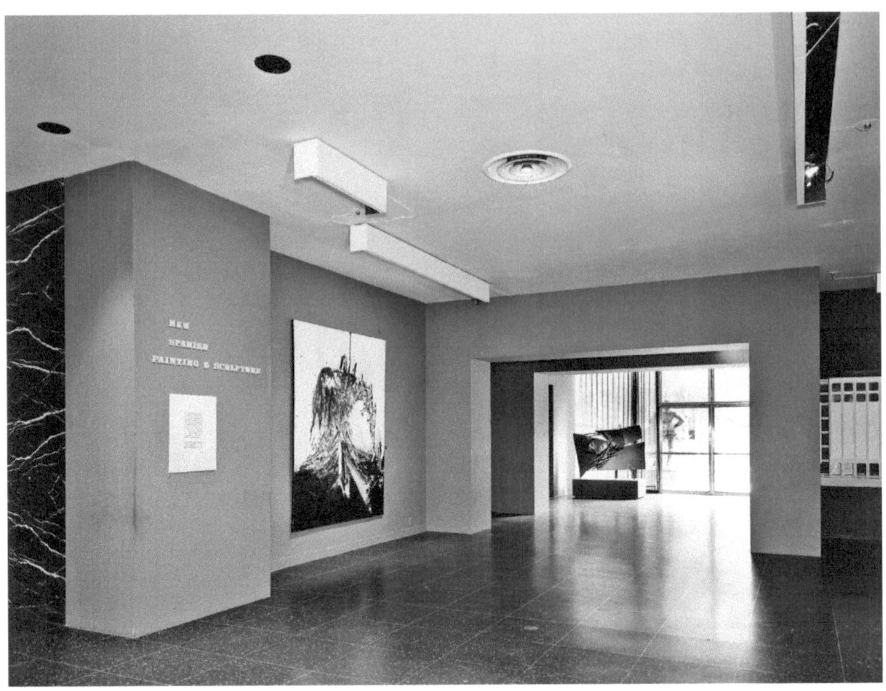

FIGURE 5.1 Installation view of the exhibition *New Spanish Painting and Sculpture*. MoMA, NY, 20 July 1960–28 September 1960.

Five | Make it New,
Make it Over

In the late summer of 1960, MoMA hosted a major survey of late modernism from Spain, curated by O'Hara.[1] *New Spanish Painting and Sculpture* was O'Hara's first major commission held at MoMA, in quick succession after his Frankenthaler retrospective at the Jewish Museum, and his first show as Assistant Curator of Painting and Sculpture. In the catalogue acknowledgements, an enthused Porter McCray noted that 'the vigorous and highly individual work ... produced by a considerable number of Spanish artists of the generations following Picasso, Miró and González' had been displayed to international audiences in a spate of recent shows over the preceding half-decade.[2] Significantly, this generation enjoyed remarkable successes at the São Paulo and Venice biennales, in 1957 and 1958 respectively. MoMA's group exhibition, for its part, represented 'the first major survey of the Spanish avant-garde to be presented throughout the United States'.[3] At least on the surface, many of the artists exhibited in *New Spanish Painting and Sculpture* were aligned with the so-called 'lingua franca' of gestural abstraction, as understood and critiqued in my second and third chapters. The exhibition accommodated a range of styles, in O'Hara's words, from 'the freedom of figurative reference in [Rafael] Canogar's powerful action-paintings', to 'Bauhaus and Constructivist researches in [Jorge] Oteiza's sculpture' and Manolo Millares' 'enigmatic encrustations from burlap, dipped in whiting, or bandage-like swathes, painted and splattered' (Figure 5.1).[4] This 'School of Spain' was an eclectic group. O'Hara stressed that the exhibition was intended, above all, to indicate 'the diversity of the stylistic tendencies and preoccupations by which some of the leading figures are exploring and developing their individual idioms'.[5]

O'Hara framed those exhibited as fresh contributors to an international language of modern art, and stressed the 'special qualities' and 'special flavor' of a Spanish artistic tradition that, for some time obscured from view by civil and world wars, these artists had refashioned.[6] In one turn of phrase that will echo throughout this chapter, O'Hara identified 'the actuality of an intensified historical atmosphere present quite tangibly in the works' of the represented painters and sculptors.[7] Twenty years after the country's ruinous Civil War, at a time when histories continued to be contested by the victorious and the defeated, we might wonder how this could have been any different. It goes without saying that any given 'historical atmosphere' often reveals more about the society that was then looking backwards, that sought to abandon, reaffirm or revise sets of historical values, than it does about the actuality of those past circumstances. This was particularly so in the case of Spain during the first two decades of the Francoist military dictatorship. So, when O'Hara made a case for the historical and geographical specificities of Spanish art, it seemed clear that he was offering a statement not only on the contemporary condition of art production in Spain, but also on the state of the country's vexed politics in 1960. 'If the motto of American art in recent years can be said to "Make it new",' O'Hara mused, self-consciously repeating Ezra Pound's manifesto for modernist transformation, 'for the Spanish it is "Make it over"'.[8]

On the wall text of the installation's entrance room, O'Hara sketched out the historicizing imagination that was coincident with what critic José María Moreno Galván would later characterize as the *segunda vanguardia* ('second Spanish avant-garde'):[9]

> The long period of isolation which Spain underwent from the end of its Civil War (1936-39) until after the close of World War II has been followed by a period of increasingly intense artistic activity. Where a previous generation (Picasso, Miró, González) had worked largely abroad, most of the artists represented here live in Spain and devote much of their time to the propagation of contemporary esthetic ideas in their homeland. Particularly in the last five years, Spanish artists have explored modern, technical and formal innovations and in many instances developed highly personal, expressive qualities. At the same time, the muted palette common to many, the preference for dramatic presentation of the image, the sometimes brutal yet detached handling of the material, remind us that the achievements of the great Catalan painters, of Velázquez and Goya, of Gaudí in his sculpturesque architecture and plastic treatment of interiors, are not absent from the consciousness of the present generation.[10]

This wall text is characteristic of the exhibition's argument. As an introduction, it identifies artists of a new generation who had been influenced by, but had now moved beyond, the modernist traditions that had gravitated away from the Iberian Peninsula, predominantly to Paris, by the time of the Spanish Civil War (all three of the artists mentioned had emigrated to the bohemian districts of Montmartre and Montparnasse at least a decade before 1936). Like the Spanish modernists of this earlier generation, this new cohort believed in the artist's transformative role and responsibility within society, and expressed their political and aesthetic mission through collective manifestoes, self-published magazines, and small-scale group shows. But this generation, we are reminded, had resolutely remained in Spain, despite the associated costs. Dore Ashton would describe their purgatorial status as that of 'interior refugees', a reference not only to their sustained political opposition to Franco's regime (which O'Hara tellingly refuses to expressly name), but also to the lack of domestic opportunities for display.[11] As we can imagine, the post-Civil War period of Franco's 'years of victory' propaganda crusade had limited enthusiasm for avant-gardes of any kind. Genoveva Tusell García has even argued that 'modernism associated with the Republic had been erased from the map' and 'all art that was opposed to academicism was seen as insubordination – artistic, social and political'.[12] The production and display of art had become thoroughly enmeshed with the politics and cultural production of national memory.

But in framing these artists in relation to national and formal concerns, O'Hara allows postwar Spanish abstraction to participate in a precarious balancing act. On the one hand, the artists were devoted 'to the propagation of contemporary esthetic ideals' and practiced 'modern, technical and formal innovations'. Their work contributed to the continental development of *Art Informel*, and were championed by Tapié.[13] On the other hand, these predominantly non-figurative artists were heirs to the canonical protagonists of the Spanish Golden Age, with Diego Velázquez, Francisco de Zurbarán and Francisco Goya front and centre; and that there was something singularly *Spanish* about their 'muted palette' (which was to say browns, greys, sombre greens, ochres, slates) finished with a 'brutal and detached' touch. O'Hara relies here on romanticized ideas of Spanish art and 'Spanishness' – the Spain of recalcitrant insularity, cruel treatment of subject, perched on the periphery of European modernity – that had been consistent since the collapse of its empire in the nineteenth century, but had taken on new inflections under Franco. Was O'Hara falling into a critical trap, not only by promulgating outdated, Anglo-Saxon stereotypes of Spanish culture, but also by lending his voice to a narrative of Spain as open to international trends but fundamentally defined by national *difference*, that had become the cornerstone of Francoist foreign policy by 1960?

This chapter will attend to these concerns. First, it will provide an account of the organization, content and reception of *New Spanish Painting and Sculpture*, and make a case for its importance as a singular event that both introduced postwar Spanish abstraction to the United States and contributed to a wider reciprocal process of Iberian–American cultural exchange at a critical moment for Cold War geopolitics. This chapter will evaluate O'Hara's curatorial practice as he articulated the specificities of modern Spanish abstraction. This is essential to understand a neglected corpus of O'Hara's poems, written during his first visit to Madrid in August 1958 and his second in spring 1960, that are his version of Poems for Spain. I argue that O'Hara internalized the 'intensified historical atmosphere' identified in his curatorial research, and in so doing sought to address how imaginations of the past can provide a model for present commitments, personal and political; how 'official' constructions of national identity were threatened, hybridized and transformed by the flows of global cultural capital; and, in a similar manoeuvre to Motherwell's *Elegies to the Spanish Republic* series, works that O'Hara curated at MoMA in 1965, O'Hara's elegies written in and on Spain can be recognized as a useful means to memorialize and articulate internationalist solidarity.[14]

I. The 'Second Spanish Avant-Garde' in 1960: From *Dau al Set* to *El Paso*

In his *Studio International* interview with Edward Lucie-Smith, at a time in October 1965 when the global success of American art seemed all but secured, O'Hara is demonstrably uncomfortable with his questioner's style of enquiry:

> EDWARD LUCIE-SMITH: [. . .] do you think American art has separate characteristics which make it American?
>
> FRANK O'HARA: That's a horrible question.
>
> LUCIE-SMITH: I know but it's difficult to put it any other way.
>
> O'HARA: I know. Does one think that Tàpies' paintings are that way because he's Spanish?
>
> LUCIE-SMITH: No, that's not quite it. Even more than that. Do you think of Tàpies as a kind of provincial in relationship to New York?
>
> O'HARA: Oh no. Not at all. No, I think the work of Tàpies in New York, as in France or in Spain or in Italy, is an absolute fact of contemporary art. See, the general mistake, I think, is in thinking of these things in terms of nationalities. There *is* modern art.[15]

In the transcript, Lucie-Smith sought, first, to essentialize and define distinct national characteristics within postwar art (although he leaves it to O'Hara to suggest what these might be). The interviewer then placed those working within the parameters of set national characteristics or styles into a geographical model that was increasingly – lazily, if not always chauvinistically – defined as central New York and the peripheral concentrations of avant-garde 'schools' in European metropolises. The implication was that there was something uniquely *American* that had made the country's recent success. And although a vociferous champion of American abstract painting, O'Hara disagrees. His statement on 'the general mistake' belies an exhaustion with the overheated critical discourse around nationality and postwar art that had become commonplace. His internationalism, and we will return to this word's political nuances shortly, seems characteristically unshakeable: 'there *is* modern art'. But O'Hara's assertion is also a little awkward: surely the curator is not so uninterested in difference and differentiation as to lump the global scenes of contemporary art all together? How can modern art, as he put it, be both a phenomenon that was international or internationalizing, at the same time as determined, as surely it must be, by regional variance and formal specificity? Why did O'Hara's 1960 MoMA show, *New Spanish Painting and Sculpture*, still maintain the logic then, at least nominally, of a national art? Ultimately, *did* O'Hara think that Tàpies' paintings were a particular way because he was Spanish?

The painter and sculptor Antoni Tàpies, generally recognized as the pre-eminent avant-garde artist to have remained in his home country throughout *la dictatura*, makes for an interesting case. The son of a Catalan nationalist lawyer father who served briefly with the Republican government and a devout Catholic mother who secured for her child a conservative religious education, Tàpies came of age in a Spain still coming to terms with the conflicts and cultural contradictions of its post-Civil War settlement. From his tubercular childhood, he was fascinated by Zen Buddhism; as a young man, he strongly admired Goya, especially the late 'Black Paintings' at the Prado, and read Jean-Paul Sartre and existentialism. After briefly studying law, Tàpies channelled these eclectic influences into an artistic vocation, and developed an intensely tactile 'matter' style that would characterize his artistic output throughout the 1950s. From the vantage point of 1975, the art critic John Russell noted that these 'matter' artworks 'seemed to have been not so much painted as excavated from an idiosyncratic compound of mud, sand, earth, dried blood and powdered minerals' and that, in their 'seigneurial dignity', appeared 'particularly Spanish'.[16] Take, for instance, *Graffiti on Blackish and Ochre Relief* (1957), a loan from Chicago collector Morton Neumann for the 1960 MoMA exhibition. In this mixed media work on canvas, Tàpies combined paint with an austere treasury of materials that formally linked his paintings with the marked, defaced and ruined topography of Catalonia, streets that appeared to physically document the violence and repression of Franco's rule. 'We have had much *graffiti* in contemporary painting,' O'Hara noted, 'but when Tàpies uses them he gives us the wall, too, or a piece of the wall, a relief, a fresco.'[17] O'Hara respects the fact that this work, one of four on show in 1960, may be radically of its time, insofar as it utilized the contemporary formal vocabularies of gestural mark-making, the iconography of the street, and the *objet trouvé* – but there was a distinct *pastness* being evoked simultaneously. O'Hara was adamant that Tàpies' art – and, indeed, the art of the *segunda vanguardia* more widely, appealed to a tradition of artistic practice that was interested, as in the relief or fresco, in the public, the tactile and, most importantly, in the collective virtues of storytelling. For O'Hara, as for Russell and so many other critics writing from 1955 until Franco's death two decades later, there was a general sense that narrative was particularly, peculiarly *Spanish*. These artists told a story of Spanish history. Or this was how 'Tàpies in New York' was presented by MoMA.

Tàpies spent short bursts of time on French government scholarships in Paris, and was taken under the wing of the expatriate community of Spanish (Catalan) exiles, chiefly Pablo Picasso and Jean Miró, whose political grievances remained far too vehement for any return back to Francoist Spain.[18] Alongside his cousin Modest Cuixart, whose recent paintings, for O'Hara, 'relate to the thick golden halos of fifteenth-century Catalan saints', Tàpies was a founding member of the avant-garde collective *Dau al Set*. The collective had collaborated since 1946 in Barcelona, but was formally established two years later, under the leadership of poet Joan Brossa.[19] *Dau al Set* translates as 'the seventh face of the dice' in Catalan – then a prohibited language and one that, when published in print, was punishable with a custodial sentence. But armed with the printing-press means of Joan-Josep Tharrats, *Dau al Set* produced a little, eponymous magazine that, as implied by its anomalous *nom de guerre*, was heavily indebted to the automatism of Surrealism and the aleatory aesthetics of Dada. 'Tharrats, the most intellectual', wrote O'Hara, 'is a headlong expressionist, astral, destructive of order', as we can readily recognize in his represented artworks which have a violently cosmic atmosphere.[20]

Dau al Set only formally exhibited twice, in Barcelona: the first exhibition, collaboratively organized with the *Cobalto 49* group, was held under the cover of 1949 Christmas observance at the Institut Français, then one of the few outlets for intercultural exchange in Spain; the second, at the Sala Caralt, was a more ambitious survey that brought together the eclectic strands of the movement, but by this stage the group was slowly dissolving. *Dau al Set* would continue to publish until 1956, including a special issue on Paul Klee, by which time any coherent network of international Surrealism had been all but dispersed. In spite, or perhaps because of their secrecies and scattered membership, O'Hara stressed the enduring importance of this Catalan avant-garde:

> [. . .] it is difficult to imagine the importance which the founding of *Dau al Set* . . . held for the future of Spanish art. At that time the frontiers of esthetic communication were all but closed to innovation and experimentation. The artists involved in this publication . . . set out to rectify this situation and, what is more important, to give the emerging Spanish avant-garde, few in number at that time, a mouthpiece and a showplace. While the overall tone was Surrealist, other movements were not neglected, nor was there ignorance of the auras of Picasso, Miró, and Torres-García, among others. But *Dau al Set* went further, nourishing and stimulating esthetic aspirations beyond the point of influence of any one artist, drawing attention to the medieval masterpieces of Catalan

art, as well as to relevant modern masters such as Klee. Not until the founding of the group *El Paso* . . . in 1957 was there another such historic moment in the development of contemporary Spanish art, though there were in the interim other movements, groups, and alliances of individual artists.[21]

I will briefly cast light on a sample of those vanguards who emerged in the decade or so around the 1950s, during which competing groups attempted in different ways to identify the continued relevance of historical Spanish painting to their respective projects.

The fate of abstraction, which had generally become the preferred style for those strategically opposed to the ideological didacticism of 'official' art and academicism, was tested out across Spain. *Equipo 57*, founded in 1957 in Paris but also operating out of Córdoba, were loosely affiliated to the Communist Party of Spain, and committed to a socially conscious artistic practice. The signatories of their manifesto argued that, especially under the conditions of dictatorship, art must be 'a political solution', must stand against an aesthetics of art-for-art's-sake, and derided Spanish *Informalismo* (often associated with Tàpies and *El Paso*) as complicit with the very regime it sought to critique on account of its bourgeois and individualist attitude.[22] Linked to the Social Realist *Estempa Popular* (Popular Print, or EP), *Equipo 57* agreed with EP's unofficial spokesman, the communist painter José García Ortega, that art should contribute to a process of 'national reconciliation'.[23] The School of Altamira, established in Santander in 1948, was interested above all in the interplay between representational and non-representational composition as researched in the region's prehistoric cave drawings, and was made up of a loosely defined cast that included the art theorist Luis Felipe Vivanco and the sculptor Ángel Ferrant. The Valencian group *Equipo Crónica* might serve as a further case, although one that did not properly emerge until 1964, when they had eschewed the reigning dominance of abstraction by fusing a Socialist Realist imaginary with Pop that returned Spanish art to the problem of figurative representation which was then, albeit in a very different guise, still associated with the 'official' academicism of the Franco regime. The collectively produced works often satirized canonical works from Spanish art history, such as the *Guernica '69* series (1969), which sees Roy Lichtenstein-esque cartoon explosions amid Picasso's monumental lament for the Basque town destroyed by Luftwaffe air power, and *La salita* (1970), a revision of Velázquez's *Las Meninas* set in a stylish apartment with inflatable animals and resting pets.

O'Hara's catalogue does gesture more widely to the prevalence of 'prodigious' artists, regretting how 'unfortunate' it was that they could not be included, but he fundamentally identifies two ('at least two') important groups in 1960: the 'recognition accorded [to *El Paso*] . . . made it seem that there was not just one Spanish School, but at least two: the School of Barcelona [*Dau al Set*] and the School of Madrid [*El Paso*]'.[24] O'Hara doubts whether there was 'such factional hiatus in actuality' and queries whether 'the rumored divergence' was just another ploy 'formulated in Parisian critical circles'.[25] But if *Dau al Set* positioned themselves as custodians of Catalonia's rich Surrealist tradition, especially that of Miró, then *El Paso* ('the step', or 'the pass'), from Madrid, defined their contribution within the more recent development of gestural abstraction. Seven of the eight signatories of the 1957 *El Paso* summer manifesto were included in *New Spanish Painting and Sculpture*: Antonio Saura, Manuel Rivera, Rafael Canogar, Luis Feito, Manolo Millares and Pablo Serrano. Juana Francés, the only woman member of the collective, was conspicuously absent.[26] Manuel Chirino and Manuel Viola, both included in 1960, joined the *El Paso* constellation a little later, and Viola's *Homage to Rothko* (1959) was a last-minute addition to O'Hara's show (Figure 5.2). In both title and composition, this painting made clear the Madrileño artists' formal debt to American abstraction. Like Rothko, Viola experimented with the compositional strategy of the 'turpentine burn' whereby the artist applied high-density solvent onto a rag that was then used to scrub and massage the surface. This process blended colours into complex composite hues, as well as removing hard boundaries between figure and surrounding colour. Unlike Rothko,

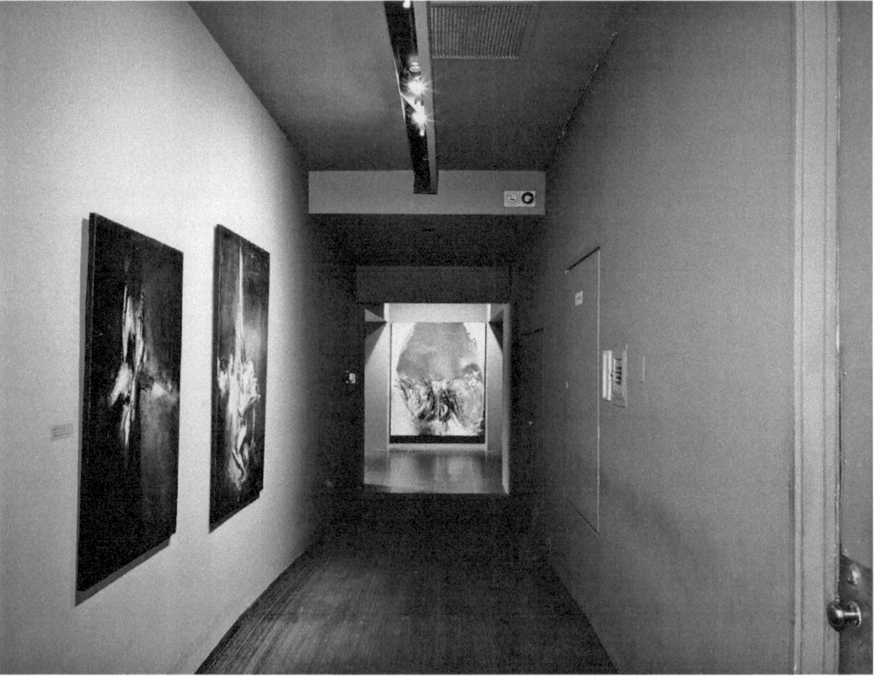

FIGURE 5.2 Installation view of the exhibition *New Spanish Painting and Sculpture*. MoMA, NY, 20 July 1960–28 September 1960.

whose structural tension was invariably realized through a rectangular lateral axis, Viola's paintings – including his *homage* – relied on a dynamic, centrifugal energy that was often completed by scraping the underside of a knife in a fierce but controlled motion. We cannot be certain what the precise relationship was between Viola and Rothko, whether they ever met or corresponded (both seem unlikely), nor whether *Homage to Rothko* was composed (or named as such) especially for the 1960 exhibition. Whatever the circumstances, the overt formal linking aligns with the sense of artistic abstraction beyond borders that was central to *El Paso*'s articulation of itself. The *El Paso* manifesto was resolutely internationalist, hostile to the autarkical and philistine cultural scene under Franco, and conscious of the oppositional radicalism of historical Spanish painting, as we can see here in three choice statements (reprinted achronologically):

> We are moving towards a revolutionary vision – within which our dramatic tradition and our direct expression are present – and which responds historically to universal activity. [. . .]
>
> Conscious of the futility of discussing the terms *abstraction/figuration, constructive/expressionist art, collective/ individualist art, etc.*, we believe that our purpose is to present authentic and free art, open to experimentation and research without borders and not subject to exclusive and limiting canons. [. . .]
>
> *El Paso* was conceived because a group of different painters and writers united and, through their different means of expression, understood the moral necessity to generate some action in their country.[27]

The manifesto prefigures O'Hara's characterization of postwar Spanish abstraction as open to international artistic influence but defined, in the main, by a national/historical difference. The signatories' purpose may have been to express an art 'without borders', but the language of a Spanish 'dramatic tradition' that responded 'historically' demonstrated how Spanish art history, even one commandeered by the Right, could be oppositional: in short, to affect change within Spain itself. But what kind of society were these painters oppositional towards? How free were the conditions for art-making under the Franco dictatorship? How do concerns around the display of the Spanish avant-garde affect our present focus, *New Spanish Painting and Sculpture*?

II. Abstraction and Cold War Cultural Politics under Franco

A brief chronology proves instructive here. O'Hara, again from the catalogue: 'The isolation of Spain culturally and economically from the period of its tragic civil war until after World War II is well-known.'[28] Franco's autarkical regime was isolated by the Western bloc in the postwar anti-fascist consensus, and was not permitted to be a member of the United Nations, nor allowed to participate within early efforts towards European integration.[29] During this time, from 1945 until around a decade later, with a markedly agrarian economy on its knees and with vastly diminished continental allies after the defeat of the Axis powers, the Francoist state needed to focus minds. It did so, as has been well documented, through a programme of internal repression and propaganda during a phase that was antagonistically proclaimed as the 'years of victory'.[30] Plaques and Catholic monuments commemorating those who died during the Civil War were erected across Spain by Franco's *Comisión de Estilo en las Conmemoraciones de la Patria* (Commission on the Style of Patriotic Commemoration), which also dictated procedural and stylistic guidelines. The 'glorious fallen' remembered only those who had died 'for God and Spain' on the Nationalist side, not the other half of the nation who had been killed fighting for the democratically elected Republican government.

The most lasting and contested symbol of this process was the construction of Valle de los Caídos ('Valley of the Fallen'), Franco's monumental memorial that is, today, one of the most disputed sites in Spain.[31] The architecture of this Catholic basilica is expressly Baroque, modelled as it was on the royal palace El Escorial, and was intended to express restoratively 'the grandeur of the monuments of old, which defy time and forgetfulness'.[32] The Valle de los Caídos was the most absolute symbol of the Francoist conservative cultural policy of National Catholicism implemented by Falangist intellectuals and artists. Aptly poeticized by Manuel Machado, brother of fellow poet Antonio (the subject of O'Hara's last poem, an elegy), in his anti-avant-garde sonnet 'Tradición' (1943), we note the importance of the past to this wider project:

> Reject vain pseudo-science, Spain of mine,
> return from your tradition, as you ought,
> for only God can fashion worlds from naught.[33]

In part to deflect from the deprivations of the present, and in part to garner support for a nostalgic and aggressive foreign policy that looked to expand south, Spaniards were to be reminded of their imperial past and a rich, unique cultural tradition distinct from the rest of Europe. The cultural utility of what Paula Barreiro López characterizes as the 'Baroque phantom', which 'represented the aspirations of the war's victors and was used in official rhetoric to justify what the regime called the Holy Crusade against communism, liberalism and democracy', was common parlance.[34] This return to historical models was believed to provide a link to intransigent religious and hierarchical order, and to cohere patriotic sentiment for the politically and economically isolated Spanish nation. Various anachronistic clichés accompanied the construction of 'Spanishness' and with them the fetishization of specific icons and symbols: the Baroque sensibilities of dramatic *tenebrismo* and defiant Catholicism, associated as it was with the Counter Reformation; the austerity and geometric rigour of the Herrerian architectural style, in particular the royal palace El Escorial; the Castillian landscape; Saint Teresa of Ávila, beatified for her devotion and mysticism; and the link between the royal and the sacred as proclaimed by the Habsburg monarchy, which ruled during the period of great colonial expansion and trade during the Spanish Golden Age.

Each of these themes is dealt with in O'Hara's meditation on love, monumentalism, and the Baroque sensibility, 'Places for Oscar Salvador' (1958). Addressed to O'Hara's Madrileño tour-guide, translator and, briefly, lover, the lyric memorializes their intense affair by counterposing touristic antics against symbols of Francoist architectural and spiritual power. Well-known for his sociability and knowledge of recent developments in artistic circles, Salvador was thanked in the *New Spanish Painting and Sculpture* catalogue for his 'expert guidance through the studios of Madrid'.[35] Curator and critic Luis González Robles, who advised O'Hara as he prepared for the exhibition, described Salvador as a translator with great 'loyalty and affection' – perhaps a knowing nod to the open secret of their clandestine relationship.[36]

The poem begins at El Escorial, the paradigmatic architectural model for the new Spain cast in the image of the past. The Baroque royal palace has come to embody, as Olivia Muoz-Rojas had explained, 'quasi-metaphyiscal properties' that symbolize *españolidad* ('national essence') and symbiotically bind imperial Spain, the monarchy and Catholicism. Against this backdrop, O'Hara curates a self-consciously clichéd *Spanish* scene of Zurbarán-esque 'tombs' and 'a vault', that is set against sexual overtones in which a 'burning landscape' is the backdrop for a 'sun lunch' with 'sweet martinis and sangria' (CP, 308). The lovers construct 'a basilica of privacy' with their 'tongues', presumably through forbidden kissing as well as conversation (CP, 308). The hagiographic symbol of Hispanic Catholicism since the Golden Age, Saint Teresa emerges in this sexual theatre since her 'heated manuscripts' are housed at El Escorial's monastic archive (CP, 308). The Counter-Reformation mystic Teresa might be most familiar as the subject of Gian Lorenzo Bernini's *Ecstasy of Saint Teresa* (1647–1652), the sensual iconography of which is possibly O'Hara's allusion here, but she was also anointed as the patron saint of Francoism, 'La Santa de la Raza'.[37] At the 1937 Paris World's Fair, where Picasso's *Guernica* (1937) was also on show in the Republican Pavilion, Josep Maria Sert's painting *Intercesión de Santa Teresa de Jesús en la Guerra Civil española (An Intercession by Saint Teresa of Jesus in the Spanish Civil War)* (1937) was displayed in the Vatican Pavilion. Miriam Basilio, who has contributed widely to studies on the visual ideologies of Francoism, notes: 'Employing a baroque idiom evoking Spanish masterpieces, [Sert] further reinforced the work's gravitas and leavened the painting's politically loaded content.'[38] If, in the reactionary Francoist imaginary, Teresa represented a reassuringly constant personification of Castilian religious virtue, as an intervening force in the fight for traditional social values, for O'Hara her manuscripts' 'inks as dry as yesterdays', reveal instead a stasis, figured as a marker of the past-as-past, which is juxtaposed against the radical present of the poem's moment (CP, 308).

Later, in a stanza entitled 'Plaza de España', O'Hara berates 'an enormous multiform past' that 'comes crashing down in its astute immobility' (CP, 308). O'Hara playfully overcompensates for the impending end of his brief but intimate union with Salvador by toying with the desire for commemoration while asserting the undesirability of fixing feelings of possibility into a monument: 'we have quixotically become a building' (a reference to the Plaza de España and to Cervantes' hero Don Quixote, who is remembered there through statuary). By then listing what their imaginary monument is not, or rather not yet – 'ruins' or a 'banquet' or 'a case of typhus' – O'Hara reveals an ambivalent desire to protect the love affair at the same time as recognizing that this would only subsume it into the radically undesirable 'past' with its 'astute immobility' (CP, 308). It seems obvious that the poet is all too cognizant of the fact that any attempt to monumentalize their togetherness, or to fix it for posterity, is as idealistic and impractical as Cervantes' protagonist, and he seems to recognize that little that is desired can be achieved by doing so – diminished libidos, or 'the horns of day', included (CP, 308). O'Hara resolves by acknowledging their vulnerability and inability to mediate the past: 'more than I ever love the past / I love our waiting' (CP, 308).

A comparable manoeuvre occurs in his elegy for V. R. 'Bunny' Lang, 'The "Unfinished"' (1959), in which O'Hara evades the elegiac pitfalls in 'impersonating some wretch weeping' by juxtaposing personal responsibility in the intervals of mourning against markers of a Spanish historical scene:

> everybody thinks if you go, you go up
> but I'm not so sure about that because the fault of my generation
> is that nobody wants to make a big *histoire* about anything
> and I'm just like everybody else, if an earthquake comes
> laughingly along and gulps down the whole of Madrid
> including the Manzanares River and for dessert all the royal tombs
> in the Escorial I'd only get kind of hysterical about one person
> no Voltaire me
> (CP, 317)

In satirizing Voltaire's 'Poème sur le désastre de Lisbonne', O'Hara proposes that even a catastrophe like the wholesale destruction of Madrid is insufficient to persuade him that a personal mourning is any less serious. Why should all these signifiers of longevity persist, he asks, when Lang did not? Her premature death is a kind of end-of-history moment in itself: it is the death of the world as he knows it. O'Hara is suggesting that when fantasizing on the destructibility of monuments and even whole cities, we encounter our own fragility. Not because they are perennial and we are not (despite the best efforts of all of those Philips of Spain who erected great sepulchres to posterity at El Escorial, or Franco at Valle de los Caídos) but because, as Jacques Derrida theorizes on our 'love of ruins', they 'have not always been there, they will not always be there, they are finite'.[39] I am then, for the most part, in agreement with Marjorie Perloff who argues that '[p]hotographs, monuments, static memories – "all things that don't change" – these have no place in [O'Hara's] world'.[40] And yet, of course, these things do have a place in the poet's world, not because they do not change, but because they do. The radical revision of, say, monuments to historical events or Civil War ruins, especially in a Spain that was then obsessed by monumental constructions of meaning, necessarily entails the manipulation of history to meet the political realities of the present.

As discussed, the Baroque played a central part in the construction of Francoist national identity. However, despite the campaigns of Francoist cultural elites to isolate historical features and transpose them onto and into the present, and to stress the unchanging or timeless properties of a singularly Spanish national identity, the needs and demands of state cultural policy were forced to respond to the febrile geopolitical atmosphere of the Cold War 'containment' years. This was 1960, after all, not 1940. Franco's Spain recognized the importance of building new alliances abroad to transition from a relatively isolated economy (largely imposed by necessity after the defeat of the Axis powers), to one that permitted limited capitalist enterprise and secured foreign investment. The regime also identified the political advantages that could be achieved in positioning itself as a strident anti-communist ally to the Western bloc in the recalibrations of the Cold War. This rehabilitation was realized in 1953 with the signing of the bilateral Pact of Madrid with Washington (the same year as the Concordat with the Vatican), despite the ongoing reservations of more proximate powers within the Western bloc, especially France. United States martial infrastructure was permitted to operate on the Iberian Peninsula, from Naval Station Rota to Zaragoza Air Base, as the Franco regime received extensive military and economic support. Over a seven-year period after the Pact's ratification, a figure close to $500 million was provided in grants from the United States Congress to Franco's Spain. At the decade's close, the now infamous black-and-white photographs of two ageing generals, Caudillo Franco and President Eisenhower, embracing, grinning and conducting a military inspection, were widely reprinted on newspaper front-pages and circulated throughout Spain. The anti-fascist postwar consensus had ultimately given way to the strategic imperatives and pragmatic alliances of anti-communist consolidation in western Europe.

Despite being directed primarily by the necessities of Cold War bifurcation, this new relationship between Madrid and Washington had familiar ramifications for the circulation of cultural enterprise and capital. As was the case across the beneficiary nations of the Marshall Plan (Spain was the only western European country excluded), various American cultural imports were now able to profit from widespread domestic distribution. It was also an opportunity for artists, writers and filmmakers working in Spain to address the subject of national identity amid Americanization. From the Spanish perspective, films like Luis García Berlanga's quietly subversive *¡Bienvenido, Mister Marshall! (Welcome Mr Marshall!)* (1953) demonstrate how even trite stereotypes of and by Americans and Spaniards could be potent forces within the definition of local and national identity amid globalizing economic forces.[41]

Many of O'Hara's poems written in and on Spain (1958–60) address the predicament of 'authentic' local Spanish culture amid Americanization and are often informed by his observations after travelling for his curatorial work. In his poem 'A Little Travel Diary', dated 14 April 1960, O'Hara sketches the train journey he shared with Ashbery towards San Sebastián, where the sculptor and former Real Sociedad goalkeeper Eduardo Chillida had his studio, and then northeast to Biarritz, where Ashbery would conduct doctoral research on Raymond Roussel at the writer's family villa. Unusually for one of O'Hara's business trips for MoMA, the pair's jaunt was not planned well in advance.[42] O'Hara amalgamated clichés of American and Spanish culture into a bizarre and cinematic spectacle:

> [. . .] in Spain they said nothing for foreigners
> as we head in our lovely 1st class coach, shifting
> and sagging, towards the northwest, while in other compartments
> Dietrich and Erich von Stroheim share a sandwich of chorizos
> and a bottle of Vichy Catalan, in the dining car
> the travelling gentleman with linear moustache and many
> many rings rolls his cigar around and drinks Martini y
> ginebra, and Lillian Gish rolls on over the gorges
> with a tear in her left front eye, comme Picasso [. . .] (CP, 357)

That he pastes Marlene Dietrich into a neighbouring carriage (and has her sipping on such a transparently *Spanish* touristic token as Vichy Catalan) shows O'Hara's recourse to American frames of reference even, or especially, when captivated by the train journey's local sights and tastes. Although both were Hollywood icons, Dietrich was a major anti-fascist campaigner, while Von Steinberg, an Austrian-born Jew, was staunchly critical of Nazism.[43] The reader cannot help but see Dietrich, her face lit, in Josef von Sternberg's *Shanghai Express* (1932), a film of foreigners playing foreigners on trains during civil war. This was not the first time O'Hara referenced Dietrich, a favourite among his silver-screen icons, in a surrealist fashion. In his 1953 play *Awake in Spain*, written while he was on sabbatical from MoMA as a Fellow with the Poets' Theater in Cambridge, O'Hara dramatized a sultry

Dietrich trying to persuade the King of Spain (disguised as Joan of Arc) to 'fight from Paris' via Granada, after she had assaulted his royal courtier with a musical saw.[44] This moment immediately follows a 'foreign intervention [by] the famous Portuguese warrior, George Hartigan' (Grace Hartigan's not-so-secret pseudonym) and the ensuing disagreement between the King and the Generalissimo over who should lead the fight-back to save the nation.[45] *Awake in Spain* is an eccentric play, and one that does not reward being taken too seriously.[46] However, it is curious that so many of its themes, facetiously presented as they may be, strike a chord with the political conversation that surrounded the 1960 exhibition seven years later and the degree to which, as in 'A Little Travel Diary', American and Spanish cultural identities were playfully essentialized and then spliced together. The theatre sets themselves were presented like a cliché mock-up of Franco-era aestheticized landscapes, with its 'Spanish palaces full of ropes, artichokes, globes, and flames', 'very Baroque' architecture, and decorated with a giant reproduction of El Greco's *View of Toledo* coloured in bright red.[47] In another scene, the Generalissimo gets anxious about the cultural influence of the United States among his enemies, when he exclaims: 'I'm so worried about the jails, they're full of Thanksgiving dinners.'[48]

In 'A Little Travel Diary', the allusion to Spain's most famous modernist expatriate, Pablo Picasso, recalls his *Weeping Woman* (1937) – only with the First Lady of American Cinema, Gish, stepping in for Dora Maar. This portrait, which now hangs in Tate Modern, responded to the specific anguish of the Luftwaffe's aerial bombardment of Guernica, and has since become a universal symbol for the terror and suffering endured by civilians during total war. Picasso had shown his first overtly political work, *The Dream and Lie of Franco* (1937), eighteen prints and an accompanying prose poem, together with his iconic mural *Guernica* (1937) at the Spanish Pavilion in exile at the 1937 World's Fair in Paris. In the 1960 catalogue, O'Hara quipped that 'France may claim Picasso but Spain, in a sense, owns him' due to his 'looking backwards, [seemingly] always to have clung to [his] identification with the Spanish people'.[49] *Guernica* spent 42 years on extended loan to MoMA, having been originally lent by the artist to tour the United States to raise money for the Spanish Refugee Aid (SRA), and was stored for some time along a corridor from O'Hara's third-floor International Program offices. Picasso's history painting was, no pun intended, thoroughly, totally in the background at MoMA in 1960. But whereas Picasso expressed solidarity from his comparatively uncomplicated pedestal as an expatriate in France, the avant-garde within Spain was thrown into an ideological conundrum by the wider international rehabilitation of Spain and the new Pact of Madrid relationship.

Many supporters of the dictatorship had for some time respected and even highly valued the achievements of postwar Spanish abstraction, and recognized the political utility in a radically de-politicized aesthetics onto which political values could be projected. This was true, as has been well discussed, in the liberal cultural establishments' uses for Abstract Expressionism in the United States.[50] In the work of the *segunda vanguardia*, with its stripped-back austerity of subject, *tenebrismo* palette, and vigorous expressivity, Franco's reform-minded cultural elites identified a modern incarnation of the pictorial legacy of the Baroque and the Spanish Golden Age. Barreiro López writes:

> Despite these artists' manifest connections to contemporary currents in European art, their works were nevertheless presented as the essence of the Spanish spirit – in its austerity modern yet traditional. This corresponded to the image of the country that the regime sought to export: a modern Spain that does not denounce its roots.[51]

In the acknowledgements for the *New Spanish Painting and Sculpture* catalogue, McCray stressed the blossoming cultural exchange between MoMA and major Spanish museums that were predominantly under the remit of the Ministry for Cultural Affairs, a Francoist institution that had, by the late 1950s, taken the lead on the state's liberalizing agenda. 'The Museum of Modern Art', wrote McCray, in typically open-handed tone,

> welcomes the opportunity that this exhibition affords of reciprocating in some degree the generous hospitality of institutions in Spain and the warm response of the Spanish public to American art when our Museum presented *Modern Art in the United States* in Barcelona in 1955 and *The New American Painting* in Madrid in 1958.[52]

Installing *The New American Painting*, recounted in a review by Mercedes Molleda and reprinted for the *finale* text on the show's homecoming to New York, 'required sawing the upper part of the metal entrance door of the building the night before the inauguration' to bring in two 'enormous' paintings by the show's 'transoceanic guests' – Pollock and (the exhibit's only woman artist) Hartigan.[53] *The New American Painting* was shown at The Museo de Arte Contemporáneo for less than a month in the summer of 1958 to mostly buoyant reviews. It is worth noting that Franco attended both exhibitions – *Modern Art in the United States*, which attracted over 60,000 visitors, and *The New American Painting* – presumably in order to keep up diplomatic appearances in accordance with the new Pact of Madrid relationship.[54] In his 1958 Director's Report to the Council of the International Program, as preparations for 1960 were well underway, McCray reported to the trustees of the International Program:

> Interest has been very intense in Spain since our showing of MODERN ART IN THE UNITED STATES in Barcelona in 1955; Spanish artists were especially attracted to that show, and I think it is safe to say that the work of American artists has had an important influence on their work. THE

NEW AMERICAN PAINTING was requested by Madrid museums and cultural officials who had seen our selection of the IV São Paulo Bienal in the fall of 1957. Mr. d'Harnoncourt and I went to Madrid to install the exhibition in the Museo de Arte Moderna, and the mid-July opening took place in the presence of the American Ambassador, and an important group representing the diplomatic and cultural life of Madrid. To understand the enormous stir caused in art circles by the show, we must remember that the traditional dichotomy between avant-garde and conservative art movements has been widened in Spain by the relative isolation in which Spanish artists have been working during recent years. Our show, therefore, had the effect of supporting the younger Spanish artists in their own efforts to revitalize their art and to make contact with important art movements outside Spain.[55]

McCray had a point. In 1955, Spain was unable to boast of a single artist chosen for Andrew Carnduff Ritchie's major MoMA survey *The New Decade: 22 European Painters and Sculptors*. 'Not every European country has produced distinguished artists', snarked Ritchie, and why 'one country rather than another provides a fertile soil for artists must remain an open question'.[56] But by 1960, there was an extraordinary roster of Spaniards with international accolades. In 1957, Jorge Oteiza was awarded the Grand Prize for Sculpture at the 4th Bienal de São Paulo by a jury commissioned by Alfred Barr. More success, and more talk of artistic opposition to the Franco regime, came the following year at the *29th Venice Biennale* when Tàpies was awarded the David E. Bright Foundation Award for Best Painter. But other critics stressed, as O'Hara would in 1960, the 'special qualities' of distinct 'Spanishness' that characterized these new achievements. The Valencian polymath critic and leftist Vicente Aguilera Cerni enthused on his country's representation as a whole: 'Spain intervened in the polemic of the Biennale in the best way possible . . . by forcing recognition (as afforded by critics from all over the world) of the power and tremendous *Spanishness* of its young and non-conformist voices.'[57] Cerni, the philosopher-poet of *Dau al Set* who went on to win the International Critics Prize at that year's Biennale, had long argued for the Spanish avant-garde's importance as a social force, and resisted claims for art's formalist autonomy. Cerni was also the first Spanish author to write a book on contemporary American art, and was among the candidates that the United States Embassy in Madrid proposed for the Foreign Leaders Program in 1958.[58] All of these international victories were engineered by Robles, described by Barreiro López as 'a skillful diplomat with an interest in new artistic currents' whose agenda, while retaining an air of independence from the regime, was to stress the modernity of Spanish *Informalismo* at the same time as their specific 'Spanishness'.

In short, the Francoist cultural establishment had recognized the political utility in promoting abstract and avant-garde art within its wider 'developmentalist' strategy of modernization. According to this attitude, radical opposition could be neutralized by being permissible to the state: if, in other words, that opposition took the form of a modernist programme that cultural elites believed to be largely disconnected from the taste and understanding of most Spaniards, but was framed within a celebrated Baroque tradition. As Guilbaut reminds us, 'art could be politicised only if it was apolitical'.[59] Besides, opportunities for display were mostly abroad, where the regime saw the greatest opportunities for recognition, and scarcely within Spain itself, where Francoist elites remained sceptical of the benefits of showing these artists. Invariably, however, the international avant-garde's dilemma within Spain itself, positioned against the regime but eschewing expatriation, with diminished opportunities for domestic display due to a lack of state funding and restrictions on the art market, was real. 'Considering the stunted Spanish art market of those years', noted Manuel J. Borja-Villel, who would become the Director of the Museo Reina Sofia in Madrid, 'an opportunity to exhibit abroad, even if through official channels, was the only realistic choice for an avant-garde artist to make.'[60] Jorge Luis Marzo was less sympathetic. For him, these were the actions of a 'collaborationist avant-garde', pure and simple.[61] Regardless, it was O'Hara who made the selections for *New Spanish Painting and Sculpture*, even if he relied on the biases of advisors on the ground in Spain. Anticipating any possible criticism, McCray stressed the exhibition's independent ambitions:

> Last Sunday, during a day's visit in Madrid I met with a group of these artists who expressed a strong preference that the exhibition be independently selected by the Museum without any association with their government.[62]

This did not, however, fully prevent criticism of too close an approach between O'Hara and the Spanish cultural authorities in Madrid. With the political stakes as high as they were, controversy beckoned.

III. 'Spaniards Aplenty': Criticism of *New Spanish Painting and Sculpture*

Only in 1960, when *la dictadura* had strategically assumed a new mantle as an anti-communist ally to the United States and had made repeated overtures to international audiences to prove that philistinism was not in charge, does New York host not one but three shows of 'avant-garde' art from Spain. Pierre Matisse's gallery on 57th Street was first with an exhibition of works by the El Paso 'gang of four' Millares, Canogar, Rivera and Saura (15 March to 9 April 1960); followed by the Solomon R. Guggenheim's *Before Picasso; after Miró* (12 June to 16 October), curated by its Director, James Johnson

Sweeney; and, finally the major anthological survey at MoMA, *New Spanish Painting and Sculpture*, which opened on 20 July.[63] O'Hara's catalogue essay was indebted to Sweeney's comparatively brief introduction, where the artists' 'range stretches back through Goya, through Velázquez, Zurbarán and medieval Catalan painting to the cave art of Altamira'.[64] It seemed that the phantom of a supra-linear trajectory of Spanish history, revitalized for the present and with incredibly specific referents to a 'national' art and the Baroque, had arrived and was a ubiquitous theme presented to the New York art public.

The city's two leading institutional tastemakers may have put on parallel shows that had thematic overlap before, but some observers were suspicious. The *New York Times*' critic John Canaday (well-known for his cynicism towards the Abstract Expressionists), wrote two articles in the summer of 1960 with the sarcastic titles 'Spaniards Aplenty' and 'Art: More from Spain. Modern Museum Show Follows Guggenheim's'.[65] More damningly, O'Hara's sometime colleague, Natalie Edgar, wrote an essay in *Art News* asking: 'Is there a new Spanish School?' Edgar's tone is scornful, and argues that if we accept the that the aesthetic merits of postwar Spanish abstraction were limited at best, which she encourages us to do, then the preponderance of interest in New York in 1960 was down to alternative factors:

One question is raised by the shows of postwar Spanish painting now at The Museum of Modern Art (to sept. 25), the Guggenheim Museum (to oct. 16) and several New York galleries – Why are there so many? . . . the paintings themselves are based mainly on *virtuosity,* their *intrinsic significance seems negligible.* Yet anything which is the focus of so much attention gains an aura of importance. Why, then, have museums and dealers with a responsibility for the creation of public taste given such importance to the new Spanish movement? . . . Only a glance is needed to plumb their depths: there are no undercurrents, no deeper, more allusive meanings to puzzle the viewer. And they are done in the familiar styles of Tenth Street – Kline, Pollock, etc. with a little French and Italian added.

Furthermore, the sheer talkability and saleability of a new school, readymade, whole-born as Athena from Zeus, with his historians, poets, manifestoes, organisations, influences, religious significances, based on a tradition of Goya and Velázquez is enormous. The fact that these paintings are stylish subject matter for the "taste bureaucracy" cannot be discarded as a major attraction.

Postwar Spanish painting is not an avant-garde movement at all, but rather a provincial aberration. Remember that it is limited by the conditions of dictatorship; the free environment necessary for a genuine avantgarde movement is missing.[66]

Even in 1960, it had become clear to New York critics, many of whom had been despondent about their government's rehabilitation of Francoist Spain, that an exhibition of this kind was incongruous with the political situation in the country. The free conditions for art-making under dictatorship were absent. Edgar was suspicious, above all, of the 'readymade, whole-born' packaging and promotion of the artists.[67]

It might be true to say, however, that Edgar's opposition was grounded as much in a distrust of curatorial narratives that linked style with locality – 'the familiar styles of Tenth Street' – and steamrolled over formal diversities, as in the specific case of Spain. Writing more recently in 2013, and with Edgar's precedent in mind, María Dolores Jiménez-Blanco and Robert Lubar, two distinguished art historians working today in Spain, make a convincing argument against this moment in New York in 1960. Their position is that major American museums not only showed a dynamic Spanish avant-garde in line with the efforts of Francoist cultural policy, but also fell back on a narrative of a national art open to foreign influence and partnership but fundamentally placed within a tradition of national difference. Jiménez-Blanco singles out O'Hara's catalogue introduction for criticism:

> The preface to the catalog *New Spanish Painting and Sculpture* displays every stereotype of Spanish art as traditionally seen from an anglosaxon perspective: Spain as an exotic, isolated, backwards country whose strong artistic personality is based on originality rather than refinement; and Spain as the birthplace of powerful artists who were forced to immigrate [sic] in order to develop their creative vision. . . . In contemporary art-historical genealogies, mainstream narratives have always followed the dictates of The Museum of Modern Art. The goal of the actions taken by the Spanish Foreign Affairs Ministry was to focus international attention on young Spanish Informalist painters and to consolidate the idea of a Spanish art open to international trends, but also *different* from them. With great approbation, The Museum of Modern Art lent its institutional weight to this discourse. For decades, even Spanish art historians believed the story.[68]

Jiménez-Blanco makes a compelling case by isolating O'Hara's efforts to explain the postwar avant-garde's 'special qualities' within Spain's cultural heritage. It seems, in this regard at least, that O'Hara's 1960 exhibition was somewhat consistent with Franco's cultural diplomacy, and that O'Hara himself, albeit with a non-aligned naïveté, had gone some way in serving Franco's interests in the cultural sphere. However, Jiménez-Blanco relies on an interpretation of the artworks exhibited as radically depoliticized, a view that she stresses was shared by the regime and was therefore acceptable to be promoted as such. It is a view of the display of art that cares much about cohering institutional ideology, and less about the works' formal properties, or the ways they might articulate a quieter subversion. Let me provide two brief examples that go some way in supporting a different view of the artworks themselves.

Canogar's gesturally abstract *Toledo* (1960), the homage to the artist's hometown that welcomed visitors to *New Spanish Painting and Sculpture*, might be best understood as an abstract landscape, a monochrome rendering of the city's palace-fortress, the Alcázar, that was a contested Civil War site. Thick impasto heaves the painting upwards and concentrates around the build-up of paint in the work's centre-ground, resembling the stone fortification, and set against a dull all-grey background that suggests horizon and sky. During the siege of Alcázar in 1936, much of the rebel-held citadel and former royal residence was destroyed by Republican artillery; a little over two months later, Nationalist forces and the Army of Africa put down the siege, led by Colonel José Moscardó who, in the hagiographic narrative of the site, sacrificed his hostage son for 'God and Spain'. As Basilio notes, 'the Alcázar became central to the new regime's mythic retelling of history' as *gloriosas ruinas* ('glorious ruins') and was later promoted as a tourist destination and 'site of memory that linked Spanish military and imperial history with Franco's Civil War victory'.[69] Franco gave a speech at the Alcázar on 28 September 1939, during which he celebrated Colonel Moscardó as a modern-day El Cid (Rodrigo Díaz de Vivar), the medieval conqueror of Valencia, and claimed that: 'History repeats itself . . . But when attempts are made to erase history, a new history is written; when the glory of these stones is attacked, a greater one arises from its ruins.'[70] The painting, then, must be seen within this history, and its politicized revisions. Rather than promoting a homogeneous narrative of history, endlessly re-emerging and endlessly reaffirming a nationalist teleology of place, might Canogar's *Toledo* be re-appropriating the Alcázar to destabilize those histories? In the Francoist version of history, selected events and figures are compared to the present to establish a false continuity. Canogar's painting, then, connects the contemporary formal vocabulary of the international *Informel* with recent Spanish history in an ambivalent way that undermines the coherence of the Alcázar as a stable nationalist monument. In this respect, I am largely in agreement with Noemi De Haro-García and Julián Díaz-Sánchez, who have argued that 'the incorporation of Spanish tradition and its famous characters into the work of anti-Francoist intellectuals undermined the regime's control over it'.[71]

To take another example, Antonio Saura's *Imaginary Portrait of Goya* (1959–60) is, according to O'Hara, 'close in its adamant recognition of terror to Goya's own *Dog Buried in the Sand* in the room of "Black Paintings" in the Prado, a room which contains much that is pertinent to other recent artists' (Figure 5.3).[72] The artist corroborates this link, and the 'point of departure' for the series that this painting inaugurates 'was the Goya "Dog appearing" from the "Black Paintings" at the Prado'.[73] Saura connects these images with phases of movement, renewal or adventure, 'the birth of a child at the moment of emerging from its mother's womb, or more recently of an astronaut emerging from his capsule', and observes in both his and Goya's work the 'deserted landscape' – or merely 'space' – from which 'a being emerges ... I have always thought of this head as Goya himself watching "something happen".'[74] This final statement relates to an important point, and to the politics of display within a climate of intensified historicism.[75] As is widely known, Goya's 'Black Paintings' produced at his Quinta de Sordo estate represent the elderly artist's retreat from courtly painting, as the works feature despondent scenes of infanticidal cannibalism (*Saturn Devouring His Son*, 1819–1823), extreme provincial poverty (*Two Old Men Eating Soup*, 1819–1823) and, perhaps most troubling of all, the vista of two men alone, trudging knee-deep in a swamp, about to pummel one another to certain death with cudgels (*Fight With Cudgels*, 1819–1823). This painting has been seen as a premonition of the political and cultural dissection into 'two Spains', a phrase made famous by Antonio Machado, which found its most terrible manifestation in the country's Civil War. Saura's revitalization of Goya's dog, as a 'witness', stands as testimony not to a celebrated national culture but to a corrupt Spanish autocracy. Goya was painting during the Napoleonic invasion, at a perilous time for his beloved liberals, and Saura links that national crisis to the present moment. This sense of direction and purpose lost, like the dog without its master, would have appeared pertinent to observers of Spain in 1960. 'Outlines of heads, body parts and decipherable elements appear', Saura wrote in his

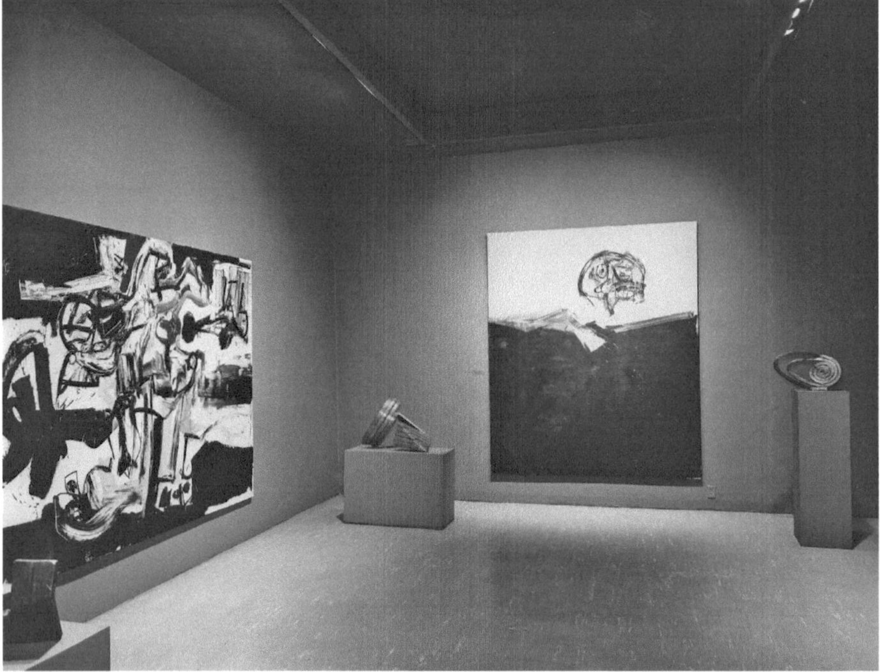

FIGURE 5.3 Installation view of the exhibition *New Spanish Painting and Sculpture*. MoMA, NY, 20 July–28 September 1960.

1958 essay 'Notes on Pollock' in *Carta de El Paso 4*, 'almost always engulfed by the landslides created by the dripping paint.'[76]

We know that O'Hara himself was enamoured with the 'Black Paintings'. In a letter to Waldo Rasmussen from the Hotel Colon, O'Hara wrote: 'I go now to lunch with Robles and Cuixart and then the latter's studio. I got to the Prado twice briefly and Goya is again my favorite painter of the whole world.'[77] Curiously, then, various references to Goya's dog appear in O'Hara's poetry of the period: in 'Places for Oscar Salvador', for example, a 'crazy artist gentler than a dog is blind' performs (CP, 308), while in 'A Little Travel Diary' O'Hara imagines being adrift on the water close to San Sebastián as forty-foot waves drench his boat and he sees 'a dead dog. . . slowly pulling out to sea' (CP, 357). 'A Little Travel Diary' should be read as a companion piece to Ashbery's 'Leaving the Atocha Station'. Both poems, against a 'locomotive landscape', employ a difficult, collagist poetic form that obscures (or otherwise makes redundant) referentiality, although Ashbery's is even more extreme; both identify a mysterious 'dog' in the distance, blind or dead (CP, 356). Marjorie Perloff and John Shoptaw are in agreement that Ashbery's poem 'reads rather like a Dada collage or *cadavre exquis* made by jumbling and cutting up' lines from other texts, with Perloff convinced that this is, really, an allusion to T. S. Eliot.[78] For her, Ashbery gestures to a passage from 'The Burial of the Dead' in *The Waste Land:* 'Oh keep the Dog far hence, that's friend to men, / Or with his nails he'll dig it up again!'[79] But we know that in between 'being wined and dined by the Spanish artists who were eager to impress Frank', Ashbery would spend hours walking the vast, subterranean picture-walls of the Prado, and we know that his travel companion was, at this time, writing an exhibition catalogue which referred extensively to Goya's 'Black Paintings'.[80] Although Ashbery offered few annotations to decode *The Tennis Court Oath*, and we should not expect him to, he has confided elsewhere that, indeed, 'the blind dog was a reference to Goya, as [he] was very impressed by his "Black" paintings in the Prado'.[81] As this demonstrates, the friends' poetic output was intimately informed and conditioned by curatorial research in Madrid. The symbol of Goya's dog provided a convenient means through which to historicize the present, not only by revealing the oppositional act of bearing witness, as in Saura's Informalist style that avoided representational criticism of the regime, but also for Goya's own superlative artistic status within the present for both poets.

While O'Hara and Ashbery toured the Basque Country in 1960, an insidious state-sponsored advertising campaign swept across Spain. Manuel Fraga-Iribarne, an author of Spain's 1978 constitution who oversaw the state's XXV Años de Paz campaign, managed a tourist drive with the tagline 'Spain is different'. A populist slogan that is now oft-quoted and self-parodied, 'Spain is different' was nevertheless tremendously successful insofar as it played up to clichés of a romanticized Spain that was exotic, anti-metropolitan, ritualistic, and, above all, *other*.[82] A tourist boom followed. Fraga-Iribarne's posters and the discourse that legitimated them were patent examples of Franco's wider foreign strategy, and the emphasis on Spain's *difference* also served other purposes. The campaign was euphemistically designed to distract from the nation's anomalous status as a western European state that was run by a fascist dictator, and sought to elide regional (or separatist) difference under the *rojigualda* which could, so it goes, accommodate difference only between national borders. Difference was perfectly acceptable, so long as it did not contradict the state's articulation of itself. In one example, cantaors and flamenco dancers (not Spanish *per se*, but from Andalusian Romani communities), perch with aristocratic poise on horseback; in another, crowds throng at *la fiesta*. These constructions, together with others that feature inhospitable landscapes and ruins, call to mind an image of the Spaniard that Immanuel Kant chided with a mix of cosmopolitan commitment and xenophobia:

> he does not learn from foreigners; does not travel in order to know other peoples; remains centuries behind in the sciences; resists any reform; is proud of not having to work; is of a romantic temperament of spirit, as the bullfight shows; is cruel, as the former *Auto da Fé* proves; and shows in his taste an origin that is partly non-European.[83]

These stereotypes of the Spaniard are conspicuously proximate to O'Hara's characterization of the artists he curated as 'different, aristocratic, intransigent, intelligent'.[84] This link between O'Hara's writing and the state's tourism propaganda might be incidental; it certainly does not convincingly confirm O'Hara as a knowing and willing collaborator with Francoist cultural officials to popularize a particular version of postwar Spanish abstraction. Exhibition archives at MoMA do indicate that O'Hara cooperated with state actors in Spain to facilitate transportation of works, although that would have been essential for customs clearance and for lender bureaucracy. Letters also reveal that some represented artists were uneasy about the increased involvement of official channels, especially through Robles, which indicates how an awareness of being co-opted by the regime was changing how some artists felt about being promoted in New York, where they had hitherto been keen to take advantage of market interest. 'Although the exhibition is not being shown under the auspices of the Spanish government', O'Hara half-heartedly reassured a concerned Luis Feito in April 1960, 'the Cultural Relations Office has offered to assist us with the assembling of the works for shipment.'[85] Elsewhere, in a letter to Waldo Rasmussen from the Hotel Colon in Barcelona, O'Hara explains how he received advice from the artists themselves:

> [Millares] said that he and the other artists always used MACARRON, which is a very expert firm in Madrid for both packing and shipping, so

if the Spanish government does not wish to use Guggenbuhl as we have suggested, perhaps Porter or Miss Dudley will wish to suggest that MACARRON be used.[86]

These kinds of decisions, essentially those that enable the exhibition to be materialized, may seem innocent enough, although they betray wider anxieties about the independence of the *segunda vanguardia* in an international arena. Robles was important not only as a mediator between MoMA and the artistic communities in Spain but was also at least in part responsible for several inclusions. Just three and a half months before the opening, Robles was 'thinking rigorously' and felt 'morally obliged' to tell O'Hara that, while the list as it stood was 'of high standards', it was 'incomplete'.[87] O'Hara appeared to have taken his concerns at face value, as Jorge Otieza and Antonio Suárez were both subsequently shown on Robles' recommendation, and the other suggested artists – Ángel Ferrant, Vicente Vela and Carlos Plannell – were all given special mention in the catalogue text. Robles wrote to O'Hara:

> I think the selection you have indicated should be oriented in another direction, especially since the Pierre Matisse Gallery is already launching the same values as The Museum of Modern Art such that nothing new is being discovered. What is worse, since the names are the same Matisse can say with pride that he discovered them and that The Museum of Modern Art is merely following his lead. This is an important consideration. Something similar occurred to me when I began to organize the exhibition at the Musée des Art Decoratifs. At that time Paris insisted that the exhibition should include very few artists, and given the unlikely coincidence that these were the same ones who were exhibiting in Parisian galleries, I was quite suspicious.[88]

O'Hara's independence was scrutinized by many of the represented artists, such as Manolo Millares, who put down his concerns in a letter to Pierre Matisse: 'What you told me about Sr. Robles being entrusted with this affair surprised me, especially since O'Hara promised me that he would be in charge of everything. I'm beginning to see that this exhibition of Spanish Art is not on a very good path, which truly concerns me.'[89] Millares' misgivings increased later in the year, when the exhibition travelled to the Corcoran Gallery in Washington DC: 'They say that the Spanish Ambassador sponsored it. If this is true I am very displeased. I don't want us to be placed within certain political lines.'[90]

It might appear accurate, then, to accuse *New Spanish Painting and Sculpture* of being an exhibition that stood as a platform to promote a particular version of Spanish art history that supported the Francoist cultural programme of the 'developmentism' period. Barreiro López outlines this well:

The official agents of the Francoist regime could not have been more
pleased by the integration of Spanish movements in such a narrative.
With endorsements from a great number of intellectuals from 'free
countries', the specificity of the Spanish informel became firmly established
because of its international character as well as its link to the Baroque
tradition, which the regime had been trying to vindicate, with a great deal
of contradictions since the end of the Civil War.[91]

The political and aesthetic outcomes of the exhibition, then, remain
ambivalent. On the one hand, I would argue that many of the artists
represented were aware of efforts to co-opt their work by the regime, and
several paintings address the dilemma of politicizing historical Spanish
painting by this generation of artists. On the other, Barreiro López is correct
in positioning *New Spanish Painting and Sculpture* as an event that
contributed to a favourable image of Spanish cultural life under Franco, and
one that was consistent with the national discourse it promoted to
rehabilitate the nation during the Cold War. Further, it is perfectly plausible
that O'Hara, who had little exposure to postwar Spanish art before his
initial research trip in 1958, acted naïvely in taking Robles's instructions for
selections, as well as adopting the then-dominant critical discourse – even
'every stereotype' of Spanish culture 'from an anglosaxon perspective' – on
the recent emergence of the *segunda vanguardia* in his catalogue.

In a separate but related observation, however, it is worth remembering
that throughout his autobiographical and art writing, O'Hara strikes a
resolutely anti-Francoist attitude, as here from the *Autobiographical
Fragments*: 'At any rate we are now approaching 1940 at a leisurely pace
and my next political memory was that of revulsion at having been made to
pray for Franco's success during the Spanish Civil War when I was in grade
school and didn't know which side was which.'[92] O'Hara also addressed the
injustices of the Spanish Civil War, its aftermath, and the consequences for
international abstraction in his writings on Robert Motherwell, whose
career was intimately linked to the historical consciousness of the Spanish
Civil War and its memory.

IV. Elegies to the Spanish Republic

Writing in the catalogue introduction to his 1965 *Robert Motherwell*
retrospective at MoMA, which then travelled to various museums in the
United States and Europe, including the Whitechapel Art Gallery in London
the following year, O'Hara notes that the 'first foreign political event to
engage [Motherwell's] feelings was the Spanish Civil War, that perfect mirror
of all that was confused, venal and wrong in national and international
politics and has remained so'.[93] A statement that echoes his own
autobiographical reflections on being made to pray for Franco at grade

school, O'Hara stresses the enduring injustice of the Civil War felt by those outside of Spain. 'No account of the period', continued O'Hara, 'can ignore Motherwell's role as an internationalist.'[94] Motherwell's defining *Elegies to the Spanish Republic* comprised over 150 abstract works between 1949 and 1991 and this series was complemented by several others, including *Iberia* (1958), first produced after his honeymoon in Madrid with Helen Frankenthaler – not to mention the earlier works *Spanish Picture with Window* (1941), *The Spanish Prison (Window)* (1943–44) and *Little Spanish Prison* (1943–44). Each of these three paintings nominally refer to the experience of Republican prisoners held during the Civil War and see thin Mondrian-esque lines and rectangles in an informalist rendering. Another painting, also included in O'Hara's 1965 retrospective, *Spanish Painting with the Face of a Dog* (1958), is a loose reworking of Goya's menacing *El Perro* that was the model, as I have noted earlier, for Saura's *Imaginary Portrait of Goya*, which the Spaniard produced the following year.[95]

Elegies tend to be poems, and it is possible that the Spanish Civil War was mourned more in verse than any other political event of the twentieth century. Motherwell's *Elegies* were themselves first imagined as an accompaniment to critic Harold Rosenberg's poem 'A Bird for Every Bird' and were originally published in the single-issue experimental magazine *possibilities*, which Motherwell co-edited with Rosenberg in 1948. The poem is a surrealistic sketch in informal quatrains and three stanzas, coloured by the stylized Spanish tinge of 'the white and the black'.[96] The final quatrain appeared above the ink-on-paper sketch. In this first version of the *Elegies*, two blocked-out rectangles separate a small ovoid on the left, as two ovoids are separated by a central rectangle and a third on the far-right of the picture. A thin vertical line divides the two ovoids on the right. None of the shapes touch the bottom of the canvas. O'Hara stressed this schema's overlying complexity, and noted that the *Elegies* have been 'variously interpreted as male verticals and female ovoids, as bulls' tails and testicles hung side by side on the wall of the arena after the fight, and as purist juxtapositions of rectangular and curvilinear forms'.[97] However read, the design soon became a dominant one for Motherwell, who reproduced it in subtly altered forms for the next two decades, defending the series insofar as he believed there 'ought to be an elegy (a funeral lament) for the original Republic'.[98] Like O'Hara, Motherwell's sense of his elegy ambivalently oscillates between public and private expressions of mourning. 'The *Elegies* record private feelings', reflected the artist, 'nevertheless they are about a public event – and to me the event was political.'[99]

In the first of these painted constructions in series, which were consistently monumental in scale (often in the region of 1.85 × 3.50 metres), the artist named the work *At Five in the Afternoon,* a refrain lifted from Federico García Lorca's own elegy 'Llanto por Ignacio Sánchez Mejías' ('Lament for Ignacio Sánchez Mejías'). Of the poem's 52 lines, 28 stress the time of day that locates the poem at a particular moment, the moment when Sánchez

Mejías, matador, writer and darling of the Generación del 27, was struck down by a bull in Manzanares on 11 August 1934 (Figure 5.4). The repeated temporal locator is disconcertingly persistent, as though marking time, perhaps the tolling of a funeral bell, or the involuntary and incessant interruptions that relive a traumatic event. Motherwell's process of naming *At Five in the Afternoon* is a well-rehearsed anecdote within Abstract Expressionism's compositional history. It also further embeds the making and meaning of Motherwell's series with the persistent task of remembering the Spanish Civil War through that conflict's poet-martyr García Lorca.[100] Motherwell claimed that as he worked on this first elegy, he wanted to communicate a peculiarly 'Spanish sense of death' in addition to a painterly mood board that spoke to his 'Mexican wife [first wife, Maria Emilia Ferreira y Moyeros], bullfights, travel in Mexico, documentary photographs of the Mexican revolution, Goya, Santos, dark Hispanic interiors'.[101]

As I have previously discussed, O'Hara assisted in a curatorial capacity on the major 1958 travelling show *The New American Painting*. Many of the facts surrounding Motherwell's representation at this exhibition remain unclear. What we are certain of, however, is that one of the *Elegies* was packed and transported to Madrid, for the first time.[102] The regime authorities steadfastly refused to exhibit *Elegy to the Spanish Republic XXXV* unless Motherwell changed the title as a condition of inclusion; unsurprisingly, Motherwell promptly refused. This expression of political and artistic solidarity naturally endeared Motherwell to the Spanish painters, with whom he maintained long friendships, especially with Tàpies and Saura. The latter's obituary for Motherwell in the Spanish daily *El País* appears to corroborate this interpretation of events, when he wrote: 'I very well remember how in 1957 [sic], I protested against the non-inclusion of one of his *Elegies to the Spanish Republic* in an exhibition of American Abstract Expressionism, held in Madrid.'[103] Robles, however, disputes any controversy: 'Nor did Motherwell's painting Elegy for the Republic [sic], which I showed [Franco and his cultural officials] one day, produce any laughter; it's something that people had warned me about, having problems, but nothing happened, it was all much simpler than that; what is important is the paintings, whether they are good or not.'[104] The *Elegies* were not reprinted in the official catalogue, although there is some disagreement as to whether the painting was shown for a short time and then censured and removed.[105] However, correspondence between officials within MoMA to both Robles and Motherwell himself suggests the controversy, or what McCray described as the 'Motherwell situation', had more serious implications for MoMA policy in relation to the Franco regime.[106] In a letter to be held 'in confidence', McCray told Robles of 'a very unpleasant experience with Motherwell about his Elegy' and noted that 'the title [. . .] as you know, we sought to change for the Madrid exhibition'.[107] In this regard at least, McCray appeared to be willing to operate with a high degree of flexibility 'in relation to the Spanish political situation' in order to show

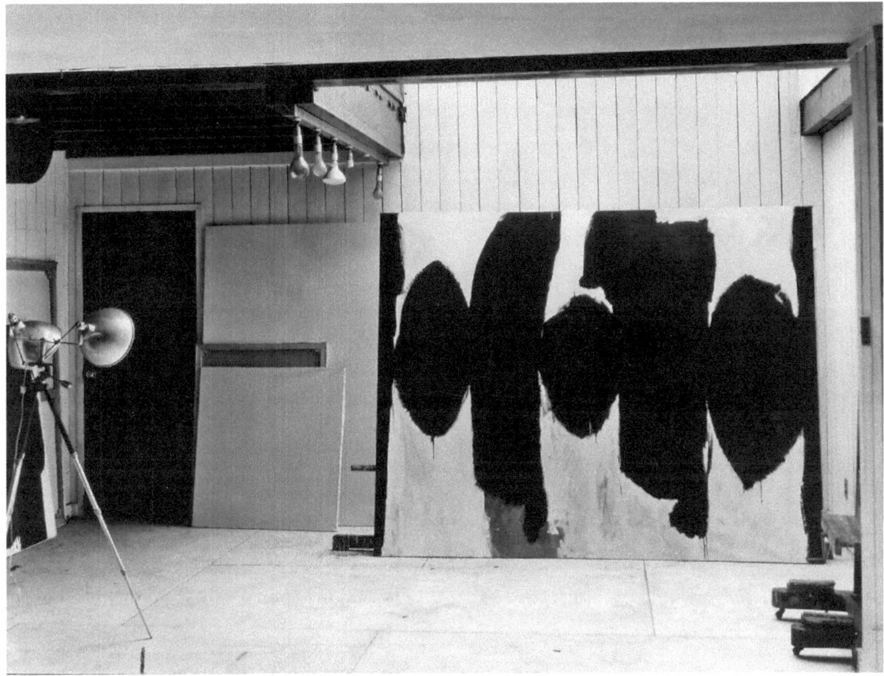

FIGURE 5.4 Robert Motherwell's *Elegy for the Spanish Republic XXXV*, in his E. 94th Street studio, 1957–58. Photograph by Sidney Janis Gallery.

the full selection. Despite ongoing fears that Motherwell, who was then in Spain, over 200 hundred miles away in St. Jean-de-Luz with Helen Frankenthaler, would 'raise Hell in Madrid' McCray reassured René d'Harnoncourt that his letter 'pacified his anger and that love and good painting had removed some of [Motherwell's] anguish and that he was putting the whole matter out of mind'.[108] O'Hara, on the other hand, shared Motherwell's anguish. 'Anne Hecht has been told by the Spanish translator', O'Hara warned Susan Senior earlier in June 1958, 'that we may expect trouble over this title [*Elegy to the Spanish Republic XXXV*] and suggested we call the painting *Elegy XXXV*. [. . .] Dorothy Miller feels as I do that this is establishing a very dangerous precedent and one which is against our usual policy in the past.'[109] While he does offer some reservations insofar as this *Elegy* was 'the major Motherwell in the exhibition and we [the International Program] would hate to have it withdrawn for political reasons', O'Hara concluded: 'I personally think it should remain exactly as is.'[110] Not only did O'Hara believe the work should maintain the original title – which, he explains, cannot be changed in any case 'without the artist's permission' – but that efforts should be made to maintain MoMA's curatorial independence and display the painting regardless of interference from cultural officials loyal to the regime.[111] Unsure if they will travel onto San Sebastián, Barcelona, the Costa Brava, the French Riviera, or even St. Ives in Cornwall, Frankenthaler writes: 'Anyway, considering the title of Bob's pictures we might be lynched if we appeared at the opening here, in Madrid! Or, they'll probably throw us out of the Ritz for painting all night in the hotel rooms. Olé, we're splendid.'[112] If Frankenthaler's exuberance was marked by the passions of her honeymoon, it was also marked by a genuine defiance against Francoist repression of those artists for whom Motherwell defended so publicly.

Like Picasso, Motherwell was a passionate supporter of the SRA. Founded in 1953 by Nancy MacDonald, SRA assisted displaced peoples, often but not always conflict veterans, who had fled to France. SRA maintained an office in New York City and coordinated aid efforts in France from Paris, Toulouse and Montauban. Its committee read like a who's who of the international Left, and included Albert Camus, Christopher Isherwood, Hannah Arendt and Sonia Orwell. Around twenty letters exchanged between Motherwell and MacDonald, now held by the Dedalus Foundation Collection, demonstrate that the painter was commissioned to create paintings and lithographs, often untitled but with the organization's name given in subtitles, to raise funds for the SRA's campaigns. It should be remembered that, over the course of the McCarthy period, the Truman administration's suppression of the former members of the Abraham Lincoln Brigade, not to mention the Pact of Madrid rapprochement phase, such activities were suspect. Although we cannot be certain, it seems likely that one such painting, completed in 1966, was donated on the occasion of a 1966 Tibor de Nagy exhibition and fundraiser. O'Hara would contribute an elegy in support, as John Bernard Myers remembered:

> My last collaboration with Frank took place in 1965 [sic] when I asked him to write a poem for a benefit exhibition that I was arranging for Spanish Refugee Relief [sic]. He was particularly sympathetic to the many painters and sculptors he had known in Madrid and he well understood their difficulties under Franco. The poem he wrote was entitled *A Little Elegy for Antonio Machado* and in it Frank expressed his concern for the plight of the Spanish people living in their world of pain and alienation, as had the poet Machado. It was printed as part of the catalogue. I wish I still had a copy.[113]

'Little Elegy for Antonio Machado', dated 27 March 1966, was the last poem Donald Allen assembled for *The Collected Poems* and, according to Bill Berkson, was the last one O'Hara ever wrote.[114]

It is difficult to read the poem outside of this truth, in part since Machado's own final verse writings were retrieved from his overcoat in the days after his death. In fact, as he was preparing for the Myers benefit in the weeks before his own death, O'Hara 'sent around a photograph of the [Pablo]

Serrano bust' of Machado and, after Barr asked whether applicable sculptures were available, there were then tentative efforts to acquire the bust as a memorial to O'Hara himself.[115] O'Hara's poem serves as another elegy, a remarkably similar function to that performed by Motherwell's *Elegies*. 'Little Elegy for Antonio Machado' will provide the conclusion to this chapter, and is worth quoting at length:

> Now your protesting demons summon themselves
>   with fire against the Castilian dark
> and solitary light
>   your mother dead on the hearth
> and your heart at rest on the border of constellary futures
>
> no domesticated cemeteries can enshroud your flight
>   of linear solarities and quiescent tumbrils
> vision of the carrion
>   past made glassy and golden
> to reveal the dark, the dark in all its ancestral clarity
>
> where our futures lie increasingly in fire
>   twisted ropes of sound encrusting our brains
> your water air and earth
>   insist on our joining you
> in recognition of colder prides and less negotiable ambitions
>
> we shall continue to correct all classical revisions
>   of ourselves as trials of ceremonial worth
> and purple excess
>   improving your soul's expansion
> in the night and developing our own in salt-like praise
>   (CP, 557)

This poem is, principally, a commissioned lament for Machado who had by the 1960s become, alongside Federico García Lorca, the great martyr-poet of the Republican defeat in the imaginations of foreign intellectuals and leftists. Through its funereal atmosphere and chiaroscuro imagery – 'the Castilian dark / and solitary light' – the poem retraces the final period of Machado's life through a fragmentary and often difficult build-up of visual set-pieces. After the Civil War broke out in July 1936, Machado was evacuated with his mother and uncle first to Valencia, and then along the coast to Barcelona. As Franco's forces closed in on the few remaining Republican strongholds in Catalonia, Machado fled across the French border to Collioure, where he would die in February 1939, just three days before his mother. It is she who lies, in O'Hara's words, 'dead on the hearth'.

There is an unapologetic internationalism to the whole scene, and O'Hara tells us that 'no domesticated cemeteries' can properly take account of Machado's 'flight'. The poem's only margin of division is not a geographical one – not between Spain and France, nor areas occupied by military forces loyal to Franco or the Republic – but a temporal one that takes on utopian proportions: 'on the border of constellary futures'. The experience of recent Spanish history, O'Hara suggests, in the light of its Civil War, its International and Abraham Lincoln Brigades, and as a kind of universalizing event that spoke to 'all that was venal and wrong . . . and has remained so', was not a national but an international experience. While I am largely in agreement with Andreas Huyssen insofar as it 'is important to recognize that memory discourses', at their core, 'remain tied to the histories of specific nations and states' and that 'the *political* site of memory practice is still national, not post-national or global', those memory discourses are also complicated by a global register and reality.[116] It is clear that O'Hara's curatorial dilemmas around historical revisionism earlier in the decade resurfaced in 'Little Elegy for Antonio Machado' and its quest for memorialization. The original version of the poem, shortened for the Tibor de Nagy publication, included a penultimate stanza – with '[? / to move]' handwritten in the margin ruminating on the relative virtues of acceptance and returning to revisit or revise:

> you sank the cadavers in the dusk to free the air
>   by embracing them and therefore also us
> moving in your space
>   accepting your grandeur
> as a necessary condition of the purple correction
>   (CP, 491)

This stanza celebrates Machado's 'grandeur', his sacrifice and commitment to political freedom, and positions 'us' as those who are now charged with taking up and remembering the 'space' left by the Civil War's lost poets. But in the poem's evasive images – why, for one, is the 'correction' coloured by purple? – O'Hara encouraged the reader to scrutinize the manner and the means by which we look to correct or revise histories, especially those that might not be our own, and what colours and shades we choose to frame subjects, even or especially those whom we believe history has since vindicated. The final stanza addresses this quandary most succinctly:

> we shall continue to correct all classical revisions
>   of ourselves as trials of ceremonial worth
> and purple excess
>   improving your soul's expansion
> in the night and developing our own in salt-like praise

Those 'classical revisions' vault from a principled effort to redress a propagandizing historical imagination to 'of ourselves', suggesting that it is in the personal *as well as* political that we must assume a corrective attitude to the past. Once more, the adjectival conditioning of 'praise' as 'salt-like' – Machado dying by the Mediterranean? – obfuscates the elegiac tone towards a supra-temporal space in which Machado's soul expands into the future, while we must be wary of the distractions of merely 'ceremonial worth' and lurid 'excess'. In this regard, O'Hara's poem follows Machado's aesthetics of time in which, as Norma Louise Hutman has explained, 'Machado endeavours to represent temporal totality: past glories, dissatisfaction with the present and desire for a better Spain', all the while 'bearing testimony to decadence but also challenging the present to redeem itself'.[117] O'Hara shares a comparative pursuit. The Spanish past was a compelling and useful subject for O'Hara to understand his present, both for his curatorial practice and in the modes of political remembrance so important to those closest to him. History not only enabled him to make it new, but to make it over.

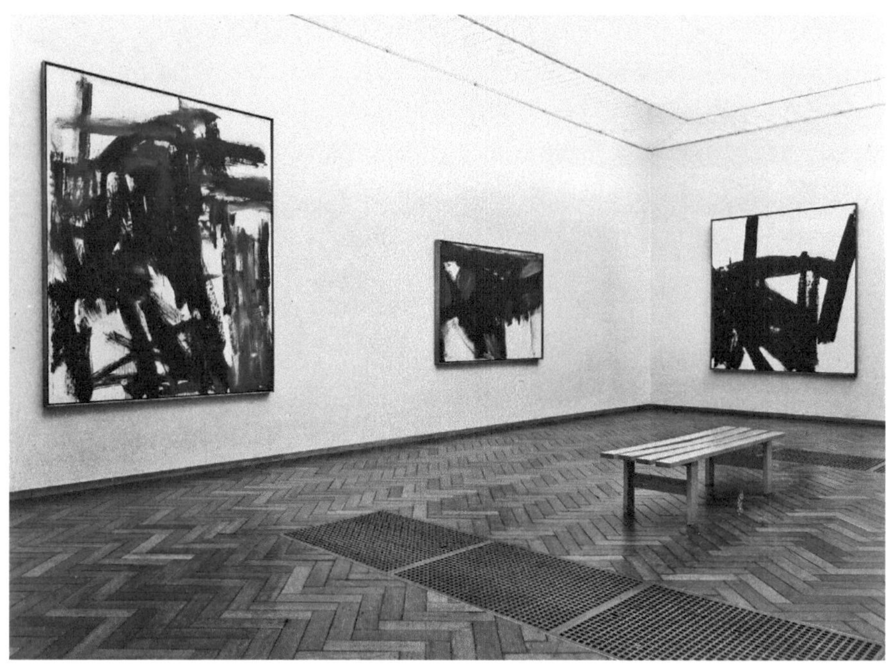

FIGURE 6.1 Installation view of the exhibition *Franz Kline* at the Stedelijk Museum, 1963.

Six | The Slightest Loss of Attention Leads to Death

Many of the single-artist exhibitions that Frank O'Hara curated were marked by the death of their principal subject. Tragically, all were close friends. Jackson Pollock's fatal car crash in 1956 meant that O'Hara's major exhibition on the artist, *Jackson Pollock 1912–1956*, was reframed as a posthumous retrospective. *Franz Kline*, which toured museums in Italy and the Netherlands in 1963, was assembled only after Kline's death the previous year. 'His death occurred at the apex of his career', Kline's *New York Times'* obituary ran, 'at a time when the avant-garde movement of which he was so conspicuously a member had achieved the dominant position in New York sales rooms and had affected the international scene in painting more decisively than any previous American movement in the arts.'[1] On 23 May 1965, at dusk near Bennington, Vermont, sometime after 8.45pm, David Smith descended a winding driveway in his Dodge truck, lost control on a curve and careened off an embankment into a ditch, ultimately colliding with a grove of trees and a power pole. When the ambulance carrying his body arrived at Albany Medical Center, he was already dead. Smith was 59 years old, and this tragedy came a full year before O'Hara opened the first major travelling retrospective of his work. It should also be noted that it would be O'Hara's own death in 1966 that delayed the first major Willem de Kooning retrospective at MoMA, which was already well in motion after the artist explicitly trusted only O'Hara to take on the project. 'I liked him immediately, he was so bright', De Kooning reflected: 'Right away he was at the centre of things, and he did not bulldoze. . . It was his manner and his way.'[2] The appeal for a Dutch museum to collaborate on a retrospective of the Netherlands' greatest modernist painter after Piet Mondrian was obvious. The Stedelijk Museum in Amsterdam had an ambitious new director, Edy de Wilde, who looked to New York for artists to invigorate his programme. At the reception dinner for the *Franz Kline* retrospective, which opened at the Stedelijk on 20 September 1963, De Wilde turned to O'Hara and stressed with a whisper his desperate 'longing' for a De Kooning retrospective (Figure 6.1).[3] De Wilde got his wish, but it turned out to be

O'Hara's last commission and ultimately opened, in Amsterdam and then New York, only after O'Hara's death.[4]

I. Franz Kline in Turin and Amsterdam

Franz Kline was De Wilde's inaugural exhibition, and he was eager to emerge from his predecessor Willem Sandberg's shadow and put his own stamp on the Stedelijk by transforming the museum into a major European centre for advanced art. De Wilde's first mission was to balance current developments in international painterly abstraction with the Museum's national collection of Dutch art. O'Hara reported back to Rasmussen after the Kline opening that 'everyone was very impressed at the unprecedented move on De Wilde's part of removing the Van Goghs from their traditional position in the large room at the head of the stairway in order to install the big late Klines there'.[5] Choosing what those 'big late Klines' would be, and where they could be borrowed from, was not simple. Kline had died of rheumatic heart disease, just ten days before his 52nd birthday the previous May, and the loss was particularly painful for O'Hara. 'I saw how difficult it was for Frank', reflected Rasmussen, 'to cope with selecting the work of an artist to whom he had felt so close and whose loss he still grieved.'[6] In an interview-essay included in the exhibition catalogue entitled 'Franz Kline Talking', the material of which was collated over three studio visits in 1958, O'Hara compares Kline's monumental mode of gestural mark-making to 'love', and in a surprising evocation of national exceptionalism, with a touch of Ralph Waldo Emerson's capacity for abstracting strength, to 'the virtue of the American dream of power, that power which shuns domination and subjection and exists purely to inspire love'.[7] O'Hara had addressed 'Poem (I will always love you)' to Kline, surely one of the most lyrical and compelling poems that he ever dedicated to an artist, which was featured in a photogravure as part of the pair's contribution to the *21 Etchings and Poems* project in 1960, alongside other poets and artists including Helen Philips and André Verdet, and published in an illustrated book by Morris Gallery in New York. Written by hand, O'Hara's poem oscillates between declarations and denials of affective commitment – 'I will always love you / though I never loved you' – to an enthusiastic celebration of Kline's paintings that feels like a no-holds-barred embrace, as 'the passion that enlightens / and stills and cultivates' (CP, 271). Kline was a painter who never forgot his roots in the gritty coal country of eastern Pennsylvania, and his paintings can feel like thunderclaps in an open landscape: his mature abstractions are atmospheres of ferocious solitude. It is this sense of immediacy, of something intensely felt but swiftly gone, and of something profoundly experiential between painting and body, which enlivens O'Hara's poem: 'I thought it was outside disappearing / but it was disappearing in my heart' (CP, 271).

The *Franz Kline* exhibition checklist counts 67 works, from early collages dated to the mid-1940s to the artist's late works from 1961, the year that

Kline fell ill and gave up painting.[8] After the critics dismissed his more recent forays into incorporating colour and grey into his previously monochrome palette, these large-format, vertically orientated and black-and-white compositions returned Kline to the bold gesturalism of the paintings that led to his initial success in 1950. It was these late works of his signature style that De Wilde had positioned at the top of the main staircase, including *Shenandoah Wall* (1961). The composition of *Shenandoah Wall* is resolutely horizontal, encouraging us to orientate the painting as a landscape study of the cascading valleys of Shenandoah National Park, with jutting vertical lines organized around a straight, thick, central line reaching to the upper and lower perimeters of the canvas. *Shenandoah Wall* was also the subject of one of O'Hara's most extraordinary critical assessments. He described the painting as 'fiercely humane [in its] sweeping inclusiveness', suggesting it represented 'a frontier which fate was to prevent the artist from crossing into who knows what other land of promise?'[9] But by choosing *Shenandoah Wall* for the exhibition, O'Hara inadvertently propelled himself into the messy orbit of Kline's probate and posthumous division of works. Two of Kline's patrons, Sidney Janis and Charles Egan, had been at loggerheads in a long-running legal dispute over the painting.[10] The retrospective enfolded O'Hara into the trust of Elizabeth (née Parsons), a former ballet dancer who had modelled in Frederick Whiting's drawing classes in London when she met her husband. Now a widow, and suffering from schizophrenia, Elizabeth Kline asked O'Hara to serve as an informal envoy by keeping her abreast of any international exhibitions of her late husband's work, especially because she felt that the executors gave her 'no information whatsoever'.[11] In response, O'Hara enclosed copies of his catalogues from Amsterdam and Turin, and informed Elizabeth that he had seen 'in Rome a beautiful small exhibition of Kline in the Galleria La Tartaruga on the Piazza del Popolo, consisting of five paintings from the collection of Baron Giorgio Franchetti, and several drawings'.[12] Kline was also represented by 'five paintings in the exhibition "54/64: Painting and Sculpture of a Decade"', organized by the Tate Gallery the following year.[13]

In Amsterdam, the Kline retrospective entailed working closely with several curators, museum officials and technicians, in what would be O'Hara's first single-artist exhibition held abroad since *Jackson Pollock 1912–1956* five years earlier. Whereas he had shared the responsibilities for the Pollock show's catalogue with Sam Hunter, O'Hara was free to make more executive decisions this time round. Logistical and material compromises in a large-scale retrospective of this kind were par for the course. 'Two of the Panza Klines [lent by Giuseppe Panza di Biumo of Milan] were reframed the morning before the opening and fitted miraculously well!', O'Hara wrote with gusto on 25 September, and 'the other two will be done today or tomorrow'.[14] He was satisfied with the 'quite well done' cases by Züst-Ambrosetti (two, containing two paintings each), 'but unfortunately, though the wood is good and heavy, they are both prodigies of nails which have to be yanked out for each unpacking and hammered back in for each transport'.[15] O'Hara worked closely with the resident curator Louis Gans, an eccentric figure who would resign from the Stedelijk just a few months later, in December 1963. (An activist as well as a curator, Gans left to implement what he called his 'Gans plan', an ambitious national effort to promote the accessibility of modern art for communities who are often excluded from galleries and museums, principally by affordable art sales at the bohemian Bols Taverne on Rozengracht.) Supported by the carpentry team, O'Hara and Gans altered the cases to approximate as closely as possible to MoMA's own boxes with metal fittings and bolts for opening. 'If this operation does not work out well enough', O'Hara cautioned, 'I will have to have new ones made in Turin, but they will certainly suffice for that trip, and I don't want to cause any delay in shipment.'[16] As this demonstrates, O'Hara thrived as part of an international cross-institutional team, and by 1963 had become adept at managing major exhibitions in collaboration with European partners. The Kline retrospective travelled to the Museo Civico di Torino, the Palais des Beaux-Arts in Brussels, the Kunsthalle Basel, Museum des 20. Jahrhunderts in Vienna and eventually closed at the Whitechapel Art Gallery in London.[17]

When the exhibition was shown at the Museo Civico di Torino, critics saw Kline's canvases in philosophical terms (Figure 6.2). In a review for *Stampa Sera*, Angelo Dragone linked, as many critics have before and since, Kline's 'big strokes put down haphazardly' with 'the symbols of some mysterious Oriental writing'.[18] For Dragone, whether it was an early painting like *White and Black* (1949) or a late one like *Riverbed* (1961), Kline's paintings 'seem to isolate a single figurative element, which becomes almost a symbol destined to express in its "gigantism" a whole which remains hidden in it'.[19] Many critics commented on the size, scale and monumentality of Kline's canvases, something that was often linked by overseas reviewers, in contradistinction to the inflections of O'Hara's interpretation of gesture as 'love', to Kline's *Americanness* and his interest in the vast industrial landscapes of Pennsylvania. Marziano Bernardi did write a review for *La Stampa* that was much indebted to O'Hara's catalogue, tracing as he did Kline's formal relationship to Rembrandt van Rijn, Johannes Vermeer, Jean-Baptiste-Camille Corot and Édouard Manet, as well as 'the American romantic landscape artists, [Ralph Albert] Blakelock and [Albert Pinkham] Ryder', before arguing that no 'matter what judgement the public passes, the exhibition . . . is of exceptional interest'.[20] O'Hara felt that the gallery space in Turin functioned particularly well for this showing (Figure 6.2). He worked closely with his stern and business-minded co-curator Vittorio Viale, whom O'Hara admired. The two figures were photographed enthusiastically greeting guests at the opening, and listening to dignitaries' speeches (Figure 6.3). For O'Hara, the exhibition 'looked very good, better actually than Amsterdam. Less grand and formal, more pwerful [sic] and moving and getting at you.'[21]

In Dutch-language newspaper reviews that were ultimately not translated for the MoMA press archive, Diederik Oostdijk notes that most were 'polite-positive', and 'almost without exception agreed with O'Hara's lyrical

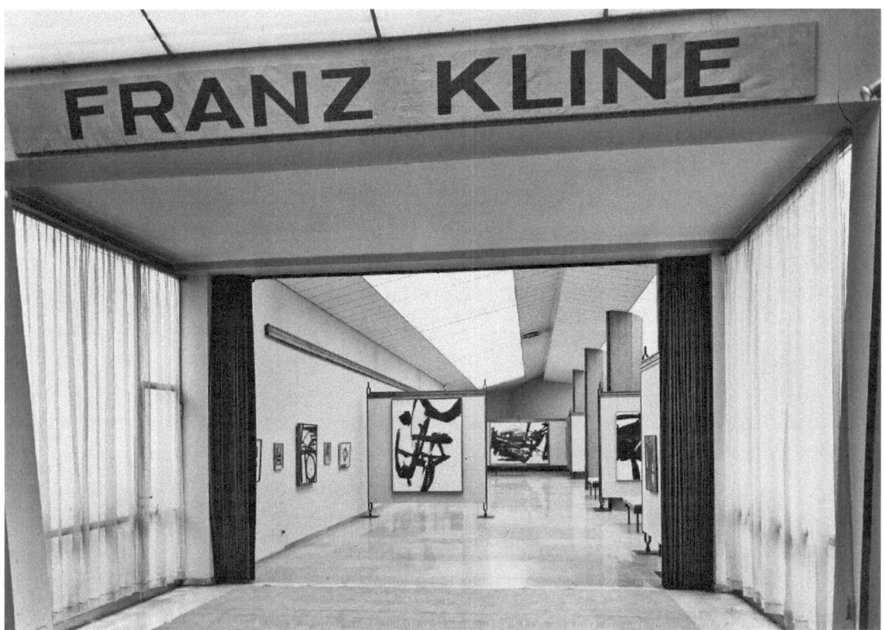

FIGURE 6.2 Installation view of the exhibition *Franz Kline* at the Museo Civico di Torino, 5 November 1963–1 December 1963.

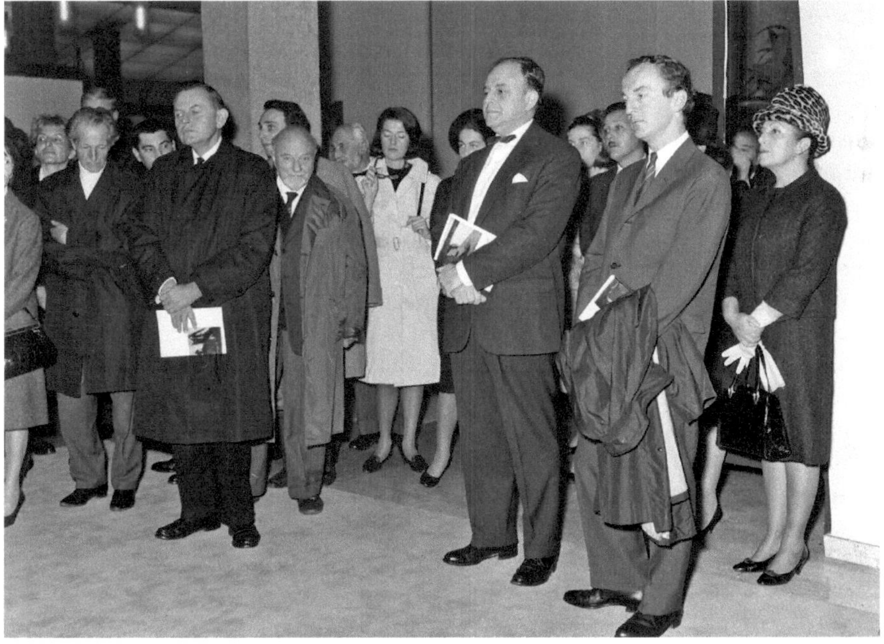

FIGURE 6.3 Frank O'Hara, second from right, with unidentified guests at the exhibition *Franz Kline* at the Museo Civico di Torino, 1963.

text about Kline from the catalogue' as a principal source of understanding the significance of this body of work.[22] Local grievances and the tense Cold War climate in 1963 coloured criticism. The popular art writer Godfried Bomans, for instance, dedicated his weekly column to challenging Lambert Tagenbosch, the reviewer for the daily morning newspaper *De Volkskrant*, and the incomprehensible 'delight with which [Kline's] works were viewed'.[23] Instead, the devoutly Catholic Bomans argued that the wild abstract marks betrayed not gestural joy and embodied expression but existential emptiness, something he associated with secularization and the absence of God. The title of his essay – 'The Burst Bomb' – chimed with widespread anxieties about the threat of nuclear war which, if any subject could be identified in these pure examples of abstract painting, was this angst. Bomans's conclusion was that Kline 'took the final plunge' and that critics have tried to shove 'a piece of lyric in a hole that wants to captivate attention by being a hole', an absence or a void.[24] Many critics have understood Kline's canvases as some kind of response to 'the bomb'. Later, the American art historian Robert Rosenblum wrote that, 'by 1945, after Hiroshima, this worship of primeval nature reached even more mythic extremes, as if after the apocalypse, the Abstract Expressionists needed to re-experience the first days of creation, turning as they did to images of molten energies, unformed matter, lambent voids'.[25]

To promote the Kline exhibition, O'Hara was interviewed by the young writer and artist Jan Cremer for The Hague-based weekly newspaper *Haagse Post*, who ran an article entitled ' "A New Manner": Dutch days with Kline and O'Hara'. While Cremer remains relatively little-known outside of his native Netherlands, in 1963 he was at the beginning of a long career as a writer, artist and inveterate traveller who moved freely within international subcultural and avant-garde circles.[26] His breakthrough was the fictionalized autobiography *Ik, Jan Cremer* (1964) which was first translated into English by R. E. Wyngaard and Alexander Trocchi, and was described by one critic as having 'blood and sperm . . . dripping off it'.[27] Together with Simon Vinkenoog, Cremer gained a reputation as an *enfant terrible*, a pioneer of Dutch beatnik poetics who would spend several years of the 1960s in New York, where he resided for a time at the Chelsea Hotel, and wrote *Made in U.S.A.* (1969) about his bohemian experiences and affairs.[28] Cremer's article ' "A New Manner": Dutch days with Kline and O'Hara' was ostensibly his personal account of the Kline exhibition, but it was more than that. The article introduced an important new friend and collaborator into O'Hara's life.

It was at the start of his 'grand tour' of European cities that O'Hara arrived in Amsterdam on 15 September 1963, a city he immediately described as 'very beautiful, the canals marvelous and filthy and calm'.[29] Alongside Amsterdam and Turin, over the course of this autumn and early winter O'Hara visited Antwerp, Paris, Milan, Rome, Copenhagen, Stockholm, Vienna, Zagreb, Belgrade and Prague. Friends often found that O'Hara cut a forlorn figure on these trips for MoMA, as Patsy Southgate recalled:

The one time I got some sense of Frank being in some kind of pain or uncertainty was the time he was packing to go to Europe and Czechoslovakia. There was something very tragic about him. He was all alone in this huge apartment with his tiny suitcase, sort of not knowing what to bring, not wanting to leave. His loneliness suddenly came across very strongly. He was packing these formal clothes. In formal circumstances he always dressed well. But when he was in a tuxedo he had a fake smile that broke my heart. It indicated to me that he was extremely strained. Here he was going to a place where there would be all strangers in formal situations. It didn't come easily to him. I realized how really alone he was.[30]

However, it is also true that O'Hara enjoyed travelling on museum business, as his commitments allowed for an extensive route through Europe. He joked that 'one of the ironies of my "life" is that the only time I'm not broke is when they send me somewhere and I have a per diem'.[31] Travelling to install and supervise exhibitions also gave him access to emerging European art and artists. In Amsterdam, O'Hara was accompanied by the well-connected American-Dutch painter Michael Francis Podulke, and they visited several studios of younger Dutch and American painters. It was Podulke who had introduced O'Hara to Cremer, who subsequently pitched an article on the Kline exhibition to the *Haagse Post*, in which he relied heavily on O'Hara's catalogue essay for biographical facts and stressed his admiration for 'the meanest tongue in New York'.[32] To prepare for the article, O'Hara walked Cremer around the exhibition and, in photographs taken by the controversial Dutch photographer Wim van der Linden, posed in front of several artworks, including *Shenandoah Wall* (Figures 6.4 and 6.5). O'Hara positions himself, in his foreshortened linen tie and wide-lapel suit, with Cremer as supporting cast, as an icon of style. Van der Linden's double portraits (and triple, in one case, with an unidentified young boy) are not in-situ shots of a curator greeting distinguished guests at the opening, or respectfully inspecting and pointing at speckles of paint up close, but photographs of a curator whose exhibition lends itself to an articulation of selfhood. Rather than the curator as an invisible presence in the making of the show, foregoing personality for the presentation of fact and objective truth, O'Hara anticipates a more modern understanding of the curator in the making of an exhibition. But O'Hara was not the only one seeking to give up institutional conventions on the veneration of art as distinct from life at this time. Speaking on Willem Sandberg (and appropriate for Edy de Wilde also, in my view), the celebrated German curator Johannes Cladders admired how Dutch curators in the early 1960s sought to stylize the exhibition as an event 'to bring art and life completely together and, therefore, to give up the institution of the museum'.[33] In short, the exhibition could be an exciting spectacle, which was importantly short-lived and temporary as opposed to the collection display (which was a kind of statement of the institution's

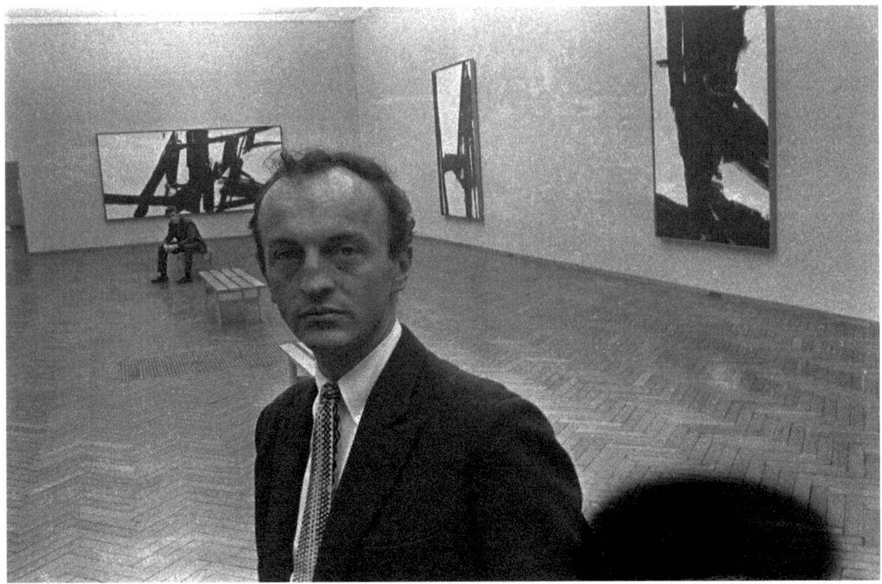

FIGURE 6.4 Jan Cremer and Frank O'Hara at the *Franz Kline* exhibition at the Stedelijk Museum, Amsterdam, 1963.

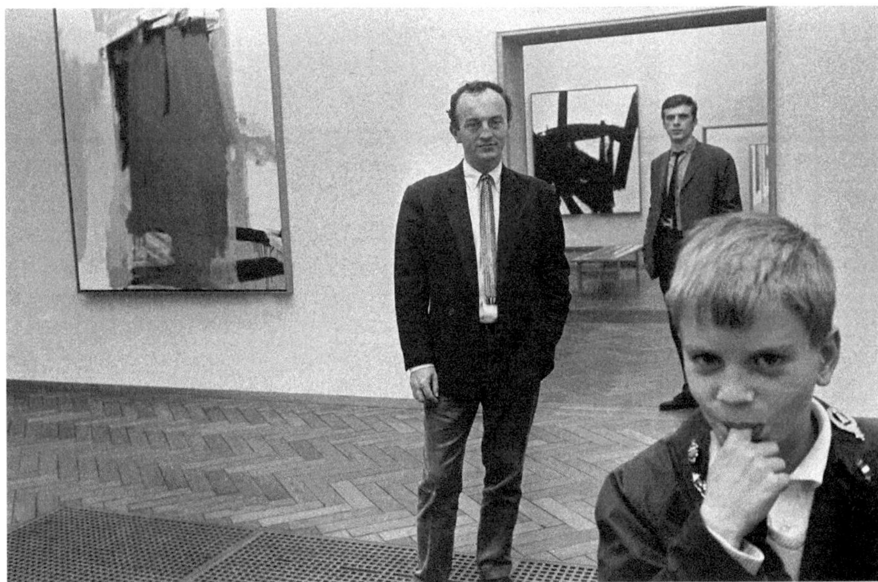

FIGURE 6.5 Frank O'Hara, Jan Cremer and unidentified boy at the *Franz Kline* exhibition at the Stedelijk Museum, Amsterdam, 1963.

identity and status, in perpetuity), and a spectacle that one could present oneself in and against as being part of that spectacle.

Following O'Hara's catalogue essay, Cremer traced Kline's career trajectory to his breakthrough exhibition at the Charles Egan Gallery in 1952; this, although not his first solo showing there, generated public recognition and enthusiasm beyond collectors. But Cremer also stressed the influence of Netherlandish art on the American painter, contrasting him with that 'famous ex-Dutchman de Kooning' and arguing that 'Kline remains an admirer of the old masters whose work he has seen in 1960 in the Rijksmuseum. Kline is and remains a painter of his descent, on some of his transparent dark canvasses, meters high, the umbers are even comparable with those of Rembrandt.'[34] Cremer was not the first to make this connection. With astonishment, Dore Ashton noted how Kline 'knew about Rembrandt's visit to Hercules Seghers, that remarkable eccentric whose intimations of the nature of space were highly abstract'.[35] Elsewhere, Harry Gaugh linked Kline's early, earthily-textured figurative works, such as *The Synagogue* (1945), to the Abstract Expressionist's 'admiration of Rembrandt'.[36] More directly, Kline himself said that he 'loved' Rembrandt in the 'Franz Kline Talking' that accompanied O'Hara's catalogue because, he reflected, '[y]ou go through the different phases of liking guys who are not like you'.[37] But by placing Kline within a tradition of the Dutch masters, Cremer was attempting to do more than situate this challenging abstract painter into more familiar art historical contexts for his readership.[38] Cremer emphasized the relational nature of art, in which a pure abstractionist like Kline could follow the interplay of figure and foreground in an Old Master like Rembrandt.

As suggested by Cremer's subtitle, 'Dutch days with Kline and O'Hara', his essay was as much about the poet and his career, style, and manner of being as it was about the subject of his exhibition at the Stedelijk – a digression, we might presume, that led Cremer's editors at the *Haagse Post* to think it lacked reasonable journalistic distance. In a more personal account ultimately omitted from the final edit, Cremer stressed the importance of his own encounter with the American poet: 'O'Hara remained in Amsterdam. Not at all the prototype of the poetry and jazz-loving young Amsterdamers who admire "beatniks" or "hipsters"; this modern American poet gave less ground for comment than beatnik Ted Joans who the evening after the opening assembled lots of people in the jazz-night-club Sheherazade.'[39] Cremer was referring to a 'jazz poetry reading by Greenwich Village's own Ted Joans', as O'Hara recalled, 'who dedicated a poem to Franz at the event and advised the whole nightclub to get over to the Stedelijk, man'.[40] O'Hara had earlier been incredulous when a newspaper clipping described Kline and himself as 'one of the "American Negro artists"'.[41] In a letter relayed back to New York on this glaring error, O'Hara exclaimed: 'quelle ironie!', and concluded: 'I hope the interview [with Cremer] comes out more accurate.'[42] While O'Hara had been initially apprehensive about the interview, signing off 'Well, I'm off to be interviewed (gulp)' in a letter to Rasmussen, he and Cremer got along well, and were even photographed tasting jenever and eating herring at fish stalls near the Haarlemmerbuurt port and industrial area (Figure 6.6).[43]

In another move that indicated O'Hara's self-reflexive and thoroughly comparative topographical imagination, in which the Netherlands was related back to a particular architecture or geography of New York, he mused: 'This part of Amsterdam makes one think of Manhattan [. . .] whether I would like to live here? Yes, but then only in the Havengebouw.'[44] Cremer closed his essay with a statement on their new friendship: 'Judging situations rapidly he, who himself in America is called "the meanest tongue in New York", dedicated to the Dutch writer-painter Jan Cremer his collection of poems *Second Avenue* "To the terror of Holland". And this after only two days (in Holland).'[45] If Cremer admired the older 'curator of the world-famous Museum of Modern Art, [. . .] who flew over from New York', who must have represented something close to the personification of cosmopolitan style to the younger man, then O'Hara also had reasons to be enamored with Cremer and wanted to preserve their amity beyond the brief circumstances of the Amsterdam interview.[46] O'Hara wrote home to Joe LeSueur: 'He's married and is about to have a second child (at 24!) so it's not what you think exactly, I mean not like Oscar [Salvador], though in a way more – well, no sense going into that, it requires too much theosophizing.'[47] The subtext was that O'Hara was pre-emptively defending his relationship with Cremer from the accusation that it was another heart-wrenching love affair with a younger,

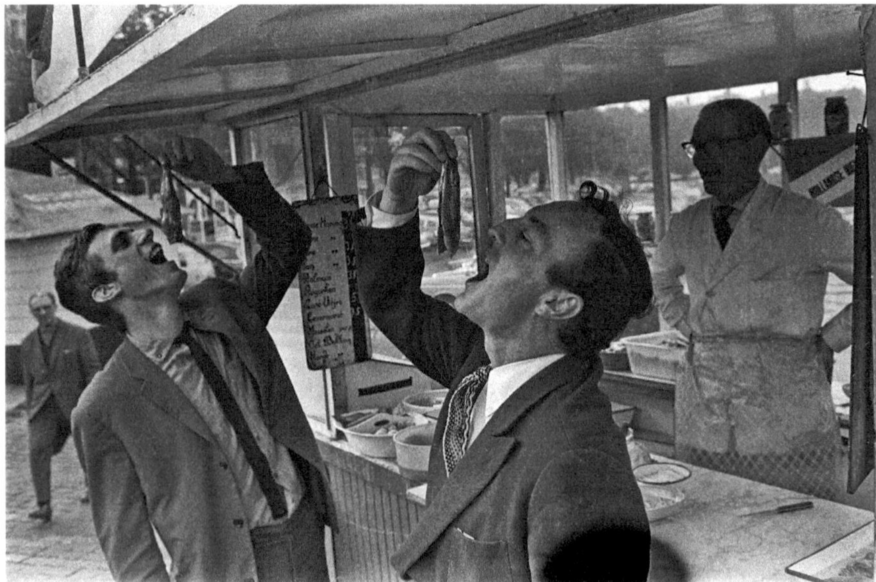

FIGURE 6.6 Frank O'Hara and Jan Cremer tasting herring at the Haarlemmerbuurt port, Amsterdam, 1963.

foreign man. And yet Cremer also fitted the type of the predominantly straight man with whom O'Hara became infatuated, but who would also prove to be an important partner in artistic exchange. There would be no time to collaborate on this trip, but before Cremer escorted O'Hara, who was to make his way to Copenhagen, in the rain, the two men agreed to work together on a new collaboration: ten poems by O'Hara, ten paintings by Cremer, which would not be ultimately realized until after O'Hara's death.

II. David Smith in Otterlo

David Smith and O'Hara had enjoyed a close if complicated relationship, with O'Hara dedicating several poems to 'the great American sculptor'.[48] O'Hara wrote 'Mozart Chemisier' on 10 August 1961, the day he left Smith's estate at the Terminal Iron Works in Bolton Landing following his first visit to research the touring exhibition that would become *David Smith: 1906– 1965* (1966). The poem is named after Smith's favourite composer and collages the topography of upstate New York with the visit of Smith's two daughters, Rebecca and Candida.[49] The non-sequitur lines evoke an atmosphere of sunny leisure, celebrating the enthusiasm for hard drinking the two men shared: O'Hara recounts enjoying 'a double carbonated bourbon on the porch' while 'back at the ranch they were serving bubbly gin' (CP, 428). The intercontinental configuration of the scene – from 'being one with Africa', to the speaker's anger as 'strictly European' and concluding with egotistical, colloquial misconceptions in 'these here America' (CP, 428) – creates a sense of overlapping terrains, as though the incongruity of Smith's industrial sculptures against the lush, rolling hills of Bolton Landing transported the speaker to many worlds at once. 'The contrast between the sculptures and this rural scene is striking', O'Hara reflected in a December 1961 issue of *Art News* , 'to see a cow or a pony in the same perspective as one of the *Ziggurats*, with the trees and mountains behind, is to find nature soft and art harsh'.[50]

O'Hara did not overtly reference Smith's sculptures in 'Mozart Chemisier' which, in addition to the works on show in the meadow at Bolton Landing, would have then included one large unfinished sculpture (welded but unpainted) housed in the studio, three others in various stages of progression, as well as 'huge piles of steel waiting to be used' outside the studio.[51] But the landscape of the poem does mirror this sense of malleable scale: of composites creating larger wholes or being diminutively returned, as the grand 'poplars' resemble an 'aspidistra' house plant beside the 'unexperienced' Lake George (CP, 428). The poem closes with what was presumably overheard dialogue, as Smith negotiates with his two daughters as they are about to leave the house:

put on your earrings we're going to the railroad station
I don't care how small the house they live in is

you don't have any earrings
I don't have a ticket
(CP, 428)

David Getsy has noted how 'Smith publicly voiced throughout his career a deep distrust of curators, art historians and collectors', and so this intimacy afforded to O'Hara was both rare and precious.[52] Carried by his irrepressible excitement for the show to be realized and brimming with praise for what he had seen, O'Hara wrote immediately to Smith after returning to New York: 'I think we have a terrific show lined up and I've been elated just thinking about it. Also I've been thinking about the new work ever since leaving, and it's staggering. [. . .] They got to me but I don't get to them. They make me feel like the world going round and round and not knowing what's going on, or, in a word, *alive*.'[53]

Four years later, in spring 1965, the pair spent a fortnight working together once again in Bolton Landing. It was there, surrounded by what Smith had called his 'girl sculptures' in a televised interview with O'Hara for *Art: New York* (1964), that they discussed the selection for *David Smith 1906–1965*.[54] 'Both Smith and O'Hara were used to good-natured but edgy banter in which artists and poets egged each other on', noted Smith's biographer Michael Brenson, 'while demanding verbal improvisations that would keep the conversation moving in ways that allowed for the formation of fresh responses without getting mired in explanation.'[55] The friendship rested on a shared belief that Smith's sculptures should not be beaten down by explanation. Smith's retrospective would be his first major retrospective organized by MoMA, but O'Hara's third on the sculptor, having overseen a touring exhibition of his sculpture in 1961 and a show of drawings in 1963. The exhibition was one of MoMA's series focusing on artists at mid-career (optimistic, in hindsight) and came at a creative time for the two men. Smith had enjoyed a productive summer during which he had made 'bigger and better sculpture', while O'Hara had been tasked with greater responsibilities in the International Program as Associate Curator.[56] These extra duties were bittersweet, as he took on the travelling exhibition after the ousting of Porter McCray, his longtime mentor, who ensured his protégé's position was protected after the 'The Revolt of the Young Turks' debacle and his subsequent resignation.[57]

Organized by the International Program, *David Smith: 1906–1965* travelled from the Kröller-Müller Museum in Otterlo, the Netherlands, to London, Basel, Nuremberg and Duisberg. Writing to Clement Greenberg, who was then one of the executors of Smith's estate, O'Hara noted that he and Rasmussen were also 'having endless negotiations with the three principal museums of Paris with no definite results' and that efforts had been made to show the exhibition at 'the newly completed Modern Museum in Belgrade' – but to no avail since 'the financial difficulties for the Yugoslavs [were] extreme'.[58] The exhibition did travel to Harvard University's Fogg

Art Museum after The Tate Gallery, and both institutions reproduced Bill Berkson's chronology of Smith. (O'Hara had commissioned the young poet, who had worked on a similar commission for O'Hara's Motherwell retrospective the previous year.) O'Hara worked closely with Jane Harrison at the Fogg Art Museum, a collaboration that ensured Smith's *Australia* (1951), the 'key-piece' which the exhibition was 'built pretty much around', was shipped in haste from London to Cambridge in time for the opening there.[59] *Australia* combines metal scraps and agricultural tool parts, and has a low centre of gravity as lines, curves, and oblongs seem to hurtle from a cubic plinth like a spring. It is for this reason, alongside its title, that *Australia* is often seen as an abstract representation of a kangaroo hurtling across a plain.

In total, the exhibition included 49 sculptures, including works from as early as 1939, although just over half (25) were produced in Smith's immensely productive final five years of his life. The exhibition would be particularly significant for presenting selected sculptures from his time in Voltri, Italy. The Italian government had invited Smith to participate in the *Festival of Two Worlds* in Spoleto in 1962; the Italsider Steel Manufacturing Company, which combined the words 'Italia' and 'siderurgia' (steel industry), gave Smith access to an abandoned welding factory in the town, as well as the support of workers. The sculptor ended up producing over 27 works in 30 days using scrap metal, objects and found materials, far exceeding the two works required as a condition of support from the Italian government. These sculptures were shown in the classical amphitheatre and thronging streets of Spoleto but had not yet reached a wider audience.[60] O'Hara surmised that across the whole exhibition these works ranged 'in importance from superb to no less than significant'.[61] After returning to the United States from Italy, Smith started work on the *Menand* series of bronzes, small painted steel pieces; on *Cubi*, a series in stainless steel that O'Hara categorized as 'heroic'; on three very large *Wagons*, a re-envisioning of one he had produced in the Voltri factory; and on the *Voltri-Bolton* series, which O'Hara defined as 'homages to the experiences and materials he had found so inspiring during his stay in Italy'.[62]

Of all the iterations of the Smith retrospective, the installation at the Kröller-Müller Museum would be the only one that O'Hara would personally attend. Indeed, it would be the last place overseas that O'Hara would visit and his final official engagement for MoMA.[63] By 1966, the gruelling exhibition schedule, his persistent struggles with alcoholism, and a prolonged spell of ill health were taking their toll. Immediately prior to the trip to the Netherlands, O'Hara was bedridden for two weeks with a virus infection in his left leg which was intensely painful, and he had to use a cane at the opening.[64] In his introductory speech at the *vernissage*, O'Hara reflected that the opening represented 'both a happy and a sad occasion for me'.[65] It is impossible to believe that this could have been otherwise. The writer and one-time De Kooning bodyguard Erje Ayden wrote, on O'Hara stricken by grief after losing his friend: 'I had never heard before a man who could describe a fellow artist so fully, making you think you knew David Smith all your life, played marbles with him, went to school with him, drank, suffered with him, shared the same women with him... And when Frank cried at the death of David Smith, self-consciously letting his tears drop into the cognac, I did the same thing.'[66]

In his speech, O'Hara continued with pleasantries, thanking attendee William R. Tyler, United States Ambassador to the Netherlands, in a way that illustrated that the exhibition was something of another diplomatic event; he expressed his delight in 'the beautiful installation' and recognized that the Kröller-Müller's 'sponsorship of [Smith's] work' was considered by the sculptor as 'one of the supreme accolades of his career'.[67] In conclusion, O'Hara moved to the cosmopolitan possibilities of Smith's practice, and celebrated the ways in which his work spoke to a kind of internationalism implicit in sculptural abstraction. 'Smith inspired in those who knew him', O'Hara resolved, 'a great faith in communicating between people and between art of all periods'.[68] The young museum director Rudi Oxenaar had recently replaced Bram Hammacher at the helm of the Kröller-Müller and, like many directors of his generation, sought to invigorate the international contacts of this provincially located (but not minded) museum. O'Hara was particularly impressed by the sculpture garden, surrounded by the woodlands of the Nationale Park De Hoge Veluwe, and remarked half in jest to Oxenaar that 'the only comparable site here in New York is Central Park itself, but alas it is not administered by a Museum'.[69] Archival photographs show the Smith works in the sculpture garden (Figures 6.7–6.8). The right environment of display for these works was essential: in Smith's words, the *Cubi* series, for instance, were 'designed for outdoors. They are not designed for Philip Johnson's building [MoMA]... Philip Johnson doesn't need me and I don't need him. Though they look pretty good inside with artificial light, I think.'[70] In the exhibition text, O'Hara emphasized the necessarily experiential nature of Smith's sculptures, best encountered on the rolling hills of Bolton Landing or the gardens at the Kröller-Müller as opposed to the clinical curation of a gallery space, and remembered his visit once more: 'one was struck by these brilliant and sophisticated stainless steel or painted structures, posed against the rugged hills and mountains, the lake in the distance, and the clouds, an assertion of civilized values not nearly so surprising in the confines of a gallery or museum, where, conversely, these same sculptures took on an aspect of rugged individualism and often an almost brutally forthright power.'[71]

Because of his grief, the landscape of the museum was difficult for O'Hara to process, and the speech itself is peppered with reflections on what might have been had Smith survived. When discussing which works would be selected from the Bolton Landing studio, Smith had urged O'Hara to 'leave room for what might yet be done', a poignant and ultimately impossible request.[72] O'Hara was sure that Smith 'would have been both gratified and inspired by the site of his installation in the park' and would have

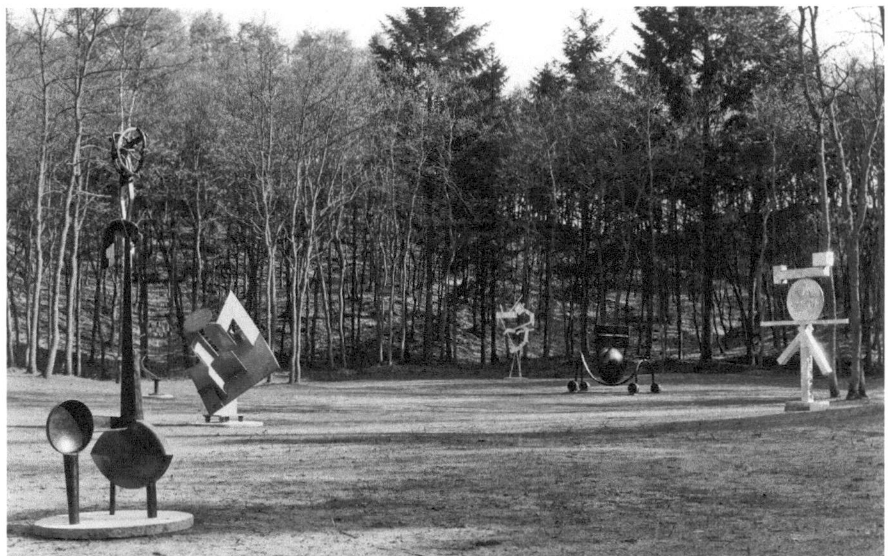

FIGURE 6.7 Installation view of the outdoor exhibition *David Smith: 1906–1965* at the Kröller-Müller Museum, Otterlo, 14 May 1966–27 July 1966. (View 1)

undoubtedly suggested, 'with his characteristic combination of humor and seriousness, that he begin immediately to work on a 12 meter high tower to challenge the trees, or a 12 meter long wagon to challenge the rhododendrons'.[73] Whatever the outcome of this challenge, O'Hara affirmed that Smith would 'probably have entitled' the project '*Kröller-Müller #1*' – such was his commitment to the specificities of the site and space he worked in, and the 'fecundity of the period so tragically terminated by his accidental death'.[74] Those imagined possibilities, while foreclosed by Smith himself, were something of a call to action by the curator, who conceived of new and transformative ways that Smith's work could be displayed.

In a letter to Joan Mitchell, O'Hara described how much he was impressed by the provincial museum, even if the neighbourhood was 'a Calvinist stronghold' populated entirely by 'elderly excursionists and little children':

It has a marvelous collection, among other things some choice Chinese sculptures, a great Cranach, a great Jongkind oil, the only Zadine I ever really admired (a huge polychrome wooden woman), and the most beautiful group of van Goghs! [. . .] The Smiths look wonderful out here in a clearing among the trees – in another nearby there's a nice big bronze of Etienne Martin in five parts (all of which you can sit on) and a big George Rickey in another one flapping in stately fashion when the wind blows. The Smiths all arrived in good condition except for chips on some of the painted zips which had to be touched up (I'd brought David's own paint – that part was quite melancholy).[75]

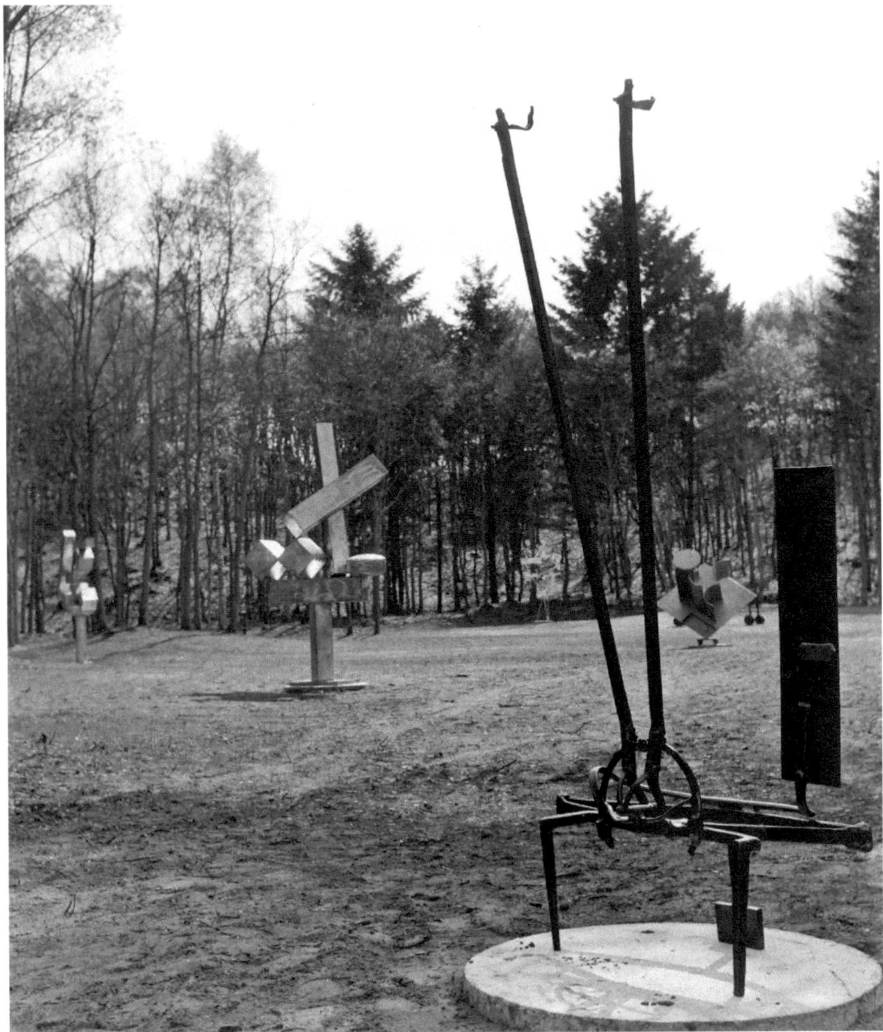

FIGURE 6.8 Installation view of the outdoor exhibition *David Smith: 1906–1965* at the Kröller-Müller Museum, Otterlo, 14 May 1966–27 July 1966. (View 2)

O'Hara recounts a touching image of friendship, loss and recuperation. The letter demonstrates how intimately O'Hara curated the works themselves, and how the proximities afforded by his relationships with artists like Smith allowed him, for a moment at least, to be there with the works themselves as the artist would. This might be described as a posthumous collaboration of sorts, in which O'Hara's curatorial prerogatives meant that he was able to at once fulfil the creative wishes of an absent friend while simultaneously contributing to the finish of the work in an embodied way. In 'David Smith:

The color of steel', O'Hara had remembered his visit to Bolton Landing earlier in 1961 and celebrated Smith's move to polychromatic sculpture in metal, in juxtaposition to Greenberg's scandalous decision to remove the paint from certain Smith sculptures.[76] Writing on this controversy, Brenson asks: 'Why were the penetrating observations of O'Hara, whose understanding of Smith was as acute in the 1960s as Greenberg's was in the 1940s, not fully acknowledged until half a century later, when Sarah Hamill and David J. Getsy wrote him into the mainstream of the Smith literature? If O'Hara had not died in 1966, at forty, while his Smith show was on tour, Smith's critical history would surely have been different.'[77]

O'Hara described the charming, anthropomorphic quality of Smith's sculptures, seeming like 'people who are waiting to gain admittance to a formal reception'.[78] He went on to note how the 'process of painting the sculptures is a complicated one', oftentimes requiring 'more than twenty coats . . . [of] rust-resistant paint of the kind used on battleships'.[79] Touching up the zips in Otterlo must have returned him to the 1961 visit and to the time when Smith's sculptures seemed only 'powerful, indomitable'.[80] These restorative gestures in the Kröller-Müller sculpture garden only affirmed O'Hara's holistic approach to curatorial practice. He believed that curating should allow artworks to breathe, to be alive, consistent with what he called the 'living situation' philosophy of the exhibition itself. It is easy, therefore, to see all of O'Hara's exhibitions as collaborations of sorts. After the interview with Smith, for *Art: New York* in 1964, O'Hara reflected on what his friend's sculptural practice meant to him:

> It's the nature of sculpture to be there. If you don't like it, you wish it would get out of the way, because it occupies space, which your body could occupy. David Smith's sculptures are – big or small, figurative or abstract – very complete, very attentive to your presence. They're generous; they have no boring views. Circle them as you may, they are never napping. They present a total attention, and they are telling you that that is the way to be: on guard. In a sense, they are benign, because they offer themselves for your pleasure. But beneath that kindness is a warning: don't be bored, don't be lazy, don't be trivial, and don't be proud. The slightest loss of attention leads to death. The primary passion in these sculptures is to avert catastrophe, or to sink beneath it in a grand way. So, as with the Greeks, Smith's is a tragic art.[81]

O'Hara's last trip abroad was an important and emotional one. But the installation of the Smith exhibition in Otterlo also perfectly typifies O'Hara's approach to curatorial practice, which he based on the principles of personal affection for the works themselves, and himself as a facilitator of cross-cultural openness that felt consistent with his approach to poetry-writing, collaboration and friendship, and not as an objective arbiter or codifier of art – or, as O'Hara might have affirmed it himself, 'presence'.

Afterword | Living Situations in New York and London

In my first chapter, I discussed O'Hara's essay 'Art Chronicle I', a review of the *American Abstract Expressionists and Imagists* at the Solomon R. Guggenheim Museum in 1961 and quoted from an important passage: 'This is all living art and the show reflects the living situation [. . .]. It depends on what you see and when it's shown and it keeps you fresh for looking and for the excitement of art.'[1] Sixty-two years after O'Hara's review, while I was in the final stages of writing this book, I also found myself halfway up Frank Lloyd Wright's winding ramp at the Guggenheim, but now looking at a portrait of O'Hara by Alex Katz. Painted using oil not on canvas but a wood panel, and at five feet tall by just over one foot wide (or 'seven-eighths life-size', as Katz put it), this cutout of O'Hara depicts the poet and curator gazing into the middle distance.[2] Smartly dressed, O'Hara is wearing a green suit jacket over a white collared shirt and patterned black-purple tie, with grey flannel trousers and black lace-up shoes. He resembles a free-standing paper doll or, as O'Hara himself described the cutouts for *Art News*, a review of himself in some ways, 'the Dummy-Board Figures which stood by English firesides of the late 17th and early 18th centuries to give burglars the illusion that the rooms were occupied'.[3] Turned away from a full-body portrait on canvas of the dancer Paul Taylor, something transfixes O'Hara's attention, but his calm and prepossessed expression suggests that he knows he is being observed. O'Hara looks as though he is quietly waiting for his friends to arrive at a cocktail party where, remarkably enough, he does not yet know anyone, so has decided to play the role of the mysterious stranger in the corner. Equally plausible, in his crisp establishment look, he is stiffening up his nerves before he is due to give a speech at the opening reception for an exhibition.

As I looked at Frank O'Hara up close, I remembered a fabled moment in the history of the New York School. When Katz had his first show of cutouts at the Tanager Gallery in 1961, *Frank O'Hara* (1959–60) was one of the featured works. Edwin Denby, the poet, art critic and mutual friend of both O'Hara and Katz, went to see his friend's show: in my mind, at least, Denby held his hands folded behind his back in an observant posture at once balletic and connoisseurial, as he is often described, and considered each cutout closely. And then, suddenly, as Denby remembers,

> I noticed out of the corner of my eye that Frank O'Hara had come in and was standing a few feet away, absorbed in the show. I quickly turned to speak to him. But he wasn't there; it was the cutout of Frank that had fooled me. A moment later with a deeper misgiving I realized that the Frank who had fooled me was only three-quarters life size. The joke— Katz's—wasn't nice at all. Quite recently, at Elaine de Kooning's studio, the same cutout fooled me again.[4]

One of the reasons why *Frank O'Hara* is so striking is its remarkable capacity to disorientate you (it depends on what you see and where it's shown). Given the fact that you can walk around this work and notice things like O'Hara's gait or poise across several vantage points, from the back and side as well as the front, or realize what it means for Katz to render his subject at a subtly different size to its actuality, which presents a remarkably more urgent demand on the viewer than the standardized rectangular-formatted wall-mounted painting, the experience jolts you. 'Though this moment of realization disrupts one aspect of the depiction's fidelity to its subject, curiously the work continues to seem correct in scale, if not in size', curator David Max Horowitz wrote in the Guggenheim exhibition catalogue: '[a]fter all, it would appear to be too big if it were larger. In this uncanny effect, *Frank O'Hara* reveals our habituation to reading images rendered in perspectival space, illustrating both the potency of this convention and its contrivance.'[5] While Katz made several cutouts of figures in the New York scene that he and O'Hara occupied, he recognized that there was a gregariousness to O'Hara: 'I think he extended himself further out emotionally than his friends', Katz wrote: 'I would love to be able to make an art with these qualities.'[6] Such was O'Hara's conviction in the art of his friends, Katz compared him to

> a priest who got into a different business. Even on his sixth martini - second pack of cigarettes and while calling a friend, "a bag of shit," and roaring off into the night, Frank's business was being an active intellectual. He was out to improve the world whether we liked it or not … the frightening amount of energy he invested in our art and our lives often made me feel like a miser.[7]

So much of the energy that Katz described was O'Hara's talent for intimacy, which was not merely the intimacy he afforded to his friends, and which is the dominant tenor of his poems, but the intimacy of enthusiasm for the creative life of those friends, which was his too.

In 1960, around the same time as Katz completed his cutout portrait, O'Hara sat for another painting by Alice Neel. Fresh from curating the travelling *Jackson Pollock 1912–1956* memorial exhibition that toured Europe and, more recently, the first Helen Frankenthaler retrospective at the Jewish Museum, O'Hara was not yet thirty-five and his ascendant career trajectory had been recently recognized with a promotion to the position of Curator in the International Program. The sixty-year-old Neel, 'three weeks younger than the century' as she liked to describe herself, was destitute with no reputation in the art world which O'Hara held in his hand.[8] Neel produced two portraits. The first, 'a romantic, falconlike profile with a bunch of lilacs', sees O'Hara at ease in a grey sweater and baby blue Oxford shirt, with his characteristic broken nose and receding hairline unable to suppress a sense of youthful composure.[9] This was still a young man in his prime. The second depicts O'Hara looking around a decade older, in a kind of insipid decline, grimacing through gritted teeth which Neel compared to 'tombstones' while 'the lilacs had withered', recalling the symbolism of lilacs as both a creative inspiration to imaginative minds and Walt Whitman's elegy for President Abraham Lincoln, thus comprising both creativity and a sense of death.[10] When O'Hara saw the picture he said, 'My God, those freckles', to which Neel responded: 'But the Fauves went that far', as if to assure her startled sitter that a portrait can offer up a sheer extremity of colour and form while retaining a fundamental likeness.[11] While abstraction then dominated the New York art scene, and O'Hara was the subject of 'abstracted portraits' by Grace Hartigan and a faceless depiction by Elaine de Kooning, he was also subject to several realist portraits, including by Fairfield Porter and Larry Rivers, such as the double-portrait that is on the front of this book. *Frank O'Hara No. 2*, (1960) is one of Neel's most striking portraits of any sitter in her *oeuvre*, and stands as one of the most accomplished works of postwar American figurative painting. Neel's second portrait 'treats O'Hara not as a glamorous, brilliant matinee idol', J. S. Marcus wrote in a review of a 2008 retrospective in Stockholm, 'but as a doomed grotesque, whose ugliness heightens his humanity'.[12] It was this second portrait that was chosen by curator Eleanor Nairne for the *Alice Neel: Hot off the Griddle* exhibition at the Barbican Gallery, in the City of London, in spring 2023.

I arrived at the Barbican on a bleak and wet Sunday morning in February with a good friend I had not seen in a while. We studied the way that O'Hara sat on the wooden and flax studio chair, with his legs crossed but his left hand hiding under a knee and his right arm awkwardly looped around the top rail as though seeking to project a sense of ease. O'Hara looks like a desperate man whose anguish is etched into the balding forehead with curled whisps of hair, as 'those freckles' that he anxiously identified half resemble an outbreak of lesions, while the third of his face in shadow resembles a red sign forewarning danger. His eyes are spinning discs that radiate a hard coldness like a far-off glacier. As we discussed the painting, bristling as it does with the kind of nervous energy carried by a carousel of regrets made the night before, we remembered one of O'Hara's best-known lines of poetry: 'The only truth is face to face . . . we fight for what we love, not are' (CP, 305). We could see O'Hara's portraits like this: truth can only be found face to face, as in the portraits by Katz and Neel. But it also rings true for his exhibitions (I think, even though I had never spent time in a museum space curated by O'Hara first hand). This was a figure who fought hard for what he loved, which is to say a small band of artists in a small pocket of New York at a particular moment in the twentieth century, and who spent a decade at MoMA trying to show people why they should love them too. In one of his more reflective pieces for *Art News*, two years after his friend's death, Ashbery wrote about O'Hara's legacy:

> If the Museum and the artists . . . are what they are today, it is at least partly because O'Hara was one of the first to think they were that. As a poet, he was able to impart existence to things merely by naming them. And he could breathe life into art, or at any rate call attention to the life that was already there, in a way which is hard to pin down but whose aura continues.[13]

While he will continue to be best remembered as a poet, O'Hara's curatorial work for the International Program, which brought him into such proximity with art, artists and cities outside of the United States, was no less significant. O'Hara shared with Smith 'a great faith in communicating between people and between art of all periods' and, in doing so, he affected the landscape of postwar modern art in his own image.

Frank O'Hara's Exhibition Record for MoMA

1956	FRANCE: Laon, Saint-Quentin, Reims, Clermont-Ferrand, Nice	*Recent American Watercolors* Eighty works by forty-one artists selected by Dorothy C. Miller; sponsored and circulated by the Association Française d'Action Artistique. Exhibition catalogue written by Frank O'Hara. Travelled to five venues in France, between October 1956 and June 1957.
1957	BRAZIL: São Paulo	U.S. Representation: *IV Bienal do Museu de Arte Moderna* The first of several official curated displays of art from the United States at perennial exhibitions abroad. The representation included two exhibition sections: first, *Jackson Pollock 1912–1956,* consisting of thirty-four paintings and twenty-nine drawings by Jackson Pollock, a memorial to the artist after his death from a car accident the previous year, and selected by O'Hara; second, twenty-three paintings and fifteen sculptures by eight artists, including James Brooks, Philip Guston, Grace Hartigan, Franz Kline and Larry Rivers, and selected by O'Hara, assisted by Porter McCray, James Thrall Soby, Dorothy C. Miller and Sam Hunter. On display in São Paulo, 22 September–31 December 1957.
1958	ITALY: Rome SWITZERLAND: Basel THE NETHERLANDS: Amsterdam GERMANY: Hamburg and Berlin ENGLAND: London FRANCE: Paris	*Jackson Pollock 1912–1956* An edition of the previous year's Bienal do Museu de Arte Moderna retrospective for Europe, and circulated between 1958 and 1959. Thirty-one paintings and twenty drawings and watercolors, selected by O'Hara but with a catalogue essay by Sam Hunter. Circulated concurrently with *The New American Painting* in Basel, Berlin and Paris. Dispersed in 1959.

	ITALY: Venice	U.S. Representation: *29th Venice Biennale* Includes four exhibition sections: thirty-six paintings by Mark Tobey, who became the first American artist since James McNeill Whistler to win the International Prize for Painting, and twelve sculptures by Seymour Lipton, selected by O'Hara, and ten paintings by Mark Rothko and fourteen sculptures by David Smith, selected by Sam Hunter. Shown at the American Pavilion, 14 June–19 September 1958.
1959	GERMANY: Kassel	U.S. Representation: *documenta 2* 144 works by forty-four American artists including painting, sculpture, prints, and a retrospective exhibition of works by Jackson Pollock, selected by O'Hara and Porter McCray. On display 11 July–11 October 1959. The quinquennial exhibition was overseen by artistic director Arnold Bode, in collaboration with art historian Werner Haftmann.
1960	UNITED STATES: New York	*New Spanish Painting and Sculpture* On display at MoMA from 20 July to 28 September 1960. The exhibition featured two to five works by sixteen artists: Raphael Canogar, Eduardo Chillida, Martin Chirino, Modest Cuixart, Francisco Farreras, Luis Feito, Manuel Millares, Lucio Muñoz, Jorge Oteiza, Manuel Rivera, Antonio Saura, Pablo Serrano, Antonio Suàrez, Antoni Tàpies, Joan Josep Tharrats and Manuel Viola. The press release (dated 25 April 1960) advertised the exhibition: 'Although individual examples of the work of some of these artists have been shown in international exhibitions such as the International Exhibit of Contemporary Painting and Sculpture at the Carnegie Institute, the Venice Biennale and the São Paulo Bienal, as well as at a Recent Acquisitions show at the Museum (Jan. – Apr., 1959), this will be the first large exhibition in this country devoted entirely to these new developments in Spanish art.'
	BRAZIL: Buenos Aires	U. S. Representation: *I International Exhibition of Modern Art* One painting each by Franz Kline, Willem de Kooning, Jackson Pollock, and Mark Tobey, selected by O'Hara. On display between 11 November and 11 December 1960.

1961	BRAZIL: São Paulo	U.S. Representation: *VI Bienal do Museu de Arte Moderna* Included four exhibition sections: thirty-four paintings and drawings by Robert Motherwell and forty-eight sculptures and drawings by Reuben Nakian, selected by O'Hara; twenty-three paintings by eleven artists, a group show selected by William C. Seitz; and twelve prints by Leonard Baskin selected by William S. Lieberman. On display between 10 September and 31 December 1961.
1962	GERMANY: Karlsruhe, Hamburg, Berlin, and Essen ENGLAND: York, London, Nottingham, and Bristol SCOTLAND: Edinburgh BELGIUM: Brussels THE NETHERLANDS: Rotterdam AUSTRIA: Vienna PORTUGAL: Lisbon NORWAY: Oslo SWEDEN: Lund SWITZERLAND: Basel YUGOSLAVIA: Zagreb and Belgrade ITALY: Rome	*Drawings by Arshile Gorky* Fifty-five drawings, selected by O'Hara, from works from Gorky's estate. Circulated to Tokyo, Japan, before briefly returning to the United States, and then on to various destinations in Europe. Shown concurrently with *Robert Motherwell: Works on Paper* in Buenos Aires, Argentina; Caracas, Venezuela; Bogotá, Colombia; and Mexico City, Mexico, between November 1967 and June 1968.
1963	THE NETHERLANDS: Amsterdam ITALY: Turin BELGIUM: Brussels SWITZERLAND: Basel	*Franz Kline* 67 works of paintings, drawings, collages, and gouaches, selected by O'Hara, circulated in Europe between September 1963 and September 1964.

	ENGLAND: London YUGOSLAVIA: Belgrade, Rijeka, Maribor, and Ljubljana GREECE: Athens INDIA: Bombay, Trivandrum, Madras, New Delhi, Lucknow, Ahmadabad, Calcutta, and Patna CEYLON (SRI LANKA): Colombo AUSTRALIA: Sydney, Newcastle, Melbourne, and Perth NEW ZEALAND: Christchurch and Auckland	*Abstract Watercolors by Fourteen Americans* Fifty-four works by fourteen artists, selected by O'Hara, and displayed between June 1963 and June 1966.
1965	UNITED STATES: New York	*Robert Motherwell* On display at the Museum of Modern Art between 1 October and 29 November 1965. One of O'Hara's most significant retrospectives, he begins his catalogue essay with the mythical anecdote of Apelles leaving his sign on the wall, and asks, in relation to Motherwell's *Lyric Suite*: 'Does art choose the artist, or does the man choose art?'
	FRANCE: Paris; GERMANY: Berlin, Baden-Baden	*Modern Sculpture: U.S.A.* Marquee display at Musée Rodin, and then German showings. Seventy-one works by twenty-two sculptors selected by René d'Harnoncourt and O'Hara, circulated between June 1965 and April 1966.

	ITALY: Spoleto	*Recent Landscapes by Nine Americans* Thirty-two works by nine painters, selected by O'Hara. Originally circulated as a smaller version, *Recent Landscapes by Eight Americans*, the exhibition was displayed at the *Festival Of Two Worlds*, Spoleto, between 24 June and 18 July 1965. Returned to U.S. for continued domestic circulation in 1965. While O'Hara was unable to attend the festival, which included the extraordinary participation of an ageing Ezra Pound, he was also asked by Gian Carlo Menotti to select the American poets for Settimana della Poesia and chose Bill Berkson, Barbara Guest, Tony Towle, John Ashbery, Allen Ginsberg, Gregory Corso, Lawrence Ferlinghetti, Robert Lowell, Charles Olson, John Wieners. Menotti refused to invite Ginsberg and Corso because of the scandal they had caused at the festival a year or two before. Lowell declined.
1966	THE NETHERLANDS: Otterlo ENGLAND: London SWITZERLAND: Basel GERMANY: Nuremberg and Duisberg	*David Smith* Forty-eight sculptures, selected by O'Hara. Circulated between May 1966 and May 1967. O'Hara found this memorial exhibition of his friend, who had died the previous year, particularly difficult to curate, especially when he had to touch up some of Smith's sculptures using rust-resistant paint in the gardens of the Kröller-Müller Museum in Otterlo.
	UNITED STATES: New York	*Nakian* Major retrospective of Reuben Nakian held at the Museum of Modern Art, which ran between 20 June and 5 September 1966. Featured 105 sculptures and 34 drawings. In his catalogue text, O'Hara wrote: ' Nakian has created a remarkable oeuvre since the mid-'forties through all these trials of temperament and of will; or perhaps, because of his harsh self-criticism and his insistence on continuing into the present the classical values of grandeur and nobility (in a non-academic sense), one might say more accurately that a remarkable oeuvre has survived to poise itself against certain contemporary values that offend him.'

THE NETHERLANDS: Amsterdam ENGLAND: London BELGIUM: Brussels GERMANY: Essen ITALY: Turin	*Robert Motherwell: Works on Paper* Works on paper. 103 paintings, collages and drawings, selected by O'Hara, and adapted from *Robert Motherwell* retrospective, MoMA, 1965. On travelling display for much of 1966, from January to October. Also circulated as a smaller version with the same title, to Buenos Aires, Argentina; Caracas, Venezuela; Bogotá, Colombia; and Mexico City, Mexico, November 1967–June 1968.

NOTES

Introduction | Curating Modern Life

1   Frank O'Hara, letter to Joe LeSueur, 19 November 1963, box 3, fol. 29, Allen Collection of Frank O'Hara Letters (ACFOL), Archives & Special Collections at the Thomas J. Dodd Research Center, University of Connecticut Libraries. This letter was also published alongside an aerial photograph of a central square in Belgrade, supplied by the Yugoslav State Tourist Office, in an edition of 500 entitled *Adventures in Poetry* by The Poetry Project, St. Mark's Church In-the-Bowery, New York.

2   Ibid.

3   Ibid. This book is written in British English, except when providing a direct quotation from American English.

4   Ibid.

5   Ibid.

6   Ibid.

7   Ibid.

8   Ibid.

9   Ibid.

10   Frank O'Hara, letter to Lawrence Ferlinghetti, Amsterdam, 25 September 1963. Letter reprinted in Frank O'Hara, *Lunch Poems: Expanded 50th Anniversary Edition* (San Francisco: City Lights Books, 2014), n.p.

11   John Ashbery, 'Introduction', in *The Collected Poems of Frank O'Hara*, ed. by Donald Allen (New York: Alfred A. Knopf, 1971), p. x. Together with The Club, an artist-run speaker series and informal hangout, the Cedar Tavern was a bar and restaurant located at 24 University Place, which became an important social centre for the Abstract Expressionist artists and affiliated musicians, poets, dancers and critics.

12   Each of the members of the so-called New York School, an often-misleading nomenclature, had extensive and significant creative investments elsewhere. Ashbery, of course, spent most of the decade between 1955 and 1965 in Paris, where he was correspondent for *Art News*. Schuyler studied at the University of Florence between 1947 and 1948 and, a year later, stayed with his illustrious, well-connected friends W. H. Auden and Chester Kallman at their home in Ischia. It was there that Schuyler typed out most of the poems in Auden's *Nones* collection as well his translation of Jean Cocteau's play *Les Chevaliers de la Table Ronde*. From 1951, Kenneth Koch spent two years in

France and Italy. Barbara Guest, whose poetry has been described by Anthony Manouos as 'urbane, cosmopolitan, and refined', showing all the markings of 'the psychological dislocations and restless imagination of the perpetual traveller', spent long periods in London and Paris. These facts can sometimes be forgotten, and literary critics of the New York School have been slower and arguably less ambitious than their art historian counterparts to push beyond the geographical limits of that movement. O'Hara was also distrustful of the name, 'New York School'. Writing on Alex Katz in the second of the three 'Art Chronicles' for *Kulchur* magazine in 1962, O'Hara argued Katz was 'one of the most individual sensibilities in the New York School – which is to say that his work is original and he lives in New York'. We might assume he had a similar view of this designation for the poets too. See Frank O'Hara, 'Art Chronicle I–III', in *Standing Still and Walking in New York*, ed. by Donald Allen (Bolinas: Grey Fox Press, 1981), p. 136.

13   John Yau, 'At the Movies with Weldon Kees and Frank O'Hara', in *The Passionate Spectator: Essays on Art and Poetry* (Ann Arbor: The University of Michigan Press, 2006), p. 18.

14   See Rod Mengham, 'French Frank', in *Frank O'Hara Now: New Essays on the New York Poet*, ed. by Robert Hampson and Will Montgomery (Liverpool: Liverpool University Press, 2010), 49–58; Lytle Shaw, 'Gesture in 1960: Toward Literal Solutions', in *Frank O'Hara Now*, ed. by Hampson and Montgomery, pp. 29–48.

15   Frank O'Hara, back cover of *Lunch Poems* (San Francisco: City Lights Books, 2014).

16   See Olivier Brossard, 'Frank O'Hara's Poetry, a "Whitman's Birthday Broadcast with Static"', *Revue Française d'Études Américaines* 2, No. 108 (2006), 63–79.

17   Author unknown, 'Frank O'Hara, 40, Museum Curator/Exhibitions Aide at Modern Art Dies – Also a Poet', *New York Times*, 26 July 1966, p. 35.

18   Peter Schjeldahl, 'Frank O'Hara: He Made Things and People Sacred', *Village Voice*, 11 August 1966, n.p.

19   T. J. Clark, *Farewell to an Idea: Episodes from a History of Modernism* (New Haven: Yale University Press, 1999), p. 394. In this study on modernist aesthetics, which concludes with two chapters devoted to Pollock, Clark made the case to 'trust the beginnings, then; trust the epigraphs [O'Hara's 'After Courbet' provided this chapter's epigraph]. Trust Freud, and Stevens, and Frank O'Hara' (p. 13). For the place of O'Hara as poet in Clark's criticism, see also Ellen Levy, '"The Deep Ludicrousness of Lyric": The Poet in T.J. Clark', *Genre* 45, Vol. 1 (2012), 9–27.

20   Morton Feldman, *Give My Regards to Eighth Street* (Cambridge: Exact Change, 2001), p. 105.

21   Shaw, 'Gesture in 1960: Toward Literal Solutions', p. 43 n33.

22   Frank O'Hara, 'F. Y. I. #371 (The Nun)', *Poems Retrieved*, ed. by Donald Allen (San Francisco: Grey Fox Press, 2003), p. 201. Concerned above all with the entrances and exits that separated MoMA and New York, the poem later presents a far less beatific image of the museum: 'and I am back at work / now I will have to wait till four o'clock for something / interesting to happen / this isn't Manhattan this is hell.'

23 Very few single-curator biographies or compilation of projects have been published, although interest over the last twenty years has seen a small number of examples. We might trace the first of these to *Alfred H. Barr, Jr. and the Intellectual Origins of The Museum of Modern Art* by Sybil Gordon Kantor (MIT Press, 2002), although this was largely an account of Barr's work as the first Director of MoMA, much less about his curatorial career or practice. In 2007, the archive-heavy edited collection *Harald Szeeman: Individual Methodology* was published on the famous Curator of the Kunsthalle Bern, and arguably the first of the jet-setting international curators (although O'Hara began organizing exhibitions a year before Szeeman!). More recently, Michelle Elligott, MoMA's Chief of Archives, Library, and Research Collections, published *René d'Harnoncourt and the Art of Installation* in 2018, through MoMA's publishing arm. While I do not explicitly focus on d'Harnoncourt's relationship with O'Hara in this book, he was a very important curator (and later Director) at MoMA. In contrast, the excellent *Joanna Drew and the Art of Exhibitions* by Caroline Hancock (Skira, 2019), focuses on Drew's impressive career at the Arts Council of Great Britain and her 'blockbuster' Picasso retrospective at the Tate Gallery in 1960.

24 See Claude Cernuschi, 'Jackson Pollock at MoMA: On the Surface and Under the Rug [a review of Kirk Varnedoe with Pepe Karmel, *Jackson Pollock* (New York: The Museum of Modern Art, 1998)], *Archives of American Art Journal* 38, No. 3/4 (1998), 30–38. O'Hara is barely mentioned in the reviewed monograph by Varnedoe, and I like to think that Cernuschi has looked to redress this.

25 Archival and collections-based research gathered over the course of the book includes material from the following institutions: the Donald Allen Collection of Frank O'Hara Papers, the University of Connecticut at Storrs; the Museum of Modern Art Archives, New York; the Archivio Storico delle Arti Contemporanee, Venice; the *documenta* Archiv, Kassel; the Hochschule für Bildende Künste Library & Archive, Berlin; the Amerika Haus, Berlin; the Terra Foundation for American Art Library & Archive, Paris; Archives des expositions du Musée d'Art Moderne de la Ville de Paris; the Dedalus Foundation Archives, New York; the Rockefeller Archive Center, Tarrytown; the Joan Mitchell Foundation Archives, New York; the Beinecke Research Library Archives, New Haven; the Stedelijk Museum Archives, Amsterdam; the personal papers of Jane Freilicher and Al Leslie; the Whitechapel Art Gallery Archive, London; the Tate Archives, London; the Archives of American Art, Smithsonian Institution, Washington DC; the New York Public Library Berg Collection; the Fundacão Bienal de São Paulo Archives, São Paulo [digital correspondence].

26 All considered, though, it would be wrong to say that O'Hara has not been understood through the archive at all. While a comprehensive published collection of his letters sadly remains an unlikely prospect at least for the present moment, the Donald Allen Collection of Frank O'Hara Letters has been an important resource since at least the publication of Brad Gooch's 1993 biography, *City Poet: The Life and Times of Frank O'Hara*. The Frank O'Hara Papers at the Museum of Modern Art Archives, and to a much-lesser extent the International Council/Program Papers, have also been widely consulted.

27　In *Whitman, Melville, Crane, and the Labors of American Poetry: Against Vocation* (Oxford: Oxford University Press, 2019), Peter Riley has also identified this self-portrait doodle, in which it 'has become paradoxically and self-consciously aware of its own state of distraction' as one 'eye stares back and out at us, and the other on some information regarding Franz Kline' (p. 175). As this suggests, Riley's recent book on American poets and their day jobs does touch on O'Hara and his labours at MoMA, although the focus is on his profession as curatorial assistant and administrator within the context of neoliberal distractedness and not on the exhibitions themselves. Instead, O'Hara's approaches to work feel a little like an afterthought, as a six-page coda entitled 'Why I am not Talking about Frank O'Hara'. See also Jason Lagapa, 'Frank O'Hara and the End of Bureaucracy', *Arizona Quarterly: A Journal of American Literature, Culture, and Theory* 75, No. 1 (Spring 2019), 1–22.

28　Lou Stoppard, 'Everyone's a Curator Now', *The New York Times* <https://www.nytimes.com/2020/03/03/style/curate-buzzword.html> [accessed 10 February 2024].

29　Bruce W. Ferguson, Reesa Greenberg, and Sandy Nairne, *Thinking about Exhibitions* (London: Taylor & Francis), p. 167.

30　Recent critical attention has been directed to the urgency of questions of 'care' in contemporary curation. See *Curating with Care*, eds. Elke Krasny and Lara Perry (London: Routledge, 2023).

31　Frank O'Hara, 'Art Chronicle I', in *Art Chronicles 1954–1966* (New York: George Braziller, 1975), p. 67.

32　Wherever possible, and in the interests of consistency across European languages, I have provided a translation of named travelling exhibitions in American English in order to be consistent with MoMA records.

33　Frank O'Hara, 'Recent American Watercolors' catalogue essay, I.A.566, The International Council and International Program Papers (IC/IP), The Museum of Modern Art Archives, New York (MoMA Archives, New York).

34　Frank O'Hara, 'Helen Frankenthaler', in *An Exhibition of Oil Paintings by Frankenthaler* (New York: The Jewish Museum, 1960), p. 6.

35　Andrew Epstein, '"A fine day for seeing" – Frank O'Hara at the Museum of Modern Art, New York', *Apollo: The International Art Magazine* (30 October 2019) <https://www.apollo-magazine.com/frank-ohara-museum-of-modern-art/?fbclid=IwAR3piKEHhv7tDKVkiw4WgHnNTEuPwktW3ifs5e33HnzfRw3yJeFp9vQkJUo> [accessed 30 October 2019].

36　Mary Ann Caws, 'The Lunchtime Room at MoMA', in *zeta: rivista internazionale di poesia e ricerche* (Udine: Unione Stampa Periodica Italiana, 2020), p. 65.

One | This is All Living Art

1　Frank O'Hara, 'Edward Lucie-Smith: An Interview with Frank O'Hara', in *Standing Still and Walking in New York*, ed. by Donald Allen (Bolinas: Grey Fox Press, 1975), 3–28 (p. 11).

2 James Schuyler, 'Poet Among Painters', in *Homage to Frank O'Hara,* ed. by Bill Berkson and Joe LeSueur (Bolinas: Big Sky, 1988), p. 82.

3 Grace Hartigan, notes for Tibor de Nagy memorial, 15 April 1994, box 28, Grace Hartigan Papers, Special Collections Research Center, Syracuse University.

4 Saul Nelson, *Never Ending: Modernist Painting Past and Future* (London: Yale University Press, 2024), p. 182.

5 Under James Thrall Soby's direction, MoMA had bought Pollock's *She-Wolf* (1943) from his first solo show at Peggy Guggenheim's Art of this Century Gallery that same year and had over the course of the 1940s purchased individual paintings by Motherwell, Willem de Kooning, and Adolph Gottlieb. While Willem de Kooning's *Painting* (1948) was bought by MoMA in October 1948, it was not until Blanchette Hooker Rockefeller acquired de Kooning's *Woman II* (1952) from the Sidney Janis Gallery in 1953 (although not officially bequeathed to MoMA until 1955), the same year as O'Hara's sighting of *The Persian Jacket* being bundled through the doors, that the museum began collecting Abstract Expressionism coherently and in earnest.

6 John Quinn, one of the architects of MoMA's institutional vision and a collector who had the largest single-person collection of European modern art in the world in the 1920s, believed MoMA would 'act as a feeder to the Metropolitan in much the same way as the Luxembourg does to the Louvre'. John Quinn, in a letter to John Cotton Dana, 26 January 1914. Reprinted in Hugh Eakins, *Picasso's War: How Modern Art Came to America* (New York: Random House, 2022), p. 64.

7 Alfred H. Barr Jr., 'Paintings from the Museum Collection: Opens Museum of Modern Art's 25th Anniversary Year Celebration,' press release, 12 October 1954, p. 4.

8 Grace Hartigan, *The Journals of Grace Hartigan, 1951–1955,* ed. William T. La Moy and Joseph P. McCaffrey (Syracuse, NY: Syracuse University Press, 2009), p. 55.

9 Louis Menand, *The Free World: Art and Thought in the Cold War* (New York: Farrar, Straus and Giroux, 2021), p. 153.

10 O'Hara worked at the front desk from winter 1951 until spring 1954 and then returned in 1955 to join the International Program: first as a special assistant to Porter McCray; in 1960 became Assistant Curator; in 1965 Associate, and in 1966, the year of his death, Curator.

11 Porter McCray, oral history interview, 17 September 1977, Porter McCray Papers (PMP), Archives of American Art (AAA), Smithsonian Institution.

12 Waldo Rasmussen, 'Frank O'Hara in the Museum', in *Homage to Frank O'Hara*, ed. by Berkson and LeSueur, p. 86.

13 Irving Sandler, 'Sweeping Up after Frank', in *Homage to Frank O'Hara*, ed. by Berkson and LeSueur, p. 78.

14 O'Hara, 'Edward Lucie-Smith: An Interview with Frank O'Hara', p. 12.

15 Frank O'Hara, 'Art Chronicle I', in *Art Chronicles 1954–1966* (New York: George Braziller, 1975), p. 1.

16 Ibid, p. 5.

17 Ibid.

18 'Frank O'Hara, 40, Museum Curator/Exhibitions Aide at Modern Art Dies – Also a Poet', *New York Times*. See also Wynn Chamberlain's painting, *Poets Dressed and Undressed* (1964).

19 Eileen Myles, in 'Eileen Myles and Jeremy Sigler Go to an Exhibition', *The Paris Review*, 27 November 2017 <https://www.theparisreview.org/blog/2017/11/27/eileen-myles-jeremy-sigler-see-show/> [accessed 1 May 2020].

20 John Yau, 'Passionate Spectator: On Frank O'Hara's Art Criticism', in *The Passionate Spectator: Essays on Art and Poetry* (Ann Arbor: University of Michigan Press, 2006), 1–1 7 (p. 2).

On the subject of pre-professionalization, it is worth noting that the two most important figures at MoMA during O'Hara's tenure – Alfred Barr and Dorothy Miller – did not pursue a full doctorate or complete major professional qualifications either. Barr was given an honorary doctorate from Harvard for his catalogue essay on Picasso in 1946, over two decades after he began work on it, and Miller only became an honorary Doctor of Letters from Smith College for services to museum connoisseurship in 1959.

21 Elizabeth Hazan, New York-based artist and daughter of Jane Freilicher and Joe Hazan, has reflected on the issue around friendship and curation: 'When I was assembling my mom's archive, I was struck by how she didn't harbour bad feelings over the inclusion of so many other of Frank's friends in the shows he curated. I never heard her say anything about it [and] it seemed so amazing that she didn't. Frank was certainly helpful to her in other ways, helping to install her first show, stretching her canvases (!) and generally championing her and her work.' Email correspondence with the author, 18 October 2019.

22 Bill Berkson, 'A New York Beginner', *Modern Painters* (Autumn 1998), pp. 51–52.

23 Nelson Rockefeller, soon to be Governor of New York (1959–1973) and then Vice-President of the United States under President Gerald Ford (1974–1977), was in many ways the embodiment of a particular kind of privilege that operated at the intersection between corporate governance, state and national politics, and the worlds of high-end modernist art lenders and collectors. Contrary to some popular conceptions, MoMA is not a public institution in a meaningful sense of the term, and its governance was never conceived as such, and certainly not in the same way that national or municipal-owned museums, such as the Tate or the Musée d'Art Moderne de la Ville de Paris, were. Many American museums established in the first half of the twentieth century were inaugurated on corporate models familiar to philanthropic and business elites and were (and often still are) controlled and managed by self-selecting boards of trustees composed of primarily rich donors, often with significant influence in politics.

24 Frances Stonor Saunders, *The Cultural Cold War: The CIA and the World of Arts and Letters* (New York: The New Press, 2013), p. 120.

25 Helen Franc, 'The Early Years of the International Program and Council', in *The Museum of Modern Art at Mid-Century: At Home and Abroad*, ed. by John Szarkowski (New York: The Museum of Modern Art, 1994), p. 110.

26 Oral History Program, interview with Porter McCray, 300 East 59 Street, New York City, 18 April 1991, p. 31, MoMA Archives, New York.

27 Ibid.

28 Nathalie Henrich and Michael Pollak, 'From Museum Curator to Exhibition Aueteur: Inventing a Singular Position', in Ferguson, Greenberg, and Nairne (eds.), *Thinking About Exhibitions*, p. 166.

29 Gooch, *City Poet*, p. 257.

30 Franc, 'The Early Years of the International Program and Council', pp. 109–110, 120–122.

31 This proposal was not the only funding application O'Hara submitted to the Ford Foundation over the course of his various careers. Together with Kenneth Koch, both of whom were represented by Grove Press, O'Hara applied for a Fellowship with The Ford Foundation Program for Poets and Fiction Writers during the 1959 cycle. In his cover letter, O'Hara made a case to 'complete a full-length libretto during the period of the grant for Ben Weber', or else Ned Rorem, Charles Turner, or Morton Feldman, and to work closely with the New York City Opera Company. 'It would be most helpful to me in testing my ideas about American prosody before these difficulties have been ironed out for performance. I am interested, too, in observing closely the problems of staging and movement which a difficult aria or an elaborate ensemble create for the singers and director, in relation to dramatic effectiveness of scenes. . . . I have wished to write a libretto for a grand opera because I feel that the medium combines my chief interests (poetry, music, painting) and, considering the present state of American theatre, is the only truly lyrical medium available to the poet at the present time.' O'Hara was ultimately unsuccessful in this application. See Frank O'Hara, 'Statement: The Ford Foundation Program for Poets and Fiction Writers', box 7, fol. 166, The Rockefeller Archive Center, Tarrytown, New York.

32 Frank O'Hara, grant proposal to the Ford Foundation, 7 March 1957, box 10, fol. 5, PMP, AAA. An annotated preliminary draft in O'Hara's handwriting can be found in Folder 5, Frank O'Hara Papers (FOHP), MoMA Archives, New York.

33 Ibid. In the same document, O'Hara argues that 'foreign countries frequently show a surprising and varied familiarity' with the literature of the United States, especially 'Hawthorne, Melville, Poe and Whitman among 19th-century authors, Lewis Dreiser, Hemingway and Faulkner among the 20th'.

34 Fritz Nemitz, 'Is there Such a Thing as American Painting? A Cross-Section from Munich', reprinted in *Hot Art, Cold War – Western and Northern European Writing on American Art, 1945–1990* (London: Routledge, 2021), p. 254. Translated by Richard George Elliot. Originally published as 'Gibt es ein amerikanische Malerei? Ein Querschnitt in München', in *Frankfurter Allgemeine Zeitung* (5 December 1951).

35 The United States government did establish a comparative organization, and at a strikingly proximate moment: The United States Information Agency (USIA, later the USIS), inaugurated in 1953 at the behest of President Dwight D. Eisenhower. Its Mission Statement was almost identical to the International Program: 'to understand, inform and influence foreign publics in promotion of

the national interest, and to broaden the dialogue between Americans and U.S. institutions, and their counterparts abroad.'

36 Andrew Berding, lecture to the annual congress of the American Foundation of Arts, October 1953, quoted in Sigrid Ruby, ed., *Have we an American Art?* (Weimar: VDG, Verl. und Datenbank für Geisteswiss., 1999), p. 119.

37 Frank O'Hara, Ford Foundation grant proposal.

38 Ibid.

39 Ibid.

40 Ibid.

41 Ibid.

42 See Greg Barnhisel, *Cold War Modernists: Art, Literature, and American Cultural Diplomacy* (New York: Columbia University Press, 2015), pp. 12–14.

43 For Dondero's speeches see the *Congressional Record,* 11 March 1949, pp. 2364–65; 25 March 1949, pp. 3297–98; 17 May 1949, pp. 6487–90; 16 August 1949, pp. 11811–14. Attitudes such as these were, if not widespread, somewhat prohibitive to a legislative agenda for the allocation of Federal funds to overseas modern art funding. In 1949, Dondero went further and asserted that 'Cubism aims to destroy by designed disorder . . . Dadaism aims to destroy by ridicule . . . Abstractionism aims to destroy by the creation of brainstorms'. See Robert C. Post, *Who Owns America's Past?: The Smithsonian and the Problem of History* (Baltimore: The Johns Hopkins University Press, 2013), pp. 39–43.

44 Alfred J. Barr, 'Is Modern Art Communistic?', *New York Times*, 14 December 1952.

45 This situation continued until 1956, when threats were made against a number of exhibitions that had been earmarked as to be co-supported by both the International Program and the USIA; at least four, in the words of McCray, 'can be approximately identified': 1. *Sport in Art*; 2. *Selections from University Collections*; 3. *Paintings U.S.A. 1900–1950*; 4. *Paintings Selected by the Artists*. McCray sounded the alarm to Rockefeller that Dondero threatened to withhold Congressional funding from these exhibitions unless 'all artists alleged as subversive or engaged in "un-American activities" be withdrawn from [these four] exhibitions now in preparation for the USIA'. Porter McCray, letter to Nelson Rockefeller, 27 May 1956, Roll 3157, Frames 1128–1129, Alfred H. Barr Papers, AAA.

46 Alfred Barr, letter to Lawrence H. C. Smith, New York, 11 April 1952, in *Defining Modern Art: Selected Writings of Alfred H. Barr, Jr,* ed. by Irving Sandler (New York: Harry N. Abrams, 1986), p. 46. See also Barr's important public-facing essay of the same year, 'Is Modern Art Communistic?', *New York Times*, 14 December 1952, p. 22.

47 Irving Howe, 'The Problem of US Power', *Dissent* 1, No. 3 (Summer 1954), p. 220.

48 Frank O'Hara, 'American Art and Non-American Art', in *Standing Still and Walking,* ed. by Allen, pp. 97. Originally featured in its Winter–Spring issue of 1959, *It Is* published 'Six Opinions on Abstract Art in Other Countries' by

Frank O'Hara, Thomas B. Hess, Paul Jenkins, Milton Resnick, William Roland and Irving Sandler.

49 Frank O'Hara, Ford Foundation grant proposal.

50 Max Kozloff, 'American Painting During the Cold War', *Artforum* (May 1973), p. 45.

51 Eve Cockroft, 'Abstract Expressionism: Weapon of the Cold War', *Artforum* (June 1974), p. 41.

52 In one of the most recent articles on O'Hara, Allison Neal argued that O'Hara 'orients his poetry within a world of global media, positioning it as a utopian lingua franca competing with a variety of other spoken and mediated forms of international communication'. See Allison Neal, 'Frank O'Hara's Voice of America', *ELH* 86, No. 3 (Fall 2019), p. 779.

53 Serge Guilbaut, *How New York Stole the Idea of Modern Art: Abstract Expressionism, Freedom, and the Cold War*, trans. by Arthur Goldhammer (London: The University of Chicago Press, 1983), p. 88.

54 See Serge Guilbaut, 'Postwar Painting Games: The Rough and the Slick', in *Reconstructing Modernism: Art in New York, Paris and Montreal 1945–1964*, ed. by Serge Guilbaut (Cambridge: The MIT Press, 1990), 30–84.

55 Guilbaut, *How New York Stole the Idea of Modern Art*, p. 9.

56 Michael Kimmelmann, 'Revisiting the Revisionists: The Modern, Its Critics, and the Cold War', in *The Museum of Modern Art at Mid-Century: At Home and Abroad; Studies in Modern Art*, ed. by John Elderfield, 38–55, p. 49.

57 Nancy Jachec, *Politics and Painting at the Venice Biennale: 1948–64* (Manchester: Manchester University Press, 2007), p. 2.

58 Ibid.

59 Ikegami, *The Great Migrator*, p. 12.

60 Ibid, p. 10.

61 'Press Release for *Twentieth Century Italian Art From American Collections*, 13 April 1960', I.B.500, IC/IP, MoMA Archives, New York.

62 The 1950s saw the exponential growth of the international exhibition, the global biennial and the large-scale perennial group exposition as an alternative to both the public museum and the commercial art gallery. The proliferation of public museums included the Institute for Contemporary Arts in London, which opened in 1947 as part of widespread cultural investment, and was significantly expanded in the 1950s; the inauguration of the Tate Gallery as a distinct entity from the National Gallery in 1955; the establishment of the Moderna Museet in Stockholm and the Louisiana Museum on the shore of the Øresund Sound in Denmark, both 1958. The various iterations of what has since been characterized as a process of *biennalization*, the global phenomenon of curated displays or 'festival-exhibitions' that operate between a kind of utopian belief in a cosmopolitan arena for the display of art and the hyper-territorialisation of the art market included – in addition to the Venice Biennale, *documenta*, and the São Paulo Bienal – the Bienal Hispanoamericana de Arte in Spain and Latin America, the Tehran Biennial in Iran, and the Paris Biennale in France (initiated by André Malraux, the French Culture Minister

and author of the 'imaginary museum' in 1959). It is also worth noting that while some of these exhibitions sound similar in scope and format to the Venice Biennale, they invariably did not subscribe to its biannual rhythm nor its representation by national pavilions. The *documenta* series that I discuss as the second case study of this chapter should be seen within this context. In 2013, the influential German-American curator René Block humorously traced the distance between the historical moment of O'Hara's curatorial work at the international biennale and our own: 'In the early 1960s . . . there were two biennials: the Venice and the Bienal de São Paulo – and every five years there was *documenta* [. . .] Since then, not even forty years have passed and today we are confronted with so many so-called biennials, triennials, and quadriennials that it's almost impossible to get an overall perspective on them.' René Block, 'We hop on, we hop off: The ever-faster spinning carousel of biennials', in *Shifting Gravity (World Biennial Forum No. 1)*, ed. by Ute Meta Bauer and Hanru Hou (Gwangju: Gwangju Biennale Foundation, 2013), p. 104. The Milan Trienniale and the Rome Quadriennale were smaller international exhibitions although, much like the Venice Biennale, sought to remodel their format as well as restore their legitimacy after being pragmatically utilized by Mussolini for propaganda during the Fascist period. The changing political conditions of the postwar period, as the Christian Democracy party sought to promote European economic integration and limit the influence of the powerful Italian Communist Party, and what these new calibrations meant for Italy's self-identification as an international centre for modern art, have been discussed by critics. See Marcia E. Ventrocq, 'National Style and the Agenda for Abstract Painting in Postwar Italy', *Art History* 12, Issue 4 (December 1989), 448–471.

63 Anglo-American critics have tended to credit Abstract Expressionist artists working in the United States as the driving force for the development of gesture painting in Western Europe in the 1950s. There is, however, a significant body of scholarship that has off-centred this history and explored the distribution and display of gesture painting from a European rather than American perspective. For example, on Italy see Germano Celant, *Roma–New York, 1948–1964*, trans. by Joachim Neugroschel (Milan: Charta, 1993); on Great Britain see Fiona Gaskin, 'British Tachisme in the postwar period, 1946–1957', in *Artists and Patrons in Postwar Britain*, ed. by Margaret Garlake (Aldershot: Ashgate, 2001), pp. 17–55; on Germany see Sigrid Ruby, 'The Give and Take of American Painting in Postwar Western Europe', *The American Impact on Western Europe: Americanization and Westernization in Transatlantic Perspective* (Washington DC: German Historical Institute, 1999), <www.ghidc.org/conpotweb/westernpapters/ruby.pdf> [accessed 15 June 2018]. The most compelling scholar on this subject is Nancy Jachec, who has written extensively on the relationship between American and European gesture painting and its consequences for the politics of internationalist commitment in the postwar period. See especially Nancy Jachec, 'Transatlantic Cultural Politics in the late 1950s: the Leaders and Specialists Grant Program', *Art History*, 26, No. 4 (2003), pp. 533–556; Jachec, ' "A Partnership of Equals": Kennedy, the European Union and the End of Abstract Expressionism as an Atlanticist Aesthetic', *Third Text* 16, No. 2 (June 2002), pp. 105–118.

64 This definition of *Art autre* was revised from the one that I provided in the chronology of events for the accompanying catalogue to *Art autre*, a spring 2019 exhibition at Lévy Gorvy, London.

65 Werner Haftmann, 'Einleitung', *documenta II: Kunst nach 1945. Malerei – Skulptur – Druckgrafik, Vol. 1* (Kassel: M. DuMont Schauberg, 1959). Translated from the German by The Museum of Modern Art, I.A.890, IC/IP, MoMA Archives, New York.

Two | The Bar Américain Continues to be French

1 Robert Motherwell, 'Reflections on Painting Now', in *The Collected Writings of Robert Motherwell*, ed. by Stephanie Terenzio (New York: Oxford University Press, 1992), 81–84 (p. 82). Motherwell gave this lecture as part of a symposium entitled 'French Art versus U.S. Art Today' in Provincetown, Massachusetts, on 11 August 1949.

2 In the first monograph on O'Hara, *Poet Among Painters*, Marjorie Perloff noted that it was 'the French influence that sets him apart from Black Mountain and the Beats, not to speak of the Confessional Poets like Lowell and Berryman, or the oracular "deep image" school.' See Marjorie Perloff, *Frank O'Hara: Poet Among Painters* (London: The University of Chicago Press, 1998), p. 30. Thomas Meyer similarly recognized O'Hara's poems as ruminations on the 'notion of surface [. . .] inherited from Mallarmé via Apollinaire, coming as it did through Dada and Surrealism'. See Thomas Meyer, 'Glistening Torsos, Sandwiches, and Coca-Cola', in *Frank O'Hara: To Be True to a City*, ed. by Jim Elledge (University of Michigan Press, 1990), p. 94. Peter Stoneley provides a compelling account of O'Hara's interactions with Frenchness, and gestures to important issues of travel, homosexuality, abjection and the poetic product as a kind of souvenir or promissory note. The framing of the article, in some respects, mirrors that of my thesis: for instance, Stoneley rightly recognizes that 'Frank O'Hara is emphatically identified with New York, and yet like other poets of the "New York School," he had considerable creative investments elsewhere' and that the 'culture of Europe was so important to him that his failure for many years to make the voyage across the Atlantic produced bitterness and envy'. Much of the argument centres on the 'mediations, substitutions, and embodiments' which are constituted as tokens or poems in O'Hara's work, and sees proper nouns become transferable exchange values, in which the domestic is supplanted for touristic signs of foreignness. Stoneley suggests that for O'Hara, Europe can never be properly apprehended or contained, never emerge as properly authentic or illusory, as seeing objects – such as the 'rocher de la Vierge' in 'A Little Travel Diary' – only reminds the poet of the limits of actual experience with an elsewhere. Despite accurately characterizing the climate of homosexuality in some aspects of New York – '[t]he most "suspect" connotation of Frenchness in the United States was of sexual and gendered "degeneracy"' – Stoneley goes on to claim that O'Hara became increasingly

disinterested in Europe as his work progressed, in part because he can imagine the fulfilment of a same-sex relationship with Vincent Warren back home. It is a leap, not least because he would go on to say, with not a little contradiction, that O'Hara was 'always preparing himself against and making up for a violence that is figured as a nationalist homophobia' in the United States all the way through his oeuvre. See Peter Stoneley, 'Frank O'Hara and 'French in the Pejorative Sense', *Journal of Modern Literature* 34, No. 1 (2010), 125–142.

3   Frank O'Hara and Richard O. Moore, 'Transcript of "FRANK O'HARA: SECOND EDITION" (a film based on USA: POETRY outtakes)', in *Homage to Frank O'Hara*, ed. by Berkson and LeSueur, pp. 217–223, p. 221.

4   Annie Cohen-Solal, *Picasso the Foreigner: An Artist in France, 1900–1973*, trans. Sam Taylor (New York: Farrar, Straus and Giroux, 2023), p. 45.

5   Barbara Guest, 'Frank and I happened to be in Paris. . .', *Homage to Frank O'Hara,* ed. by Berkson and LeSueur, p. 77.

6   This account by Guest has become well-repeated in accounts of O'Hara and France. With that said, we cannot be certain that O'Hara remembered his attitude the same way. In a letter to Guest, O'Hara also recalled this anecdote but differently in his postscript: 'P.S. I loved our evening in Montmartre and the bateau lavoir being the color of Ricard was perfect!' Frank O'Hara, letter to Barbara Guest, 90 University Place, New York, 14 September 1958, ACFOL.

7   Mengham, 'French Frank', p. 50.

8   John Bernard Myers, *Tracking the Marvelous: A Life in the New York Art World* (New York: Random House, 1981), p. 66.

9   Clement Greenberg, 'The Decline of Cubism', *Partisan Review* 15, No. 3 (Spring, 1948), p. 369. This was the first instance of a critic claiming American art to be superior to the French. With that said, this statement spoke as much to Greenberg's continued insistence on a Marxist analysis of art in terms of base, superstructure and production as much as a bald-faced assertion of national pride.

10   Menand, *The Free World*, p. 226.

11   O'Hara, 'Edward Lucie-Smith: An Interview with Frank O'Hara', p. 10.

12   Rebecca Walkowitz, *Cosmopolitan Style: Modernism Beyond the Nation* (New York: Columbia University Press, 2006), p. 9.

13   In the Lucie-Smith interview, O'Hara wrote that 'my general tendency has been to work on American shows ever since [re-joining the Museum in 1955], except for Spanish exhibitions. So I was asked to come back to work on the "De David à Toulouse-Lautrec" exhibition which was made up of masterpieces from American collections.' See ibid, p. 11.

14   Guilbaut, '1955: The Year the Gaulois Fought the Cowboy', p. 172.

15   John Ireland, 'Review: Sartre's America', in *Sartre Studies International* 20, No. 2 (2014): 76–89, p. 84.

16   Menand, *The Free World*, p. 8

17   George F. Kennan, *International Exchange in the Arts* (New York: International Council of The Museum of Modern Art, 1956), n.p.

18 Ibid.

19 Ibid.

20 Ibid.

21 Broadly speaking, the strategy of the United States and the Soviet Union to seduce the French was comparable: stress a shared history and a shared culture bound by admiration and the centrality of Paris. The United States argued for the respect of their collectors and connoisseurs; the Soviet Union the influx of avant-garde ideas from Russia, such as Igor Stravinsky and the Ballets Russes. There is insufficient space here to outline what the Soviet cultural diplomatic offensive meant in Paris, so see Richard Pells, *Not Like Us: How Europeans Have Loved, Hated, and Transformed American Culture Since World War II* (New York: Basic Books, 1997), especially p. 65. See also Richard F. Kuisel, *Seducing the French: The Dilemma of Americanization* (Berkeley: University of California Press, 1993), p. 38.

22 Gary O. Larson, *The Reluctant Patron: The United States Government and the Arts, 1943–1965* (Philadelphia: University of Pennsylvania Press, 1983) p. 111.

23 Nancy Jachec, *The Philosophy and Politics of Abstract Expressionism* (Cambridge: Cambridge University Press, 2000), p. 184.

24 We might think of several examples, and about Philip Rahv's 1939 article 'Paleface and Redskin', in which the highbrow, 'paleface', and European in disposition writers like Henry James were contrasted with the lowbrow, 'redskin' figures like Walt Whitman, who were unashamedly American and original in attitude. See Philip Rahv, 'Paleface and Redskin', *The Kenyon Review* 1, No. 3 (Summer, 1939), pp. 251–256. See also Arthur C. Danto, 'Philosophizing American Art', in *American Art in the 20th Century: Painting and Sculpture, 1913–1993*, ed. by Christos M. Joachimides and Norman Rosenthal (London: Royal Academy of Arts, 1993), pp. 21–28. See Catherine Dossin, 'Beyond the Clichés of "Decadence" and Myths of "Triumph": Rewriting France in the Stories of Postwar Western Art', in *France and the Visual Arts since 1945: Remapping European Postwar and Contemporary Art*, ed. by Catherine Dossin (London: Bloomsbury, 2019), pp. 1–22. Dossin has traced the origins of these facile but prevalence clichés in the national discourse, which are generally considered to be framed around the decadent decline of France and the uncultured materialism of the United States.

25 Clement Greenberg, 'Symposium: Is the French Avant-Garde Overrated?', in *Clement Greenberg, The Collected Essays and Criticism, Vol. 3: Affirmations and Refusals, 1950–1956* (Chicago: The University of Chicago Press, 1993): 155–157, p. 156. The editors of *Art Digest* asked Ralston Crawford, Robert Motherwell, Jack Tworkov, and Greenberg to present and defend their positions on 'advanced Parisian art and about the phenomenal critical and financial success which it has enjoyed in this country'.

26 Ibid.

27 Clement Greenberg, '"American-Type" Painting', in *Clement Greenberg, The Collected Essays and Criticism, Vol. 3,* ed. by O'Brian, 217–236 (p. 219).

28 Ibid.

29 Guilbaut, 'Postwar Painting Games', p. 31.

30 Frank O'Hara, 'Art Chronicle I', in *Art Chronicles* (New York: George Braziller, 1975), pp. 1–11 (p. 8).

31 O'Hara, 'American Art and Non-American Art', p. 98.

32 Frank O'Hara, 'Introduction', *Robert Motherwell, with selections from the artist's writings*, ed. by Frank O'Hara (New York: Museum of Modern Art, 1965), p. 8.

33 Ibid.

34 Milan Kundera, 'Die Weltliteratur: How we read one another', *The New Yorker* (8 January 2007) <https://www.newyorker.com/magazine/2007/01/08/die-weltliteratur> [accessed 10 January 2020]. See also John Davis, 'Only in America: Exceptionalism, Nationalism, Provincialism', in *A Companion to American Art*, ed. by John Davis, Jennifer A. Greenhill and Jason D. LaFountain (New York: Wiley, 2015), 317–335, especially p. 324.

35 Ibid.

36 O'Hara, 'American Art and Non-American Art', p. 97. My emphasis.

37 The term 'individualist *internationale*' was first used by the critic Pierre Descargues in a January 1948 review of Polish artists in Paris. Descargues wrote of 'the great melting-pot of minds' in Paris and stressed that it was essential to the city's international reputation for advanced art. Attributing the success of this new moment to the decline of specific national traditions, he imagined a new future from the debris, and identified 'the end of an art of, let's say, folklore, in pushing things to the extreme, and the beginning of an individualist *internationale* whose growth, seriously contested today, coincides with the birth of the École de Paris'. See Pierre Descargues, 'À la Galerie des Beaux-Arts: Les Artistes Polonais résidant à Paris', *Arts* (30 January 1948). Translation by Natalie Adamson.

38 Natalie Adamson, *Painting, Politics, and the Struggle for the École de Paris, 1944–1964* (London: Ashgate, 2009), p. 9. See also Ihor Junyk, *Foreign Modernism: Cosmopolitanism, Identity, and Style in Paris* (London: University of Toronto Press, 2013), especially the chapter 'Travelling Culture: Rilke, Rodin, and the Poetics of Displacement', pp. 12–32.

39 Frank O'Hara, 'Introduction', *Robert Motherwell* (New York: Museum of Modern Art, 1965), p. 10.

40 O'Hara, 'American Art and Non-American Art', p. 97.

41 Ibid.

42 O'Hara, 'Introduction', *Robert Motherwell*, p. 10.

43 Greenberg was clear that his version of Abstract Expressionism 'practiced by a group of painters who came to notice in New York about a dozen years ago' was nourished by the wave of expatriate artists and teachers. Hans Hofmann, who had fled Paris for New York in 1932, cultivated a 'sophisticated audience for adventurous art' in his students, who were now maintaining strong and independent styles of their own. See Greenberg, '"American-Type" Painting', p. 219.

44 Ibid., 73.

45 Pierre Restany, in conversation with Jeremy Lewison, 5 November 1997. Reprinted in Jeremy Lewison, 'Jackson Pollock and the Americanization of

Europe', in *Jackson Pollock: New Approaches,* ed. by Kirk Varnedoe and Pepe Karmel (New York: The Museum of Modern Art, 1999), 201–232 (p. 220).

46 Ibid.

47 The International Program had, by the end of the decade, collaborated with the Musée d'Art Moderne on several occasions. On Cassou's invitation and request to organize a show of 'dramatic contrasts', Andrew Carnduff Ritchie had earlier selected artists working in both abstract and figurative styles for *Twelve Modern American Painters* (1953). Painters included Ivan Albright, Stuart Davis, Arshile Gorky, Morris Graves, Edward Hopper, John Kane, John Marin, Jackson Pollock, Ben Shahn; the sculptors Alexander Calder, Theodore Roscak and David Smith. Styles ranged from Socialist Realism (Shan) to Abstract Expressionism (Pollock). According to Ritchie, the ambition of the exhibition was to demonstrate that 'each of the 12 artists chosen is one of the principal interpreters of the styles in vogue in the United States at mid-century'. Significantly, Ritchie avoided cohering a sense of collective style, and argued that 'diversity flourishes in the absence of an "official art": The emphasis lies mostly on the artist as an individual'.[1] See Andrew Carnduff Ritchie, *Zwölf Amerikanische Kunstler*, Zurich, 1953, n.p., ICE-F-3-53, box 6.8, IC/IP, MoMA Archives, New York.

48 Gay R. McDonald, 'The Launching of American Art in Postwar France: Jean Cassou and the Musée National d'Art Moderne', *American Art* 13, No. 1 (Spring, 1999), 40–61 (p. 55).

49 O'Hara, 'Edward Lucie-Smith: An Interview with Frank O'Hara', p. 4.

50 Ibid.

51 'Origin and Organization of Salute to France' policy document, I.B.59*, IC/IP, MoMA Archives, New York.

52 President Eisenhower, who had attended Kennan's speech at MoMA, wrote: 'I am sure that this exhibition, demonstrating our deep appreciation of French artistic genius, will do much to strengthen the friendship, esteem and warm understanding which have long existed between the United States and France.' President Dwight Eisenhower, letter to William Burden, The White House, 8 November 1954, I.B.54, IC/P, MoMA Archives, New York.

53 Danto, 'Philosophizing American Art', p. 22.

54 *Cinquante Ans d'art aux Etats-Unis*, Musée National d'Art Moderne, 2 April–15 May; *De David à Toulouse-Lautrec*, 20 April–3 July, Musée de l'Orangerie (all from American collections). Concerts as part of the *Salute to France* programme also featured The Philadelphia Orchestra, The New York City Ballet, a production of *Okalhoma!* as well as a theatre schedule that included *Medea* and *The Skin of Our Teeth. Cinquante Ans d'art aux Etats-Unis* then travelled as *Modern Art in the United States* to several additional venues: Frankfurt, Barcelona, Zurich, Vienna, The Hague, London and Belgrade.

55 Darthea Speyer, oral history interview with Paul Cummings, Paris, 28 June 1976, AAA.

56 Douglas Dillon, letter to William Burden, American Embassy in Paris, 27 June 1955, I.B.113, IC/IP, MoMA Archives, New York. President Coty had also

received a delegation of officials from the United States Embassy and others more directly responsible for the organization of the exhibition, such as McCray, at the Élysée Palace, when he entertained on the terrace overlooking the gardens. On another occasion, President Coty was joined by Nelson Rockefeller on a visit to the exhibition itself.

57 Ibid.

58 Ibid.

59 Frank O'Hara and others, 'Summary of French press reaction to the exhibition "De David a Toulouse-Lautrec: Chefs d'Oeuvre des Collections Americaines" held at the Musee de l'Orangerie, Paris, April 20 – July 3, 1955 [sic]', I.B.54, IC/IP, MoMA Archives, New York.

60 Pierre Descargues, article in *Les Lettres françaises*, translated and reprinted in '*50 Ans d'Art aux États-Unis,* Paris Showing: Summary of the French Press Reaction', 1 May 1956, I.B.71, IC/IP, MoMA Archives, New York.

61 *Témoignage Chrétien,* referenced in Irwin M. Wall, *The United States and the Making of Postwar France, 1945–1954* (Riverside, CA: University of California, 1991), p. 124.

62 Michel Seuphor, article in *Preuves* (a Paris-based monthly publication of the Congress of Cultural Freedom), 1 May 1956, I.B.71, IC/IP, MoMA Archives, New York.

63 Motherwell, 'Reflections on Painting Now', p. 66.

64 Ibid.

65 Helen C. Franc, letter to Lois Bingham, 26 June 1956. I.A.566, IC/IP, MoMA Archives, New York.

66 Porter McCray, letter to Dorothy Miller, 3 February 1956. I.A.566, IC/IP, MoMA Archives, New York.

67 *Recent American Watercolors,* or *41 Aquarellistes américains d'aujourd'hui,* was a collaboration between the International Program and the USIA in Paris. The costs of internally distributing the show within France were met by the AFAA. *Recent American Watercolors* featured 80 works by some 41 artists and was shown at the following regional centres: Musée des Beaux-Arts, Laon (November 1956), Musée Antoine Lecuyer, St. Quentin (8 December–8 January 1957), Musée des Beaux-Arts, Reims (15 February–15 March 1957), Bibliothèque Municipale, Clermont-Ferrand (23 March–11 April 1957), Musée des Ponchettes, Nice (15 May–20 June 1957). There were initially ambitions to show in seven regional cities instead of five and, as a result, funds were left over from the AFAA account on the project.

68 Rasmussen was worried that the two exhibitions were too similar but did note the difference in terms of historical breadth: 'Please note that the Meltzer Gallery prepared an exhibition of American watercolors for the AFAA for circulation in France under their auspices, and that of the Cultural Relations Services Division of the United States Embassy, Paris. [. . .] Works dated from 1920 to 1954 and included examples by Morris Graves, Charles Burchfield, Hans Hoffman, Reginald Marsh, Dong Kingman, William Zorach and others. 109 works in all. Title of the exhibition was CONTEMPORARY WATERCOLOR IN THE UNITED STATES (L'AQUARELLE

CONTEMPORAINE AUX ETATS-UNIS).' Waldo Rasmussen, letter to Rose Kolmetz, 26 June 1956, I.A.566, IC/IP, MoMA Archives, New York.

69 O'Hara, 'Recent American Watercolors', I.A.566, IC/IP, MoMA Archives, New York.

70 Ibid.

71 Ibid.

72 Of the works on show, O'Hara favoured several European expatriates and exiles: Giorgio Cavallon had emigrated from Italy to New York in 1920, and studied during the evenings at Hans Hofmann's School of Fine Art; another Italian, Angelo Ippolito, arrived in the United States at the age of nine, and became one of the founders of the first artist-run Downtown gallery in New York; a third first-generation immigrant, Julio Girona, was born in Cuba but had led a cosmopolitan life in Paris, Greece and Egypt, before taking classes at the Arts Student League, and settling in Greenwich Village; Richard Lindner was born in Germany, and did not move to New York until he was forty. Lawrence Calcagno and Edmond Casarella were second-generation immigrants, their families moving from Italy. While such a cosmopolitan check-list was by no means exceptional, it does suggest the trend of the 'Individualist *Internationale*' now based in New York.

73 Frank O'Hara, 'Recent American Watercolors'.

74 Frank O'Hara, 'Joan Mitchell', for the 'Recent American Watercolors' catalogue essay (unpublished), I.A.566, IC/IP, MoMA Archives, New York.

75 Joan Mitchell letter, in John I. H. Baur, *Nature in Abstraction: The Relation of Abstract Painting and Sculpture to Nature in Twentieth-Century American Art* (New York: Whitney Museum of American Art, 1958), p. 75.

76 I wrote on this subject for a paper given at the *Border Control: On the Edges of American Art* symposium at Tate Liverpool in 2017, entitled '"Borders Meandering But Determined": Becoming an Apatride with Joan Mitchell and John Ashbery (1959–1965)'. Amy Rahn's doctoral dissertation on the transnational networks of Mitchell's career between New York and Paris is currently being revised for monograph publication.

77 John Ashbery, 'An Expressionist in Paris: John Ashbery on Joan Mitchell, in 1965', *Art News* <http://www.artnews.com/2015/07/17/an-expressionist-in-paris-john-ashbery-on-joan-mitchell-in-1965/> [accessed 13 April 2017].

78 John Ashbery, 'American Sanctuary in Paris', in *Reported Sightings*, ed. by David Bergman (Manchester: Carcanet, 1993), p. 88.

79 Shaw, 'Proximity's Plea: O'Hara's Art Writing', *Qui Parle* 12, No. 2, Special Issue on the Poetics of New Meaning (Spring/Summer 2001), 143–178 (p. 154).

80 This sense of the dangers attendant with an '-esque' as a kind of politics of resemblance recalls an anecdote that features Mitchell and her partner Riopelle, a Québécois who could easily pass for Algerian were accosted one evening by two gendarmes at the height of the May 1958 crisis. The authorities demanded to see their papers whereupon Riopelle who was allegedly unwilling

or unable to produce his. When asked of his name and identity, he responded sarcastically: 'Myself.' This provocative reply led to his arrest, at which point Mitchell started protesting and she too was hauled into the police station. The lingering threat of over-reaching state violence in the poem, of police 'frisking' Algerians, speaks to the anxieties of cultural hybridity in France at this time. A year earlier, O'Hara had written to Mitchell at 77 rue Daguerre and asked: 'Your descriptions of your new quarters are marvellous, especially walking around between Arabs and machine guns, does it make you feel sort of nervous and Joan of Lorraine-ish?' Frank O'Hara, letter to Joan Mitchell, 4 November 1957, The Joan Mitchell Foundation Archives (JMFA).

81 It is clear that 'Far from the Porte des Lilas and the Rue Pergolèse' is a companion piece to 'With Barbara Guest in Paris', which was also written in Paris during O'Hara's September 1958 visit, and addressed in exclamative apostrophe to two of his close friends there. 'With Barabara Guest in Paris' also mediates resemblance in an anxious way, as the poet finds himself 'in our Pushkinesque enclosure' – another transposing of the cultural spaces of France and the Soviet Union – as 'greatness' or some kind of future poetic legacy 'sleeps outside' (CP, 310). In 'About Doctor Zhivago and His Poem', O'Hara writes: 'I cannot agree with Elsa Triolet when she recently attacked Pasternak for having betrayed Mayakovksy in writing *Doctor Zhivago*' (CP, 502).

82 Hannah Feldman, *From a Nation Torn: Decolonizing Art and Representation in France, 1945–1962* (London: Duke University Press, 2014), p. 2.

83 Darthea Speyer, letter to Porter McCray, 11 July 1957. I.A.566, IC/IP, MoMA Archives, New York. Various letters sent from McCray's office ask Speyer to clarify or substantiate these vague sentiments, but none were forthcoming. McCray's frustration was compounded by the fact that Speyer had delayed the opening of the exhibition after not properly liaising with the handling company Lérondelle, nor organizing the requisite paperwork for the receiver of customs at Orly Airport. This debacle is recorded in various letters between Lérondelle and the International Program office. See R. Lérondelle, letter to Porter McCray, 14 October 1956, I.A.566, IC/IP, MoMA Archives, New York.

84 O'Hara, 'Recent American Watercolors'.

85 At this time, MoMA was busy acquiring a haul of late work by the Impressionists, the centrepiece being Alfred Barr's purchase of Monet's *Water Lilies* (1914–26) in 1955, after being strongly encouraged to do so by Miller and Soby who were despatched to the artist's Giverny estate. 'Work that [the New York School] claimed to be fatherless – in Emersonian fashion, a self-reliant American painting – made room for the entrance of a putative precedent. Monet's Water Lilies, as free of polemic as the Americans' work was a clarion call, would come to take on a prominent role. For countless commentators, and completely in spite of themselves, these works of an elderly man were transformed into fresh young things. Such was the alchemy of art critics and historians who could turn something that was an ending – Impressionism half a century after its baptism – into a beginning, a forecast of mid-century American painting.' See Nora Lawrence and Anne Temkin, *Claude Monet: Water Lilies* (New York: The Museum of Modern Art, 2008), p. 19. See also Matthew Holman, 'How Monet's water lilies took root across the pond', *Apollo: The International Art Magazine* (17 July 2018) <https://www.apollo-

magazine.com/water-lilies-american-abstract-painting-monet-review/>
[accessed 17 July 2018].

86   Greenberg, '"American-Type" Painting', p. 228.

87   Ibid, p. 219.

88   In an essay entitled 'A Tale of Two Cities', Tom Hess wrote on this alleged
     decline: 'We all know what happened to International School of Paris Painting
     at some time in between 1939 and 1945; it ceased to exist. We know what
     happened; the evidence is plain in literally thousands of pictures by hundreds
     of very gifted, intelligent artists. . . . The nicely adjusted harmony of blues and
     roses took on a deathly look of undertaker's cosmetics. Virtuoso drawing
     strangled form instead of defining it. The secret recipes of the painter's cuisine,
     of fine cookery to Cocteau's taste, now combined to dish up cloying sauces,
     pastries that would never give rise no matter how thoroughly the dough was
     teased, the cream whipped, the crusts garnished and dusted.' See Thomas B.
     Hess, 'A Tale of Two Cities', *Location* 1, No. 2 (Summer 1964), pp. 84–111.

89   Frank O'Hara, 'Changes in Style', box 1, fol. 4, FOHP, MoMA Archives, New
     York.

90   Jeff Dolven, *Senses of Style: Poetry Before Interpretation* (Chicago: The
     University of Chicago Press, 2017), p. 164.

91   Even MoMA has recognized the limitations of Barr's causal *Cubism and
     Abstract Art* flow-chart. In 2012, on the occasion of its *Inventing Abstraction*
     exhibition, the museum remodelled the same colour-coded system and graphic
     style, but rather than the development of *influence* privileged instead the scope
     of multilateral *networks*.

92   Holland Cotter, 'MoMA, the New Edition: From Monumental to
     Experimental', *New York Times*, 5 February 2019 <nytimes.com/2019/02/05/
     arts/design/moma-expansion.html.> [accessed 15 January 2024]. See Sandra
     Zulman, 'Unpacking the MoMA Myth: Modernism Under Revision',
     Modernism/Modernity 29, No. 2 (2022): 283–306.

93   The majority of paintings displayed as part of *Jackson Pollock 1912–1956*
     were secured loans from Krasner, who took on executive responsibilities after
     her husband's death. The American Embassy in Paris paid the costs for the
     shipping of the exhibition, overseen by Speyer, and the artworks were shipped
     back gratis on the USS *American Farmer*, meaning MoMA incurred little cost
     for the show as a whole.

94   Frank O'Hara, on behalf of Porter McCray, letter to Lee Krasner, 13
     November 1959, box 1, fol. 60, Jackson Pollock and Lee Krasner Papers,
     AAA. The posthumous Pollock retrospective may have been a curatorial *fait
     accompli* after the artist's death in 1956, with figures representing institutions
     across the world keen to capitalize on the significant public interest in his work
     as a result, Arnold Rüdlinger, the newly appointed director of the Kunsthalle
     Bern, played a particularly important role. In 1957, Rüdlinger travelled to New
     York on a People-to-People Grant, a cultural exchange project supported by
     the State Department under the Leaders and Specialists Grant Program
     (LSGP), and worked closely with McCray on an ultimately unsuccessful
     exhibition specifically for the Kunsthalle Bern, but what would ultimately be

realized with the travelling-exhibitions *The New American Painting* and *Jackson Pollock, 1912–1956*. See Nancy Jachec, 'Transatlantic Cultural Politics in the late 1950s: the Leaders and Specialists Grant Program', *Art History* 26, No. 4 (September 2003), 533–555 (p. 539).

95 O'Hara, letter to Krasner, 13 November 1958, AAA.

96 Lewison, 'Jackson Pollock and the Americanization of Europe', p. 220. It would also have been an attractive exhibition proposal given that the American Embassy paid the costs of shipping, which were largely offset by being shipped back free on the USS *American Farmer*. Speyer played a significant role in organizing this, knowing that these significant reductions in the cost of the exhibition would make it more palatable for Cassou.

97 Darthea Speyer, letter to Frank O'Hara, 21 November 1958. I.A.709, IC/IP, MoMA Archives, New York.

98 Jean Cassou, 'L' introduction', *Jackson Pollock 1912–1956 et la Nouvelle Peinture Américaine* (Paris: Musée national d'Art Moderne, 1959), n.p. Exhibition catalogue.

99 Invitation to the exhibition *Véhémences confrontées*. See Matthew Holman, 'Chronology of Events', *Un Art Autre* (London: Lévy Gorvy, 2019), p. 92. Exhibition catalogue.

100 Michel Tapié, 'Des signes chargés d'un possible maximum d'expressivité', *Un Art autre*, n.p. Referenced from and translated by Karen Kurczynski, 'Ironic Gestures: Asger Jorn, Informel, and Abstract Expressionism', in *Abstract Expressionism: The International Context*, ed. by Joan Marter (New Brunswick: Rutgers University Press, 2007), p. 112.

101 Tapié was well-known for his eccentric and poetic catalogue entries that fused complex existentialist philosophy with anti-formalist readings. Pollock would complain, for instance, that not even Dubuffet could write a 'decent translation' for his first one-person show in Paris, '*Pollock avec nous*'. Letter from Jackson Pollock to Alfonso A. Ossorio, 30 March 1952, referenced in B. H. Friedman, *Jackson Pollock: Action Made Visible* (Boston: De Capo Press, 1995), p. 192.

102 Michel Tapié, 'Jackson Pollock avec nous' (February 1951), reprinted in and translated by Nancy Jachec, 'Pollock in Paris', in *Jackson Pollock: Works, Writings and Interviews,* ed. by Nancy Jachec (Barcelona: Ediciones Poligrafia, 2011), p. 78.

103 Reprinted in *Jackson Pollock, 1912–1956*, ed. by Frank O'Hara (London: Whitechapel Art Gallery, 1958), p. 5. Not everyone was happy with the catalogue as it was published, first in São Paulo, and then largely retaining its textual shape for the European retrospective. On receiving her copy, Peggy Guggenheim wrote to Alfred Barr: 'Thank you so much . . . for the Pollock Catalogue . . . With reference to these I was shocked to see no mention of Art of this Century which discovered and launched Pollock . . . Also no mention made of a show I made for Pollock in Venice in the Museo Correr's Salla Napoleonic opening July 1950 . . . These grave omissions I feel were made on purpose. However you and I are sufficiently historically minded to include everything pertaining to facts, and if you still have any regard for me please

do not let me be thus pushed out of history. . .' Peggy Guggenheim, letter to Alfred Barr, 22 October 1957. I.A.686, IC/IP, MoMA Archives, New York.

104 Sam Hunter, 'Introduction', in *Jackson Pollock, 1912–1956,* ed. by Frank O'Hara, p. 8. In 2018, the Whitechapel Gallery exhibited *Staging Jackson Pollock* (4 September 2018–24 March 2019), focusing on Trevor Dannatt's constructivist design for the show.

105 Ibid.

106 Ibid.

107 Ibid, p. 12.

108 Frank O'Hara, letter to John Ashbery, 90 University Place, New York, 19 December 1958, box 1, fol. 9, ACFOL.

109 O'Hara, telegram to Ashbery, 26 December 1958, I.A.710, IC/IP, MoMA Archives, New York.

110 James Schuyler, letter to John Ashbery, 5 February 1959, I.A.710. IC/IP, MoMA Archives, New York.

111 Ibid.

112 John Ashbery, letter to Porter McCray, Paris, 29 January 1959, I.A.710. IC/IP, MoMA Archives, New York.

113 Georges Boudaille, article in *Lettres Françaises*, Paris, 22 January 1959. Reproduced in 'Critical Reviews: *Jackson Pollock, 1912–1956* (São Paulo and Europe)', box 1, fol. 60, Jackson Pollock and Lee Krasner Papers (JPLKP), AAA.

114 Bernard Dorival, article in Paris, 28 January 1959. Reproduced in 'Critical Reviews: *Jackson Pollock, 1912–1956* (São Paulo and Europe)', box 1, fol. 60, JPLKP, AAA. On Dorival's nationalist history of the École de Paris, see Dorival, *The School of Paris in the Musée d'Art Moderne* (New York: Harry N. Abrams, Inc., 1962).

115 Pierre Restany, 'U.S. Go Home and Come Back Later', *Cimaise* 6, No. 3 (January–March 1959), p. 37.

116 In a letter to Fleischmann, McCray informed him of the O'Hara-Ashbery plan of 'an official opening at 11.30 on Friday attended by the Ambassador and other American and French officials and special guests. This is to be followed by an official luncheon at the American Ambassador's residence . . . a cocktail supper to be given by you as a member of the International Council for the creative artists of the younger generation inn Paris . . . I shall speak with Nicholas Nabokov about the possibility of having this party at his apartment.' Porter McCray, letter to Julius Fleischmann, Jr., 6 January 1959. I.A.709, IC/IP, MoMA Archives, New York.

O'Hara was particularly impressed by the final choice of location, the Closerie des Lilas, because it was 'where Apollinaire played chess with Lenin, will you ever!' Frank O'Hara, letter to Joe LeSueur, Paris, 17 January 1959, box 1, fol. 9, ACFOL.

117 O'Hara, letter to LeSueur, 17 January 1959, ACFOL.

118 In a letter to Ashbery, O'Hara wrote that the 'most exciting thing that has happened to me recently is that Big Table forwarded me an envelop [sic] the

other day and in it was a drawing from Dubuffet. It is in India ink on his stationery, about the size of this page, the head of a man, and around it is written, so it fills out the rest of the space – "Salut Frank O'Hara . . . de Paris . . . le jour de Noël 1960 . . . à vous . . . un bon jour . . . d'un ami . . . j'ai lue le poème . . . dans Big Table . . . bonne année . . . Jean Dubuffet." [Hello Frank O'Hara . . . from Paris . . . Christmas day 1960 . . . to you . . . a hello . . . from a friend . . . I read the poem . . . in Big Table . . . happy New Year . . . Jean Dubuffet].' Frank O'Hara, letter to John Ashbery, 1 February 1961, box 2, fol. 17, ACFOL.

119 Rona Cran, *Collage in Twentieth-Century Art, Literature, and Culture: Joseph Cornell, William Burroughs, Frank O'Hara, and Bob Dylan* (London: Routledge, 2017), p. 145.

120 Bill Berkson and Frank O'Hara, 'Us Looking Up to St. Bridget', in *Hymns of St. Bridget & Other Writings* (Woodacre: The Owl Press, 2001), p. 19.

Three | In Favor of One's Time

1 Frank O'Hara, 'Introduction to the United States Representation: IV Bienal, São Paulo Catalog', 24 June 1957, I.A.627, IC/IP, MoMA Archives, New York.

2 Grace Hartigan, in *The New American Painting as Shown in Eight European Countries 1958–1959* (New York: Museum of Modern Art, 1959), p. 44.

3 O'Hara, 'Introduction to the United States Representation: IV Bienal, São Paulo Catalog'.

4 Ibid.

5 Suzanne Ferguson, 'Crossing the Delaware with Larry Rivers and Frank O'Hara: The post-modern hero at the Battle of Signifiers', *Word & Image* 2, Vol. 1 (1986), pp. 27–32 (pp. 29–30).

6 Larry Rivers, 'Larry Rivers on Larry Rivers', *Art News* 60 (March 1961), p. 54.

7 Frank O'Hara, letter to Betty Parsons, 24 September 1957, I.A.618, IC/IP, MoMA Archives, New York.

8 Frank O'Hara, 'XXIX Biennale di Venezia' (unpublished draft of press release), box 1, fol. 2, FOHP, MoMA Archives, New York.

9 Given that *The New American Painting* exhibition had been shown in Milan, at the Galleria Civica d'Arte Moderna in June 1958, many Italian critics and audiences had been engaging with American gesture painting that summer. It was a shrewd move on the part of McCray to show lesser-known artists than Jackson Pollock at Venice, given that Peggy Guggenheim's patronage of the artist at the Biennale stretched back as far as 1948, when Giulio Carlo Argan organized the display of his work in the Greek pavilion. That was Pollock's first major introduction to European audiences, and he was shown alongside 136 works by 73 international artists.

10 Gooch, *City Poet*, p. 312.

11 Frank O'Hara, 'Seymour Lipton', in *Lipton Rothko Smith Tobey: XXIX Biennale Venezia 1958*, I.A.819, IC/IP, MoMA Archives, New York.

12 Ibid.

13 Frank O'Hara, 'Mark Tobey', in *Lipton Rothko Smith Tobey: XXIX Biennale Venezia 1958*, I.A.819, IC/IP, MoMA Archives, New York.

14 Ibid.

15 The American Pavilion occupies a central position within the garden of nations in the enclosed sector of the Giardini, on the perimeter of Venice's city limits. But the Pavilion was an anomaly: having been purchased outright by MoMA in 1953, it was the only national pavilion to be owned not by a government but by a private museum or gallery. O'Hara noted that it was in order 'to insure the continuous representation of American art at the Venice expositions' that MoMA felt compelled to purchase the Pavilion, suggesting that no American representation whatsoever was a possible outcome if it did not. See O'Hara, 'XXIX Biennale di Venezia' (unpublished draft of press release), box 1, fol. 2, FOHP, MoMA Archives, New York.

16 See Frances K. Pohl, 'An American in Venice: Ben Shahn and United States Foreign Policy at the 1954 Venice Biennale, or Portrait of the Artist as an American Liberal', *Art History* 4, Issue 1 (March 1981), 80–113 (p. 80).

17 'The United States Government's difficulties in handling the delicate issues of free speech and free artistic expression, generated by the McCarthyist hysteria of the early 1950s, made it necessary and convenient for MoMA to assume this role of international representation for the United States. For example, the State Department refused to take responsibility for the United States representation at the Venice Biennale, perhaps the most important of international-cultural-political art events, where all the European countries including the Soviet Union competed for cultural honours. MoMA bought the United States pavilion in Venice and took sole responsibility for the exhibitions from 1954 to 1962.' Cockroft, p. 40. With that said, Cockroft's reasoned attribution as to why the United States government did not take up overt stewardship of the American Pavilion – that it was paralyzed by McCarthyistic philistinism and beset by domestic opposition to state funding for modernist exhibitions during the period of war on the Korean peninsula – remains convincing, as I have already outlined.

18 'Paintings by de Kooning and Shahn to be shown at 27th Venice Biennale with Sculpture by Lassaw, Lachaise and Smith', press release for *27th Venice Biennale*, 4 April 1954, I.A.447, IC/IP, MoMA Archives, New York.

19 Katherine Kuh, quoted in Mary Caroline Simpson, 'American Artists Paint the City: Katherine Kuh, the 1956 Venice Biennale, and New York's Place in the Cold War Art World', *American Studies* 48, No. 4 (Winter 2007), 31–57 (p. 38).

20 Lionello Venturi, 'Foreword', in *American Artists Paint the City: XXVIII Venice Biennale*, ed. by Katherine Kuh (Chicago: R. R. Donnelley & Sons Company, The Lakeside Press, 1956), p. 6.

21 Daniel Catton Rich, 'Europe is Imitating Our Painters for the First Time – Written Statement for the Associated Press', I.A.587, The IC/IP Papers, MoMA Archives, New York. This statement, and extracts therein, was published widely in the national press between 22 and 29 July 1956.

22 Nancy Jachec, 'Anti-Communism at Home, Europeanism Abroad: Italian Cultural Policy at the Venice Biennale, 1948–1958', *Contemporary European History* 14, No. 2 (May 2005), 193–217 (p. 193).

23 Françoise Choay, 'La XXIX Biennale de Venise', *L'Oeil*, 45 (1958), pp. 34–5. Translated from the French on behalf of the author by Rebecca Digne.

24 Ibid.

25 Silvano Giannelli, 'Il Volto dell'Occidente,' in *Il Quotidiano Sardo*, 23 June 1958, Archivio Storico delle Arti Contemporanee (ASAC). Translated from the Italian on behalf of the author by Rebecca Digne.

26 The 'Idea of Europe' campaign was intended to 'strengthen cultural relations with a view to developing European culture, to make Europe a single cultural entity without thereby sacrificing its remarkable variety, to disseminate the idea of European unity and to foster the European spirit in this and future generations'. See Council of Europe, *Directorate of Information, European Culture and the Council of Europe* (Strasbourg: Council of Europe, 1955), p. 15.

27 Gian Alberto Dell'Acqua, 'Introduzione', in *XXIX Esposizione Internazionale d'Arte* (Venice, 1958), p. lxi. Translated from the Italian on behalf of the author by Rebecca Digne.

28 Lawrence Alloway, *The Venice Biennale 1895–1965: From Salad to Goldfish Bowl* (New York: Graphic Society, 1970), p. 139.

29 'U.S. Section of 29th Venice Biennale Under Auspices of International Council', press release for *29th Venice Biennale*, 25 April 1958, I.A.811, IC/IP, MoMA Archives, New York.

30 Claire Brandon, 'Abstract Expressionism and the Global Impact of the Venice Biennale in the 1950s', in *In Focus: Cathedral 1950 by Norman Lewis*, Tate Research Publication, ed. by Andrianna Campbell (2018) <https://www.tate.org.uk/research/publications/in-focus/cathedral/venice-global-impact> [accessed 23 October 2019].

31 Porter McCray, 'Introduction, US Representation at the *XXIX Venice Biennale*, 30 April 1958', I.A.832, IC/IP, MoMA Archives, New York.

32 O'Hara, 'Mark Tobey', *Lipton Rothko Smith Tobey: XXIX*, I.A.817, IC/IP, MoMA Archives, New York.

33 On Tobey's Whitmanian sensibility, see Christopher Reed, '*E Pluribus Discrepantia*: Mark Tobey's American Modernism', *American Art* 30, No. 1 (Spring 2006), 21–27.

34 In the same statement reprinted by O'Hara in the catalogue, but presented in the catalogue of Dorothy Miller's *Fourteen Americans* exhibition (MoMA, 1946), Tobey wrote: 'America more than any other country is placed geographically to lead in this understanding, and if [. . .] she has constantly looked toward Europe, today she must assume her position, Janus-faced, toward Asia. [. . .] it is not surprising to me when an Oriental responds to a painting of mine as well as an American or a European.' See Mark Tobey, 'Artist's Statement', in *Fourteen Americans*, ed. by Dorothy Miller (New York: Museum of Modern Art, 1946), p. 70. Exhibition catalogue.

35 O'Hara, 'Franz Kline Talking', p. 89.

36 Frank O'Hara, 'American Art and Non-American Art', p. 98.

37 Philip Rahv, 'Paleface and Redskin', *The Kenyon Review* 1, No. 3 (Summer, 1939), pp. 251–256 (p. 252).

38 Ibid.

39 O'Hara, 'Seymour Lipton', *Lipton Rothko Smith Tobey: XXIX*, I.A.817, IC/IP, MoMA Archives, New York.

40 Seymour Lipton, referenced in Lori Verderame, *Seymour Lipton: An American Sculptor* (New York: Hudson Hills Press, 1999), p. 46.

41 Mark Tobey, referenced in O'Hara, 'Mark Tobey.' This statement was abridged from Tobey's contribution to the catalogue for *Fourteen Americans*. In her accompanying essay, Miller laid the groundwork for the American representation outwardly committed to internationalist values: 'The idiom is American but there is no hint of regionalism or chauvinistic tendency. On the contrary, there is a profound consciousness that the world of art is one world and that it contains the Orient no less than Europe and the Americas.' Dorothy Miller, *Fourteen Americans*, p. 8.

42 Lionello Venturi, 'La sconfitta degli anziani', *L'Espresso*, 22 June 1958, ASAC. Translated from the Italian on behalf of the author by Rebecca Digne.

43 Ibid.

44 See Frank O'Hara, letter to Marian Willard, 17 February 1959, I.A.842, IC/IP, MoMA Archives, New York.

45 Mario Monteverdi, 'Usa Soprammobili per la Casa di un Robot', *Corriere Lombardo*, 11 August 1958, ASAC. Translated from the Italian on behalf of the author by Rebecca Digne.

46 Ibid.

47 Ibid.

48 Leonardo Borgese, 'Il nulla alla Biennale', *La Domenica del Corriere*, 6 July 1958, ASAC. Translated from the Italian on behalf of the author by Rebecca Digne.

49 Frank O'Hara, memorandum to Porter McCray, 1 May 1958, I.A.834, IC/IP, MoMA Archives, New York.

50 Ibid.

51 Ibid.

52 John Ashbery, 'Jan Müller', *Art News* 56, No. 2 (January 1958), pp. 16–17.

53 Jachec, *Painting and Politics at the Venice Biennale*, p. 96.

54 See Franco Russoli, 'Giovani artisti italiani e stranieri', *CB VXXIX*, p. 116. Translated from the Italian on behalf of the author by Rebecca Digne.

55 Ibid., p. 114.

56 Jachec, *Painting and Politics at the Venice Biennale*, p. 96.

57 Porter McCray, 'Director's Report to the Council: International Program', 24 November 1958, p. 2, box 10, fol. 21, PMP, Archives of American Art, Washington DC.

58 Eva Cockroft, 'Abstract Expressionism: Weapon of the Cold War', in *Pollock and After: The Critical Debate*, ed. Francis Frascina (New York: Harper and Row, 1985), p. 83.

59 When I attended a symposium entitled 'Eccentric, realist, populist, procedural: the politics of figuration in American Art, 1929–1980' at Humboldt-

Universität zu Berlin in 2018, Charlotte Klonk's plenary speech identified *documenta 2* as the first-time ordinary West Germans became aware of American art in a meaningful way.

60 Werner Haftmann, 'Einleitung', I.A.890, IC/IP, MoMA Archives, New York.

61 Ibid.

62 Ibid. Many critics were unconvinced by Haftmann's utopianism on the role of art in the transatlantic political sphere. Some, however, were just as ebullient. 'Regional boundaries are eliminated', exclaimed Swedish critic Gunnar Hellmann, and everywhere 'one finds likenesses between Germans and Britons, Poles and Americans, Yugoslavs and Spaniards'. Gunnar Hellmann, 'World Sensation in Kassel', in *Hälsinge Kuriren,* Söderhamn, Sweden, 1 August 1959, n.p.

63 See John C. Torpey, *Intellectuals, Socialism, and Dissent: The East German Opposition and Its Legacy* (London: University of Minnesota Press, 1995), especially pp. 54–59.

64 Haftmann, 'Einleitunng'. With that said, statistics on the representation demonstrate a more complex picture. Of the fifteen represented countries, two were from beyond the Iron Curtain but not Soviet (Yugoslavia and Czechoslovakia); of the 200 painters, some 176 could be properly called abstract with 638 works between them, as against twenty figurative painters with sixty-nine works.

65 Charlotte Klonk, *Spaces of Experience: Art Gallery Interiors from 1800 to 2000* (London: Yale University Press, 2009), p. 176. See also Heather Elizabeth Mathews, 'Making histories: The exhibition of postwar art and the interpretation of the past in divided Germany, 1950–1959', PhD diss., The University of Texas at Austin (May 2006), pp. 165–197.

66 Will Grohmann, 'Die neue amerikanische Malerei: Zu einer Ausstellung in der Hochschule für bildende Künste', *Der Tagesspiegel* (7 September 1958). Translation by Richard George Elliot.

67 Arnold Bode, 'Bode-Plan', MS 1954, dIM20, *documenta* Archiv (DA), Kassel.

68 Wolfgang Christlieb, article in *Die Abendzeitung,* Munich, Germany, 17 October 1959, 'Press Reactions to the Exhibition Documenta 2, held in Kassel, Germany, July 11, to October 11, 1959', I.A.894, IC/IP, MoMA Archives, New York.

69 Knud W. Jensen, 'Indtryk fra Documenta 2', in *Louisiana 1959*, ed. by Knud W. Jensen (Copenhagen: Louisiana, 1959), p. 61. Translated by Kristian Handberg.

70 Lawrence Alloway, article from *Art International,* Vol. II/7, I.A.894, IC/IP, MoMA Archives, New York.

71 Jensen, 'Indtryk fra Documenta II', p. 61.

72 Porter McCray, 'The International Council: Annual Report, 1959, Director of the International Program', box. 10, fol. 21, PMP, Archives of American Art, Washington DC.

73 Rudolf Zwirner, letter to Porter McCray, Kassel, 12 March 1959, I.A.905, IC/IP, MoMA Archives, New York.

74 Reprinted in '"Documenta II": Mecca for Art Lovers', *The Bulletin* (Bonn), 7, No. 28, 28 July 1959, p. 4, *documenta* Archiv, Kassel.

75 Ernst Goldschmidt, on behalf of the Executive Committee of *documenta 2*, letter to Porter McCray, 13 November 1958, I.A.905, IC/IP, MoMA Archives, New York.

76 Haftmann, 'Einleitung', I.A.890, IC/IP, MoMA Archives, New York.

77 Ibid.

78 'Project Proposal: U.S. Representation, *documenta II*, Kassel, Germany, 1959', 24 November 1958, I.A.905, IC/IP, MoMA Archives, New York.

79 Porter McCray, letter to Frank O'Hara, Moscow, 22 July 1959, I.A.905, IC/IP, MoMA Archives, New York.

80 Herta Wescher, article in *Cimaise* (September/December, 1959), I.A.894, IC/IP, MoMA Archives, New York.

81 McCray, letter to O'Hara, 22 July 1959, I.A.905, IC/IP, MoMA Archives, New York.

82 Five paintings (by Kline, Pollock and Tobey) were then included in a selection of works entitled 'Vaerker fra Documenta' that was shown in November 1959 in the Louisiana, the recently inaugurated Danish contemporary art museum at Humlebæk, outside of Copenhagen. See Kristian Handberg, 'The Shock of the Contemporary: *documenta II* and the Louisiana Museum', *On Curating: The documenta Issue, Curating the History of the Present (Issue 33)*, ed. by Nanne Buurman and Dorothee Richter, pp. 34–43 <https://www.on-curating.org/files/oc/dateiverwaltung/issue-33/pdf/Oncurating_Issue33.pdf> [accessed 5 January 2019]. More research should be done on O'Hara's engagement with Scandinavian museums. In the same year as the opening of the Louisiana, the Moderna Museet opened in Stockholm under the directorship of Pontus Hultén. The Louisiana and the Moderna Museet became important 'provincial' museums in the distribution and promotion of American art in Europe in the 1960s and beyond. O'Hara visited both on his trip to Europe in 1963.

83 Frank O'Hara, memorandum to Porter McCray, 19 March 1959, I.A.913, IC/IP, MoMA Archives, New York. With that said, nine Pollock loans from Lee Krasner, the artist's widow and executor, remained in Europe after the 1958 travelling exhibitions to be displayed at *documenta* 2 in 1959.

84 Pierre Restany, article in *Art International*, Vol. II/7, 1959, I.A.894, IC/IP, MoMA Archives, New York.

85 Reprinted in John Anthony Thwaites, 'Report on *documenta II*', *ARTS* (November 1959), p. 46.

86 Ibid.

87 Will Grohmann, 'The New American Painting: On an Exhibition at the Hochschule für bildende Künst', translated by Richard George Elliot and printed in *Hot Art, Cold War – Western and Northern European Writing on American Art 1945–1990*, eds. Claudia Hopkins and Iain Boyd Whyte (New York: Routledge, 2021), pp. 261–262. Originally published as 'Die neue amerikanische Malerei: Zu einer Ausstellung in der Hochschule für bildende Künste', in *Der Tagesspiegel* (7 September 1958).

88   Albert Schulze Vellinghausen, review in *Frankfurter Allgemeine Zeitung*, 25 July 1959. IA.894, IC/IP, MoMA Archives, New York.

89   Frank O'Hara, 'Jackson Pollock', in *Art Chronicles*, p. 13.

90   Ibid., p. 35.

91   Clement Greenberg, 'How Art Writing Earns its Bad Name', *The Collected Essays and Criticism, Vol. 4, Modernism with a Vengeance, 1957–1969*, ed. by John O'Brian (Chicago: University of Chicago Press, 1986), 135–144 (p. 144).

92   Frank O'Hara, memorandum to Porter McCray, 4 May 1957, IC/IP, I.A.618, MoMA Archives, New York.

93   O'Hara, 'Art Chronicle', 9–10.

94   In one of his most assured examples of art writing, O'Hara writes: 'Much has been written about Pollock's difficulties in the last three years of his life, and more has been spoken. The works accomplished in these years, if created by anyone else, would have been astonishing. But for Pollock, who had incited in himself, and won, a revolution in three years (1947–50), it was not enough. This attitude has continued to obscure the qualities of some of these works, for in *Blue Poles* he gave us one of the great masterpieces of Western art, and in *The Deep* [another work featured at *documenta 2*], a work which contemporary aesthetic conjecture had cried out for. *Blue Poles* is our *Raft of the Medusa* and our *Embarkation for Cythera* in one. I say *our*, because it is the drama of the American conscience, lavish, bountiful, and rigid. It contains everything within itself, begging on quarter: a world of sentiment implied, but denied; a map of sensual freedom, fenced; a careening licentiousness, guarded by eight totems native to its origins (*There Were Seven in Eight*). What is expressed here is not only basic to his work as a whole, but it is final.' O'Hara, 'Jackson Pollock', pp. 36–37.

95   Frank O'Hara, letter to the Editor of *ARTS*, 3 February 1959, box 1, fol. 60, Jackson Pollock and Lee Krasner Papers, Archives of American Art, Washington DC. Note that O'Hara also forwarded his *ARTS* letter to Lee Krasner, presumably in part to prove his willingness to champion Pollock's work against his critics.

96   Ibid.

97   McCray, letter to O'Hara, 22 July 1959, I.A.905, IC/IP, MoMA Archives, New York. McCray refers to O'Hara's 1959 monograph on Pollock, published by George Braziller.

98   Haftmann, 'Einleitung', I.A.890, IC/IP, MoMA Archives, New York.

99   Vellinghausen, review in *Frankfurter Allegmeine Zeitung*. My emphasis.

100   Guy Habasque, article in *L'Oeil*, September 1959, pp. 19–27, I.A.894, IC/IP, MoMA Archives, New York.

101   Reprinted in Thwaites, p. 45.

102   Alloway, *Art International*.

103   Porter McCray, letter to Frank O'Hara, 10 December 1959, I.A.914, IC/IP, MoMA Archives, New York.

104   Ibid.

105 Ibid.

106 Rudolf Zwirner, in Dieter Honisch and Jens Christian Jensen, *Amerikanische Kunst von 1945 bis Heute* (Cologne: DuMont, 1976), p. 142.

107 Erhard Gopel, review for *Süddeutsche Zeitung,* Munich, Germany, 18 July 1959, I.A.894, IC/IP, MoMA Archives, New York.

108 'UFA Wochenshcau 155/1959' (1959), box 14, fol. 7, *Filmotek Bundesarchiv* <https://www.filmothek.bundesarchiv.de/video/584345> [accessed 18 April 2023].

109 Harald Kimpel and Karin Stengel, *documenta 1955: Erste Internationale Kunstausstellung – eine fotografische Rekonstruktion* (Bremen: Edition Temmen, 1995), p. 8. Translation by Kristian Handberg.

110 Porter McCray, letter to Frank O'Hara, 10 December 1959, I.A.914, IC/IP, MoMA Archives, New York.

111 Joe LeSueur, *Digressions on Some Poems by Frank O'Hara: A Memoir* (New York: Farrar, Straus and Giroux, 2003).

112 Ibid.

113 Ibid.

114 Edith Schloss, *The Loft Generation: From the De Koonings to Twombly, Portraits and Sketches 1942–2011* (New York: Farrar, Straus and Girou, 2021), p. 90.

115 Ibid.

116 Franz Kline, 'Franz Kline Talking', in *Standing Still and Walking,* ed. by Allen, p. 89.

117 In a March 1956 letter to O'Hara, Kenneth Koch recounts a conversation he had with de Kooning at the Cedar Tavern after discussing O'Hara's poem, in which de Kooning tells Koch that 'he had always been interested in mattresses because they were pulled together at certain points and puffed out at others, "like the earth"'. See *The Collected Poems,* notes by Allen, p. 536.

118 Adrienne Rich, 'Rauschenberg's Bed', in *Later Poems: Selected and New, 1971–2012* (New York: W. W. Norton & Company, Inc., 2013), p. 363.

119 Helmuth Kotschenreuther, 'Schützenfest der Tachisten', *Erlangener Tageblatt,* 1 September 1959. I.A.894, IC/IP, MoMA Archives, New York.

120 'Documenta: Im Wolfspelz', *Der Spiegel,* 29 July 1959, pp. 50–53. Translated from the German by Catherine Dossin.

121 Robert Rauschenberg, from *Selections from the Ileana and Michael Sonnabend Collection,* ed. by Sam Hunter (Princeton: The Art Museum, Princeton University, 1985), p. 21. Exhibition catalogue.

122 Robert Rauschenberg, reprinted in Elizabeth Fullerton, 'Robert Rauschenberg', in *Art in America* (27 February 2017) <https://www.artnews.com/art-in-america/aia-reviews/robert-rauschenberg-62310/> [accessed 15 October 2023].

123 Rick Barot, 'Rauschenberg's Bed', *The Yale Review* 96, No. 1 (January 2008), 64–75 (p. 65).

124 Restany, article in *Art International.*

125 Frankenthaler was represented by three paintings at *documenta 2*: *Mountains and Sea* (1952), *Las Mayas* (1958) and *Nude* (1958).

126 Friedel Dzubas, letter to Ernst Goldschmidt, [date queried], I.A.905, IC/IP, MoMA Archives, New York.

127 Ibid.

128 Ibid.

129 Ibid.

130 Egon Vietta, letter to the Editor, *Frankfurter Allegmeine Zeitung,* 11 July 1959, p. 2. Referenced from, and translation by, Mathews, 'Making histories', p. 189.

131 Frank O'Hara, memorandum to Porter McCray, 12 February 1959, I.A.914, IC/IP, MoMA Archives, New York.

132 Ibid.

133 Yau, 'Passionate Spectator', p. 10.

134 'I can't tell you how much we appreciated the loan of this important work to Documenta or how much pleasure I has brought me for I have had it in my own office since its return from Germany. I cannot help but be less gay facing the great grey wall which now frowns down upon me.' Porter McCray, letter to Eleanor Ward, 1 May 1961, I.A.926, IC/IP, MoMA Archives, New York.

135 Judith E. Bernstock, *Joan Mitchell* (Manchester: Hudson Hills Press, 1988), pp. 46–47.

136 Ibid., p. 47.

Four | Blue Territory

1 Deborah Solomon, 'Artful Survivor', *New York Times Magazine*, 14 May 1989.

In the same interview, this was how Solomon described Frankenthaler: 'As she sits sipping tea, Frankenthaler, a thin, attractive woman of 60 dressed conservatively in a dark green sweater and a gray pleated skirt, looks like a character from the old New York world of an Edith Wharton novel. Her posture is regal, and she speaks with a precision that enhances her stately demeanor. Her face can quickly turn cold and skeptical, but when she laughs, as she often does, she conveys a youthful vigor that makes it easy to picture her in the 1950's – a promising painter fresh out of Bennington who had already begun to impress the most discerning critics of her time.'

2 Mary Gabriel, *Ninth Street Women*, p. 643.

3 Alexander Nemerov, *Fierce Poise: Helen Frankenthaler and 1950s New York* (New York: Penguin Random House, 2021), p. 145.

4 Elaine de Kooning, 'Dialogue with Rosalyn Drexler', *Art News*, January 1971 <https://www.artnews.com/art-news/retrospective/eight-artists-reply-why-have-there-been-no-great-women-artists-4245/> [accessed 2 January 2024].

5   S[am] F[einstein], 'Helen Frankenthaler', *Art Digest* 27 (15 February 1953), p. 20.

6   Frankenthaler herself described some of her works as 'private' pictures – 'menus, memos, salutations, birthday greetings', quoted in, Karen Wilkin, *Frankenthaler: Works on Paper 1949–1984* (New York: George Braziller, 1984), p. 26.

7   Julian Barnes, 'Freud: The Episodicist', in *Keeping an Eye Open: Essays on Art* (London: Jonathan Cape, 2015): 237–258, p. 241.

8   The name was also lent to Robin Lippincott's immersive 2015 book on Mitchell, *A Meditation on the Life and Art of Joan Mitchell.*

9   Anne M. Wagner, 'Pollock's Nature, Frankenthaler's Culture', in *Jackson Pollock: New Approaches*, eds. Kirk Varnedoe and Pepe Karmel (New York: The Museum of Modern Art, 1999): 181–200, p. 185.

10 Helen Frankenthaler, in 'An interview with Helen Frankenthaler', in *The New York School: The Painters & Sculptors of the Fifties Irving*, ed. Sandler (New York: Harper & Row, 1978), p. 67

11 Ibid.

12 Ibid.

13 Marjorie Perloff, *Frank O'Hara: Poet Among Painters* (London: The University of Chicago Press, 1977), p. 82. Part of Perloff's doubts on O'Hara's 'Blue Territory' as a successful ekphrastic representation of Frankenthaler's painting, centred on the fact that the critic did not believe this to be a landscape, may well be down the fact that it is vertically orientated when hung. Convention encourages us to see portraits as vertical, and landscapes as horizontal, although Frankenthaler's paintings often scupper this binary logic. See Robert Slifkin, 'Orientating Frankenthaler', *Imagining Landscapes: Paintings by Helen Frankenthaler, 1952–1976* (London: Gagosian, 2021), p. 5. Slifkin opens his essay by admitting that, in *Mountains and Sea*, of the horizontal-landscape mode, he sees a woman's face.

14 Eleanor Careless, 'risk the big gesture: Frank O'Hara on Helen Frankenthaler', unpublished conference paper delivered at *Frank O'Hara and Friends: The Day Before O'Hara Died* symposium, Institute of Contemporary Arts, London, July 2016.

15 Frank O'Hara, from 'Short Reviews (1953–55)', in *What's Wrong with Modern Art?*, ed. Bill Berkson (Austin, TX: Mike & Dale's Press, 1999), p. 19.

16 See William Empson, 'Chapter V', *Seven Types of Ambiguity* (London: Chatto and Windus, 1949), pp. 155–175.

17 Mary Gabriel, *Ninth Street Women*, p. 712.

18 John Elderfield, in 'John Elderfield and Carol Armstrong on Helen Frankenthaler | In Conversation', *Gagosian Quarterly* (2023) <https://gagosian.com/quarterly/2023/04/07/video-in-conversation-carol-armstrong-and-john-elderfield-helen-frankenthaler/> [accessed 15 January 2024].

19 Donald Judd, 'In the Galleries', *Arts Magazine* 34 (March 1960), p. 55.

20 Frank O'Hara, 'Helen Frankenthaler', in *An Exhibition of Oil Paintings by Frankenthaler* (New York: The Jewish Museum, 1960), p. 7.

21 John Elderfield, *Frankenthaler* (New York: Abrams, 1989), p. 125.

22 Helen Frankenthaler, quoted in *MoMA Highlights: 375 Works from The Museum of Modern Art, New York* (New York: The Museum of Modern Art, 2019), p. 219.

23 Frankenthaler's 'Jewishness' has received fairly scant attention in critical appraisals of her work. Nemerov mentions her Jewish identity in relation to Greenberg's ideas of 'innerlichkeit', or inwardness (Nemerov, *Fierce Poise*, p. 204) while Anna C. Chave writes that 'within the ambit of the New York School—the diving board from which she launched, as she envisioned it (with the troping to the fluid that ran deep with her)—Frankenthaler's being Jewish may have counted, if anything, as a plus. Some of the school's founding figures were Jewish—such as Mark Rothko, with whose work Frankenthaler's manifested at times a real affinity; and there was, too, what Max Kozloff termed that "old time Jewish sect called American art criticism."' See Anna C. Chave, 'Frankenthaler's Fortunes: On Class Privilege and the Artist's Reception', *Women's Art Journal* Vol. 37, Issue 1 (Spring–Summer 2016), p. 30. See also Alison Rowley, *Helen Frankenthaler: Painting History, Writing Painting* (New York: I.B. Tauris & Co., 2007), p. 102.

24 O'Hara, 'Helen Frankenthaler', p. 3. It is worth noting that, in 1989, Frankenthaler was photographed surrounded by her paintings again, but this time in a luxury advertisement for a $7,000 (the 1989 price), 18-karat Oyster Perpetual Lady Datejust Rolex watch. The advertising copy furthered the narrative that 'although Frankenthaler leads a calm, ordered life, she embraces risks and adventure in her art', which is preciously close to how O'Hara defined her work in 1960, as each painting an 'occasion of risk and paint-adventure.'

25 Careless, '"risk the big gesture": Frank O'Hara on Helen Frankenthaler.'

26 Nemerov, *Fierce Poise*, p. 201.

27 O'Hara, 'Helen Frankenthaler', p. 6.

28 Carl Belz, 'Helen Frankenthaler and the 1950s', in *Painted on 21st Street: Helen Frankenthaler from 1950 to 1950*, ed. John Elderfield (New York: Gagosian and Abrams, 2013), p. 151.

29 O'Hara, 'Helen Frankenthaler', pp. 5–7.

30 O'Hara, from 'Short Reviews', p. 19.

31 O'Hara, 'Helen Frankenthaler', p. 7.

32 Barbara Butler, 'Movie Stars and Other Members of the Cast', *Art International* 4 (February–March 1960), p. 55.

33 Ibid.

34 Robert Coates, *The New Yorker*, 36 (9 April 1960), p. 159.

35 O'Hara, 'Helen Frankenthaler', p. 7.

36 Anne Seelye, 'Helen Frankenthaler', *Art News* 59, Issue 1 (March 1960), pp. 39, 57.

37 Ibid, p. 57.

38 Sybil E. Gohari, 'Gendered Reception: There and Back Again: An Analysis of the Critical Reception of Helen Frankenthaler', *Women's Art Journal* 35, Issue 1 (2014) <https://go-gale-com.ezproxy.herts.ac.uk/ps/i.do?p=AONE&u=uniherts&id=GALE A464161900&v=2.1&it=r&sid=summon> [accessed 4 January 2024].

39 Nemerov, *Fierce Poise*, p. 205.

40 Constance Emmerich, Letter to the Editor, *Art News* 59, Issue 2 (April 1960), p. 10.

41 Everett Ellin, Letter to the Editor, *Art News* 59, Issue 3 (May 1960), p. 6.

42 B. H. Friedman, Letter to the Editor, *Art News* 59, Issue 2 (April 1960), p. 10.

43 B. H. Friedman, Letter to *Art News*, 14 March 1960, Helen Frankenthaler Foundation Archives. Cited in Mary Gabriel, *Ninth Street Women* (New York: Little, Brown and Company, 2018), p. 982.

44 B. H. Friedman, letter to Helen Frankenthaler, 8 February 1960, Helen Frankenthaler Foundation Archives. Cited in Nemerov, *Fierce Poise*, p. 202.

45 Helen Frankenthaler, Letter to the Editor, *Art News* 59, Issue 3 (May 1960), p. 6.

46 Ibid.

47 Sonia Rudikoff, Letter to the Editor, *Art News* 59, Issue 3 (May 1960), p. 6.

48 O'Hara, 'Short Reviews (1953–55)', p. 19.

49 See Sarah Chambre, 'Distant relations: The othered construction and communicability of Mona Brigstock and communities offstage', *Henry James Review*, forthcoming 2024.

50 Dan Chiasson, 'Fast Company', in *The New Yorker*, 31 March 2008 <https://www.newyorker.com/magazine/2008/04/07/fast-company> [accessed 10 July 2024].

51 *Helen Frankenthaler: A Paintings Retrospective* was organized by E. A. Carmean, Jr., director of the Modern Art Museum of Fort Worth, Texas. After its New York showing at Museum of Modern Art (5 June–20 August 1989), the exhibition travels to the Modern Art Museum of Fort Worth (5 November 1989–7 January 1990), the Los Angeles County Museum of Art (8 February–22 April 1990), and The Detroit Institute of Arts (June–September 1990).

52 Frank O'Hara, letter to Helen Frankenthaler, 16 December 1959, quoted from Gooch, *City Poet*, p. 342.

53 Helen Frankenthaler, interview with Brad Gooch, 7 April 1990. See Gooch, *City Poet*, p. 356.

Five | Make it New, Make it Over

1 *New Spanish Painting and Sculpture* was on show at MoMA from 20 July to 28 September 1960. The exhibition featured two to five works by sixteen artists (all men): Raphael Canogar, Eduardo Chillida, Martin Chirino, Modest Cuixart, Francisco Farreras, Luis Feito, Manuel Millares, Lucio Muñoz, Jorge de Oteiza, Manuel Rivera, Antonio Saura, Pablo Serrano, Antonio Suàrez, Antoni Tàpies, Joan Josep Tharrats and Manuel Viola.

2 Porter McCray, 'Acknowledgements', in *New Spanish Painting and Sculpture*, ed. by Frank O'Hara (New York: The Museum of Modern Art, 1960), p. 7.

3   Ibid.

4   Frank O'Hara, 'New Spanish Painting and Sculpture', in *New Spanish Painting and Sculpture*, ed. by O'Hara, p. 9. All subsequent references from this essay will be provided with the abbreviation: O'Hara, *NSPS*.

5   O'Hara, *NSPS*, p. 7.

6   Ibid, p. 9.

7   Ibid, p. 10.

8   Ibid.

9   I use the term 'avant-garde' in this context purposefully, and as a gesture to the way it was and is understood in Spanish art history. In Spain, 'modern art' tends to be synonymous with Modernism and with specific kinds of Modernist aesthetics that emerged in the first two decades of the twentieth century. The term *segunda vanguardia* was first used in Spanish art criticism by José María Moreno Galván to estheticize the experimental and radical art processes that had taken place from the mid-fifties. See José Maria Moreno Galván, *Pintura Espanola: La Ultima Vanguardia* (Madrid: Magius, 1969).

10 Installation view of the exhibition, *New Spanish Painting and Sculpture* (20 July–28 September 1960). Photographic Archive. IN668.1. MoMA Archives, New York. Photograph by George Barrows.

11 Dore Ashton, 'The Place of Spanish Art in Modern Experience', *YouTube* video, 9.36, posted by Meadows Museum Dallas, 3 September 2013 <https://www.youtube.com/watch?v=IoWPmc0459w> [accessed 5 January 2023].

12 Genoveva Tusell García, 'The Internationalisation of Spanish Abstract Art (1950–62)', *Third Text* 20, No. 2 (2006), 241–249 (p. 241).

13 To offer one example, see Antoni Tàpies and Michel Tapié, *Antoni Tàpies* (New York: G. Wittenborn, 1959).

14 As Frank O'Hara travelled through Spain, conducting research in support of *New Spanish Painting and Sculpture* and visiting artists' studios, he wrote a substantial corpus of poetry that in ways obvious and oblique contribute to his wider writings on Spanish history, art and politics. These would include 'Places for Oscar Salvador', 'A Little Travel Diary', 'Now That I am in Madrid and Can Think', 'The "Unfinished"', 'Avenue A', and 'Flag Day.'

15 O'Hara and Lucie-Smith, 'Edward Lucie-Smith: An Interview with Frank O'Hara', p. 7.

16 John Russell, 'Art: Recent Tàpies Work Keeps Old Spirit', *New York Times*, 15 November 1975, p. 23.

17 O'Hara, *NSPS*, p. 9

18 For a fuller biography of Tàpies' life and career, see Roland Penrose, *Tàpies* (London: Thames & Hudson, 1978). For the pre-Civil War period through the 1960s, see Antoni Tàpies, *A Personal Memoir: Fragments for an Autobiography (Volume I)*, trans. by Josep Miquel Sobrer (Bloomington: Indiana University Press, 2009). For an account of Tàpies' relationship to historicized artistic practice, see Renée Riese Hubert, 'Antoni Tàpies Between History and Mysticism', *Dalhousie French Studies* 21, Fall–Winter (1991), 101–111.

19 O'Hara, *NSPS*, p. 9.

20 Ibid, p. 10. In his *Homage to Frank Lloyd Wright* (1959), displayed opposite Cuixart's *Painting* (1959), Tharrats estheticized a violent procedure that appeared, at least on the surface, to share precious little with Lloyd Wright's brand of measured 'organic architecture'.

21 O'Hara, *NSPS*, p. 8.

22 Equipo 57, 'Manifesto of the exhibition at the Café Le Rond Point, Paris, 1957', referenced in M. González and B. Díaz, *Equipo 57* (Madrid, 1994), pp. 153–157.

23 José García Ortega, reprinted in Noemi de Haro García, 'Culture Will Set You Free: Art and Politics in Cold War Spain (1951–1964)', *Konsthistorisk tidscrift/ Journal of Art History* 82, No. 4 (2013), 287–303 (p. 292).

24 O'Hara, *NSPS*, p. 7. O'Hara found the geographical stratification of different artists laborious. 'There is a sort of East Coast–West Coast rivalry between the two cities which gets quite tiresome.' Frank O'Hara, letter to Waldo Rasmussen, Hotel Colon, Barcelona, 5 April 1960, C/E 59-3, FOHP, MoMA Archives, New York.

25 Ibid.

26 The story of Juana Francés' place within postwar Spanish abstraction has only been partly told, but the Alicante Museum of Contemporary Art's 2018 retrospective, and her inclusion in the *Action, Gesture, Paint* exhibition at The Whitechapel Gallery in 2023, indicates some curators are catching up.

27 Various, '*El Paso* Manifesto', reprinted in the preface to *Millares, Canogar, Rivera, Saura: Four Spanish Painters*, ed. by Juan Eduardo Cirlot (New York: Pierre Matisse Gallery, 1960), n.p. Exhibition catalogue.

28 O'Hara, *NSPS*, p. 7.

29 Although Spain did maintain alliances with Portugal, Argentina and some Arab-speaking nations, the country was effectively ostracized by all multilateral organizations from 1945 until 1955 during the period when the international community grappled with 'the Spanish Question'. On 12 December 1946, the United Nations General Assembly voted to exclude Spain from membership 'until a new and acceptable government is formed'. The UN declared that 'the Franco Fascist Government of Spain, which was imposed by force upon the Spanish people with the aid of the Axis Powers and which gave material assistance to the Axis Powers in the war, does not represent the Spanish people, and by its continued control of Spain is making impossible the participation of the Spanish people with the peoples of the United Nations in international affairs.' See UN General Assembly, 'Relations of Members of the United Nations with Spain', 12 December 1946 <http://www.refworld.org/ docid/3b00f08d8.html> [accessed 18 March 2020]. On the issue of 'the impact of politics on morals', written in the intervening period between Spain's isolation and rapprochement, see John A. Houston, 'The United Nations and Spain', *The Journal of Politics* 14, No. 4 (November 1952), 683–709.

30 For more on a culture of repression and fear during the period of what was named by the regime as the 'years of victory', see Antonio Cazorla Sánchez, *Fear and Progress: Ordinary Lives in Franco's Spain, 1939–1975* (Chichester: Wiley-Blackwell, 2010).

31 For more on the current purpose of Valle de los Caídos, see Jeremy Treglown, *Franco's Crypt: Spanish Culture and Memory since 1936* (London: Penguin, 2015), especially pp. 57–84. Since Treglown's book, Franco's body was exhumed from the site to widespread controversy and national debate. See Stephania Taladrid, 'Franco's Body is Exhumed, as Spain Struggles to Confront the Past', *The New Yorker*, 26 October 2019 <https://www.newyorker.com/news/daily-comment/francos-body-is-exhumed-as-spain-still-struggles-to-confront-the-past> [accessed 30 October 2023].

32 Francisco Franco, 'Boletín Oficial del Estado', 2 April 1940, 2240. Translated by Paula Barreiro López.

33 Manuel Machado, 'Tradición', reproduced in Julio Rodriguez Puértolas, 'Fascismo y poesía en España', in *Actas del séptimo congreso de la Asociación Internacional de Hispanistas,* ed. by Giuseppe Bellini (Rome: Bulzoni, 1982), p. 885. Translation by Paula Barreiro López.

34 Paula Barreiro López, 'Reinterpreting the Past: The Baroque Phantom during Francoism', *Bulletin of Spanish Studies* 91, No. 5 (2014), 715–734 (p. 716). There is an extensive literature on the subject of Francoist promotion of Baroque aesthetics, and the struggle on the part of experimental or avant-gardist artists to 'reclaim' the period's Spanish masters from their co-option by the regime. Alongside Barreiro López's essay, the following are most pertinent to this study, collated in a 2014 special issue of *Bulletin of Spanish Studies* (Vol. 91, No. 5): Noemi De Haro-García and Julián Díaz-Sánchez, 'Artistic Dissidence under Francoism: The Subversion of the Cliché', 735–754; Johannes Großmann, '"Baroque Spain" As Metaphor': Hispanidad, Europeanism and Cold War Anti-Communism in Francoist Spain', 755–771.

35 McCray, 'Acknowledgements', *NSPS*, p. 5.

36 Luis González-Robles, letter to Frank O'Hara, Hotel Wellington, Madrid, 31 March 1960, box 3, fol. 17, FOHP, MoMA Archives, New York. Translated from the Spanish on behalf of the author by Luciana von Römer.

37 From at least the moment that her sacred arm-reliquary was recovered from a Republican General in battle in 1937, Teresa was the emblem of the Francoist crusade against democracy, Jewish-Masonic conspiracy, and international socialism. Franco even received a special dispensation to keep her arm-reliquary throughout his dictatorship in his residence, the Palacio de El Pardo, for private devotion.

38 Miriam Basilio, *Visual Propaganda, Exhibitions, and the Spanish Civil War* (Surrey: Ashgate, 2013), p. 175.

39 Jacques Derrida, 'Force of Law: The Mystical Foundation of Authority', trans. by Mary Quaintance, in *Acts of Religion*, ed. by Gil Anidjar (London: Routledge, 2002), p. 278. I cannot help but be reminded of O'Hara's elegiac reading of *Blue Poles* by Jackson Pollock (1952), which is compared to Picasso's *Guernica* and was 'a painfully beautiful celebration of what will disappear, or has disappeared already, from his world, of what may be destroyed at any moment'. Frank O'Hara, *Jackson Pollock* (New York: George Braziller, 1960), p. 14.

40 Perloff, *Poet Among Painters*, p. 21.

41 *¡Bienvenido, Mister Marshall!* was a satirical take-up of the widely held yet trite stereotypes of the Spaniard and the American. Set in a 'typical' village on the eve of a visit by American diplomats representing the Marshall Plan whom the characters are eager to impress, the plot sees various Spanish 'types' – the mayor, the hidalgo, the priest, and the flamenco impresario – dreaming of American culture and its history, from the conquistadors to the common white hoods of the Holy Week and the Ku Klux Klan. Ultimately, however, the American motorcade whizzes straight through the village, and no investment is secured despite their best efforts. Berlanga was adept at skirting the regime's censors, and *¡Bienvenido, Mister Marshall!* competed at the 1953 Cannes Film Festival to the state's pleasure. The film is one example of how art and culture that had been, theoretically, critical to Francoism, was now tolerated and even received the tacit support of the regime.

42 O'Hara reported back on his itinerary: 'Oh, one rather amusing thing: it's a good thing we put that contingency item in my budget because I forget at the last moment to tell you that there is no plane service to San Sebastián from Barcelona unless you return first to Madrid so I will have to go overland from here to there, not just from San Sebastián to Paris. It's not terribly expensive, though, anyway.' O'Hara, letter to Rasmussen, 5 April 1960, FOHP, MoMA Archives, New York.

43 Intriguingly, John Davis Lodge, who supported Dietrich in von Sternberg's *The Scarlet Empress* (1934), was then U.S. Ambassador to Spain (1955–1961) and instrumental in the Pact of Madrid relationship.

44 Frank O'Hara, 'Awake in Spain', in *The Hasty Papers: Special Millennium Edition of the 1960 One-Shot Review*, ed. by Alfred Leslie (Austin: Host Publications, 2000), pp. 78–81 (p. 80).

45 Ibid.

46 The eclectic character list includes poets William Blake, Kenneth Koch and W. B. Yeats (or, rather, a character playing Yeats' Mind, and another for his Soul); New York School artists Arshile Gorky and Larry Rivers; Founding Fathers John Adams and Benjamin Franklin; European aristocrats and monarchs, real and fictional, including Princess Marie of Rumania, King, Duke, Grand Vizier, and so on. Best described as a surrealist farce, *Awake in Spain* was made up of a series of disjointed and largely un-performable vignettes.

47 O'Hara, 'Awake in Spain', p. 79.

48 Ibid, p. 78.

49 O'Hara, *NSPS*, p. 7.

50 See Michael Leja, *Reframing Abstract Expressionism: Painting and Subjectivity in the 1940s* (New Haven: Yale University Press, 1997).

51 Paula Barreiro López, *Avant-Garde Art and Criticism in Francoist Spain* (Liverpool: Liverpool University Press, 2017), p. 63.

52 McCray, *NSPS*, p. 5.

53 Mercedes Molleda, 'As the Critics Saw It', in *The New American Painting, as shown in eight European countries, 1958–1959*, ed. by Dorothy Miller (New York: The Museum of Modern Art, 1959), p. 9. Exhibition catalogue.

54 It is curious to speculate on what Franco personally thought of gestural
    abstraction – or Spanish *Informalismo* – and the answer might reasonably be
    not much, although Treglown wonders how the vanguard artists reconciled
    their anti-Francoism with their new promotion by the regime: 'Would they
    have been easier in their minds if they had known that Franco himself really
    didn't care much either way? At one of the Spanish national Biennales, a group
    of nervous officials stood with him in front of some pictures by Tàpies.
    "Excellency, this is the revolutionaries' room", one of them is said to have
    explained. "So long as this is how they carry out the revolution", he cheerfully
    replied.' Treglown, *Franco's Crypt*, p. 102.

    Luis González Robles offered another, complementary anecdote: 'Franco and I
    were opening an exhibition of artists from the States. Sotomayor [conservative
    Director of the Prado Museum] was about ten or fifteen steps behind us, beside
    the Caudillo's wife and other ministers. I turned to Franco and said to him,
    "Can I speak freely to you, Excellency?", "Of course!", he said. So then I said
    to him, "I believe you have an exquisitely academic taste." He stopped and
    asked me what I meant by that. So then I suggested that perhaps he was
    somewhat too influenced by Sotomayor's fussy academicism. [. . .] When we
    finished going around the exhibition, and just after seeing Rauschenberg and
    Rivers, Franco said to me, "This is a really fantastic experience, I'm deeply
    impressed. It is a reality I didn't know."' Jorge Luis Marzo, 'Interview with
    Luis González Robes, Government official with overall responsibility for
    contemporary art during Franco's regime', *Revista de Calor*, No. 1 (December
    1993), 28–36 (p. 31).

55 Porter McCray, 'Director's Report to the Council: International Program',
    24 November 1958, box 10, fol. 22, PMP, AAA.

56 Andrew Carnduff Ritchie, 'Foreword', *The New Decade: 22 European Painters
    and Sculptors* (New York: The Museum of Modern Art, 1955), p. 11.
    Exhibition catalogue.

57 Jorge Luis Marzo, *Art Modern i Franquisme. Els origens conservadors de
    l'avantguarda i de la política artística a L'Estat Espanyol* (Girona: Fundación
    Espais, 2008), n.p, quoted in Bartomeu Marí, 'Building a Museum in the Late
    20th Century: The MACBA Case', in *Contemporary Transatlantic Dialogues:
    Art History, Criticism, and Exhibition Practices in Spain and the United States*,
    ed. by María Dolores Jiménez-Blanco and Robert S. Lubar (New York: Centre
    for Spain in America, 2013), 103–118 (p. 108).

58 For more on the importance of this scheme as a means through which
    American art organizers relied on the support and collaboration of local
    intellectuals, see Nancy Jachec, 'Transatlantic Cultural Politics in the late
    1950s: the Leaders and Specialists Grant Program', *Art History* 26, No. 4
    (2003), 533–555.

59 Guilbaut, *How New York Stole the Idea of Modern Art*, p. 190.

60 Manuel J. Borja-Villel, 'The Changes of Taste: Tàpies and the Critics', in
    Tàpies: els any 80 (Barcelona: Ajuntament de Barcelona, 1988), p. 246.

61 Marzo, 'Interview with Luis González Robes', p. 31.

62 Porter McCray, 'The International Council: Annual Report, 1959, Director of
    the International Program', box 10, fol. 22, PMP, MoMA Archives, New York.

63 Millares himself helped organize an exhibition at the Galería Biosca, Madrid, which opened on 7 June 1960 and 'featured precisely those artists who would exhibit a month later at The Museum of Modern Art in New York'. See *La Nueva Pintura de España* (London: The Tooth Gallery, 1960). Exhibition catalogue.

64 James Johnson Sweeney, 'Before Picasso, after Miró', in *Before Picasso, after Miró* (New York: The Solomon R. Guggenheim Museum, 1960), n.p. Exhibition catalogue.

65 John Canaday, 'Spaniards Aplenty', *New York Times*, 21 June 1960; John Canaday, 'Art: More from Spain. Modern Museum Show Follows Guggenheim's', *New York Times*, 20 July 1960. See also, later in the year: John Canaday, 'The Joyless Spaniards', *Time Newsmagazine*, 8 August 1960.

66 Natalie Edgar, 'Is there a new Spanish School?', *Art News* 59, No. 5 (September 1960), p. 44.

67 Cirlot, who wrote the preface to the 1960 Matisse exhibition, stressed that the collective mentality was essential to the emergence of avant-gardes of any kind. 'The creation of the group was motivated by the need to consolidate the isolated efforts of artists situated at the extreme vanguard in their esthetic and social concepts. Frequently, movements of contemporaneous art were obliged to rely on the principle of group psychology as the only way to acquire self-consciousness and to fight against the hostility and indifference of their environment.' Juan Eduardo Cirlot, *Four Spanish Painters*, n.p.

68 María Dolores Jiménez-Blanco, 'Spanishness and Difference: The Reception of Spanish Informalism in New York, 1960', in *Contemporary Transatlantic Dialogues*, ed. by Jiménez-Blanco and Lubar, pp. 19–20.

69 Miriam Basilio, 'A Pilgrimage to the Alcázar of Toledo: Ritual, Tourism and Propaganda in Franco's Spain', in *Architecture and Tourism: Perception, Performance and Place*, ed. by D. Medina Lasansky and Brian McLaren (Oxford: Berg, 2004), 93–108 (p. 95).

70 M. Barrachina, *Propagandae et culture dans l'Espagne franquiste, 1936–1945* (Grenoble: Université Stendhal, 1998), p. 278. Translated by Miriam Basilio, and referenced from Basilio, 'A Pilgrimage to the Alcázar of Toledo', p. 102.

71 De Haro-García and Díaz-Sánchez, 'Artistic Dissidence under Francoism', p. 739.

72 O'Hara, *NSPS*, p. 9.

73 Antonio Saura, referenced in *Catalogue of the Tate Gallery's Collection of Modern Art other than Works by British Artists*, ed. by Ronald Alley (London: Tate Gallery and Sotheby Parke-Bernet, 1981), p. 671.

74 Ibid.

75 In his poem 'The "Unfinished"', O'Hara wrote: 'in the 26th Century when the Court of the Bourbons is reinstated / and heaven comes to resemble a late Goya' (CP, 317–318). If a late Goya offers only nihilism, abjection, and hysteria, then the impulse to 'excavate' and 'reinstate' is a terrifying one. Franco long justified his dictatorship as an interregnum wherein he would steward the state from leftist insurrection and return it safely to Bourbon monarchical rule on his death. The Bourbons were the royal house that ruled Spain for most of Goya's life.

76 Antonio Saura, 'Notes on Pollock', in Saura, *Visor sobre artistas 1958–1998*, trans. Isabel Adey (Barcelona: Glaxia Gutenberg, 2001): 9–14. First published in a reduced version as 'Notas sobre Pollock', in *Carta de El Paso 4* (1958).

77 O'Hara, letter to Rasmussen, 5 April 1960, FOHP, MoMA Archives, New York.

78 John Shoptaw, *On the Outside Looking Out: John Ashbery's Poetry* (Cambridge: Harvard University Press, 1994), p. 44.

79 T. S. Eliot, 'The Waste Land', in *The Waste Land and Other Poems* (London: Broadview Press, 2011), p. 67 (ll. 74–75).

80 John Ashbery, email correspondence with the author, 6 January 2017.

81 Ibid.

82 'Spain is different' has become a popularly used launch-phrase in cultural and historical studies to engage in debates around national 'difference' – racial, political, sexual – right up until the present day. The most recent example is *Is Spain Different? A Comparative Look at the 19th and 20th Centuries*, ed. by Nigel Townson (Brighton: Sussex Academic Press, 2015). The ideological implications of the 'Spain is different' tourist campaign is well outlined in Sasha D. Pack, 'Tourism and Political Change in Franco's Spain', in *Spain Transformed: The Franco Dictatorship, 1959–1975*, ed. by Nigel Townson (London: Palgrave, 2010), 47–66; Dorothy Kelly, 'Selling Spanish "otherness" since the 1960s', in *Contemporary Spanish Studies*, ed. by Barry Jordan (New York: Oxford University Press, 2000), 29–37.

83 Immanuel Kant, *Anthropology from a Pragmatic Point of View*, trans. by Robert B. Louden (Cambridge: Cambridge University Press, 2006), pp. 411–412.

84 O'Hara, *NSPS*, p. 10.

85 Frank O'Hara, letter to Luis Feito, 27 April 1960, box 3, fol. 17, FOHP, MoMA Archives, New York. It is worth noting that the same explanation was offered to other artists represented in the exhibition.

86 O'Hara, letter to Rasmussen, 5 April 1960, FOHP, MoMA Archives, New York.

87 Luis González Robles, letter to Frank O'Hara, 21 March 1960, box 3, fol. 17, FOHP, MoMA Archives, New York.

88 Ibid.

89 Manuel Millares, letter to Pierre Matisse, 6 May 1960, Pierre Matisse Papers, MoMA Archives, New York.

90 Manuel Millares, letter to Pierre Matisse, 5 November 1960, Pierre Matisse Papers, MoMA Archives, New York.

91 Barreiro López, 'Reinterpreting the Past', p. 733.

92 Frank O'Hara, 'Autobiographical Fragments', in *Standing Still and Walking in New York*, ed. by Allen, p. 31.

93 O'Hara, *Robert Motherwell*, p. 9. The process of choosing works for the Motherwell retrospective was not altogether simply. Unusually for a living

artist, Motherwell sought to limit the amount of works on display. O'Hara, however, felt differently and argued that the large number of works was necessary to demonstrate, as he put it in a letter to the artist, 'your own uniqueness, and nothing can be gained by avoiding it or trying to edit it, since it is your vitality and strength. …part of the uniqueness is a big, swinging, openminded variety of experience between you and your art where you are willing to fall on your face if necessary to get the experience in paint or in paper. We haven't included any where you did land that way, but what we have I think has the thrilling atmosphere of your willing to if you have to.' Frank O'Hara to Robert Motherwell, 26 August 1965. Archives of The Dedalus Foundation. See also Bruce Altshuler, 'Motherwell and Exhibitions', *Dedalus* <https://dedalusfoundation.org/programs/onlinefeatures/ view/ motherwell-and-exhibitions/#_edn24> [accessed 8 February 2025].

94   O'Hara, *Robert Motherwell*, p. 9.

95   As he prepared Motherwell's selection for the 1965 retrospective, O'Hara tried to cover all bases: 'We have included 8 great elegies, ranging from #34 to #102, and if you add to that *Iberia, Spanish Painting with the Face of a Dog* and *Irish Elegy* and *Africa*, the "black" side of your work is certainly well represented, if not magnificently.' Frank O'Hara, letter to Robert Motherwell, 26 August 1965, II.9, Robert Motherwell Papers, The Dedalus Foundation Archive, New York.

96   It was this monochrome palette that led Barbara Guest to dedicate her poem for Motherwell 'All Elegies are Black and White'. Motherwell also wrote an essay entitled 'Black and White' (1950).

97   O'Hara, *Robert Motherwell*, p. 19.

98   Robert Motherwell, 'A Personal Recollection, 1986', in *The Writings of Robert Motherwell*, ed. by Dore Ashton (Los Angeles: The University of California Press, 2007), 346–351 (p. 348).

99   Robert Motherwell, referenced in E. A. Carmean, 'Robert Motherwell: The Elegies to the Spanish Republic', in *American Art at Mid-Century: The Subjects of the Artist*, ed. by E. A. Carmean and Eliza Rathbone (Washington DC: National Gallery of Art, 1978), p. 101.

100 For an outline on O'Hara's relationship to the poetry of Federico García Lorca, and indeed one of the very few examples of scholarship on his relationship to Spanish culture more widely, see Jonathan Mayhew, *Apocryphal Lorca: Translation, Parody, Kitsch* (London: University of Chicago Press), pp. 122–142. See also Frank O'Hara, 'The Grand Manner of Motherwell', *Vogue* (New York), Vol. 146, Issue. 6 (1 October 1965), 206–209; 263–265.

101 Carmean, 'Robert Motherwell: The Elegies to the Spanish Republic', p. 98.

102 Frank O'Hara, 'Inventory checklist: *The New American Painting*', box 2, fol. 14, FOHP, MoMA Archives, New York.

103 Antonio Saura, 'Un artista paradigmático del siglo XX', *El País*, 18 July 1991. Translated from the Spanish on behalf of the author by Luciana von Römer.

104 Marzo, 'Interview with Luis González Robes', pp. 32–33.

105 According to Elisabet Goula Sardà, 'Miguel del Valle-Inclán, director of the library of the Museo Nacional Centro de Arte Reina Sofia (National Museum

Queen Sofia Art Centre) in Madrid says that Luis González Robles, head of Exhibitions in the Foreign Affairs Ministry at the time and hence in charge of the "New American Painting" exhibition, claimed that the Elegy had been exhibited and that Franco had seen it at the opening and was prompted to remark, "Pues yo no veo la elegía por ninguna parte" (Well, I don't see any elegy here). However, the work does not appear in the exhibition catalogue (Barr, 1958). It is probable that the painting was initially exhibited but subsequently withdrawn by the organizers.' See Elisabet Goula Sardà, '"Someone Who Did Not Forget": The Reception of Robert Motherwell's *Elegies to the Spanish Republic*', *Forma* 1, No. 77 (2009), 77–91 (p. 81). My account here answers Goula Sardà's query beyond reasonable doubt.

106 Porter McCray, letter to Luis González Robles, Parkhotel Rotterdam, 6 August 1958, I.A.718, IC/IP, MoMA Archives, New York.

107 Ibid.

108 Porter McCray, letter to René d'Harnoncourt, Geneva, 9 August 1958, I.A.718, IC/IP, MoMA Archives, New York.

109 Frank O'Hara, letter to Susan Senior, 9 June 1958, I.A.718, IC/IP, MoMA Archives, New York.

110 Ibid.

111 Ibid.

112 Helen Frankenthaler, transcription of a postcard to Frank O'Hara, 23 June 1958, I.A.785, IC/IP, MoMA Archives, New York.

113 John Bernard Myers, 'Frank O'Hara: A Memoir', in *Homage to Frank O'Hara*, ed. by Berkson and LeSueur, p. 37.

114 Bill Berkson, 'Frank O'Hara and His Poems', in *Homage to Frank O'Hara*, ed. by Berkson and LeSueur, p. 161.

115 'Last spring Frank O'Hara sent around a photograph of the Serrano bust of Antonio Machado and Alfred, in sending it back to him, noted that it was very good and asked him whether casts were available and what the dimensions were.' Betsy Jones, letter to René d'Harnoncourt, 16 September 1966. FOHP, MoMA Archives, New York.

116 Andreas Huyssen, *Present Pasts: Urban Palimpsests and the Politics of Memory* (Stanford: Stanford University Press, 2003), p. 16.

117 Norma Louise Hutman, *Machado: A Dialogue with Time, Nature as an Expression of Temporality in the Poetry of Antonio Machado* (Albuquerque: The University of New Mexico Press, 1969), p. 118.

Six | The Slightest Loss of Attention
Leads to Death

1 'Franz Kline, 51, Painter, is Dead', *New York Times*, 15 May 1962, p. 39.

2 Willem de Kooning, quoted in Peter Schjeldahl, 'Frank O'Hara: He Made Things and People Sacred', *Village Voice,* 11 August 1966.

3 The Willem de Kooning retrospective was a long time coming. At dinner after the opening of the Kline exhibition, O'Hara noted that 'de Wilde again brought up his longing for a de Kooning show'. Frank O'Hara, letter to Waldo Rasmussen, Amsterdam, 21 September 1963, I.A.1297, IC/IP, MoMA Archives, New York.

4 In the spring of 1966, O'Hara had begun work on organizing the first major retrospective of de Kooning at MoMA. Hostile to a large-scale biographical exposition, De Kooning identified O'Hara as the sole curator he trusted to take the project on. The exhibition would eventually be shelved until March 1968, when it opened for less than two months. Thomas B. Hess was drafted to curate and to write the catalogue, and was originally shown at the Stedelijk Museum in Amsterdam, with much fanfare and talk of the artist's 'homecoming' after he had become a modern master in the New World. In New York, the retrospective would display some 147 works – paintings, drawings, pastels, and collages – in eleven rooms, a far larger showing than O'Hara had envisaged. Discussions in support of a De Kooning retrospective between MoMA and the Stedelijk Museum had been ongoing since at least 1960.

5 O'Hara, letter to Rasmussen, 21 September 1963, IC/IP, MoMA Archives, New York.

6 Waldo Rasmussen, 'Frank O'Hara in the Museum', in *Homage to Frank O'Hara*, ed. by Berkson and LeSueur, 84–90 (p. 89).

7 Frank O'Hara and Franz Kline, 'Franz Kline Talking', in *Franz Kline* (New York: The Museum of Modern Art, 1963), n.p.

8 Frank O'Hara, 'Franz Kline: Exhibition checklist', I.A.1286, IC/IP, MoMA Archives, New York.

9 Frank O'Hara, 'Franz Kline', in *Art Chronicles* (New York: George Braziller, 1975), 40–52 (p. 48).

10 The ownership of *Shenandoah Wall* was contested between Sidney Janis Gallery, who had originally lent it to the Kline retrospective, and Charles Egan, who claimed that Kline had intended to leave the painting to him in his will. A lengthy court battle ensued. O'Hara wanted to credit the painting anonymously on the suggestion of Sidney Janis, but Egan objected. The *New York Law Journal* featured the controversy in its 31 March 1964 edition.

11 Elizabeth Kline, letter to Frank O'Hara, Long Island, New York, 14 December 1963, I.A.1307, MoMA Archives, New York.

12 Frank O'Hara, letter to Elizabeth Kline, 19 December 1963, I.A.1307, MoMA Archives, New York.

13 Ibid.

14 Frank O'Hara, letter to Waldo Rasmussen, Amsterdam, 25 September 1963, I.A.1297, IC/IP, MoMA Archives, New York.

15 Ibid.

16 Ibid.

17 Efforts were made by Waldo Rasmussen to show the exhibition at the Louisiana Museum of Modern Art in Denmark, the Kunstverein in Hamburg, the Wallraf-Richartz Museum in Cologne, the Musée National d'Art Moderne in Paris, Staatliche Kunsthalle in Baden-Baden, the Finnish-American Society in Helsinki,

Ausstellungsleitung München E.V. Haus der Kunst and Staadtische Galerie und Lenbach Museum in Munich, Muzeum Narodowego in Warsaw, Museo Nacional de Art Moderna in Madrid, Moderna Museet in Stockholm, Kunstnernes Hus in Oslo, Bezalel National Museum in Jerusalem, and Museum Folkwang in Essen. None were ultimately realized due to the limited scheduling opportunities for these 'provincial' museums over the summer and the relatively late and rushed planning of the retrospective after Kline's death. Galleria Nazionale d'Art Moderna would have committed to the exhibition had Rasmussen not already made an agreement with the Museo Civico di Torino, but the Roman museum did not desire the exhibition to be shown twice in Italy. Muzej za umjetnost i obrt in Yugoslavia could not afford the $1000 insurance costs to cover their budgetary proportion for shipping and installation.

18 Angelo Dragone, review in *Stampa Sera,* Turin, Italy, 4 November 1963, 'Critical Reviews, Second Showing: Turin, Italy, Museo Civico di Torino, November 5 – December 1, 1963', I.A.1287, IC/IP, MoMA Archives, New York.

19 Ibid.

20 Marziano Bernardi, review in *La Stampa*, 5 November 1963, 'Critical Reviews, Second Showing: Turin, Italy, Museo Civico di Torino, November 5 – December 1, 1963', I.A.1287, IC/IP, MoMA Archives, New York.

21 Frank O'Hara, letter to Waldo Rasmussen and Gary [?], Turin, 5 November 1963, I.A.1303, IC/IP, MoMA Archives, New York.

This letter also included descriptions of the inaugural ceremony, attended by Vittorio Viale, 'Antonio Tàpies, Michel Tapié, Accardi, Pistoi (Notizid gallery), Rudolphe Stadler, and the man who runs La Tararuga, and some reporters'. The Mayor of Turin 'gave quite a long address [by saying] that even though we may find Kline more difficult, more impassioned and expressionistic, even more disturbing, than the current mostri of Piedmontese Baroque art, where would we be without our artists – a sentiment I found quite remarkable in a mayor, if I understood him correctly'. The letter concluded with comparative reflections on his travels through the Netherlands and Italy: 'Turin as you may have guessed from Di Chirico, is full of marvelous arcades and you hardly ever get wet when it's raining unless you're going out of your way. It is terribly romantic and at the same time severe. Like with The Haggue [sic] and its paucity of canals compared to Amsterdam, I'm afraid I won't be able to forgive Milan its lack of porticos when I get there tomorrow.'

22 D. M. Oostdijk, 'Haring happen met Frank O'Hara: Transatlantische uitwisseling of veramerikanisering?' *Armada: Tijdschrift voor wereldliteratuur* 65 (December 2011), 79-90. Translated from the Dutch on behalf of the author by Yente Vaneerdewegh.

23 Ibid.

24 Ibid.

25 Robert Rosenblum, 'The Primal American Scene', in *The Natural Paradise: Painting in America, 1800–1950,* ed. Kynaston McShine, exhibition catalogue (New York: Museum of Modern Art, 1976), p. 37.

26 It is a major regret of this book that I was unable to secure an interview with Jan Cremer to discuss his friendship and collaboration with O'Hara. After

planning conversations with his dealers at Adams Amsterdam Auctions and with his wife, the indomitable Babette Cremer-Sijmons, I was not able to track him down. The last I heard he was on an ethnographic study mission in Tunisia.

27 Clara Eggink, review in *Leidsch Dagblad*, quoted in Marja Kingma, 'Ik, Jan Cremer – controversial but not banned', *British Library*, 27 September 2019 < https://blogs.bl.uk/european/2019/09/ik-jan-cremer-controversial-but-not-banned.html> [accessed 5 May 2022].

28 See Jaap van der Bent, '"O Fellow Travelers I Write You a Poem in Amsterdam": Allen Ginsberg, Simon Vinkenoog, and the Dutch Beat Connection', in *College Literature* 27, No. 1, Teaching Beat Literature (Winter, 2000), 199–212.

'When Cremer arrived in New York on a visit in 1965, O'Hara was similarly tolerant and bemused. He encouraged him to flash. At a Museum of Modern Art opening Cremer showed up in a skintight fire engine red outfit with the exotically beautiful Venezuelan sculptor Marisol on the back of his Harley. "Frank thought it was a riot", says Jim Brodey of the highjinks of Cremer, who made a big splash with Pop society that trip and began going around with Nico of the Velvet Underground. (At the same opening Brodey claims that O'Hara introduced him to Nelson Rockefeller to whom Brodey spoke in thick street slang, to O'Hara's extreme discomfort).' Gooch, *City Poet,* p. 411.

29 Frank O'Hara, letter to Vincent Warren, Amsterdam, 18 September 1963, box 2, fol. 13, Allen Collection of Frank O'Hara Letters, Storrs.

30 Patsy Southgate, interview with Brad Gooch, 14 April 1989, reprinted in Gooch, *City Poet,* p. 409.

31 Frank O'Hara, letter to Lawrence Ferlinghetti, Amsterdam, 25 September 1963. Letter reprinted in Frank O'Hara, *Lunch Poems: Expanded 50th Anniversary Edition* (San Francisco: City Lights Books, 2014), n.p.

32 Jan Cremer, 'A NEW MANNER', I.A.1288, IC/IP, MoMA Archives, New York.

33 Johannes Cladders, in Hans Ulrich Obrist, *A Brief History of Curating* (Zurich: ZRP Ringier, 2008), p. 74.

34 Ibid.

35 Dore Ashton, 'Kline as He Was and as He Is', in *Franz Kline, 1910–1962,* ed. by Carolyn Christov-Bakargiev (Turin: Castello di Rivoli Museo d'Arte Contemporanea, 2004), p. 39. Exhibition catalogue.

36 Harry F. Gaugh, *Franz Kline: The Vital Gesture* (New York: Abbeville Press, 1985), 47–48.

37 Frank O'Hara, 'Franz Kline Talking', in *Standing Still and Walking in New York*, ed. by Allen, p. 91.

38 Cremer himself raised his profile as the *enfant terrible* of postwar Dutch art when he exclaimed in a TV interview: 'Rembrandt? Who's that? I don't know anything about sports.' See Jan Cremer, interview reprinted in Manfred Wolf, 'Dutchman', *The Reporter*, Vol. 34 (1966), p. 56.

39 Cremer, 'A NEW MANNER', I.A.1288, IC/IP, MoMA Archives, New York.

40 O'Hara, letter to Rasmussen, 25 September 1963, I.A.1297, IC/IP, MoMA Archives, New York.

41 Ibid.

42 Frank O'Hara, letter to Rasmussen, 21 September 1963, I.A.1297, IC/IP, MoMA Archives, New York.

43 Ibid.

44 O'Hara, 'A NEW MANNER', I.A.1288, IC/IP, MoMA Archives, New York.

45 Ibid.

46 Ibid.

47 Frank O'Hara, letter to Joe LeSueur, Copenhagen, 30 September 1963, box 3, fol. 28, Allen Collection of Frank O'Hara Letters, Storrs.

48 A reading of this poem was chosen by O'Hara as the opening to Richard O. Moore's 1966 documentary film of his work, *USA Poetry*. See 'USA: Poetry, Frank O'Hara (1966)', *YouTube* video, 0:20, "cassandra gillig", 30 November 2012 <https://www.youtube.com/watch?v=344TyqLlSFA&t=4s> [accessed 14 March 2020].

49 In a joyful missive to Helen Frankenthaler, Smith exclaimed that it was: 'Happyest [sic] I've been sometime with my dolls.' David Smith, postcard to Helen Frankenthaler, July 1961, Collection of Helen Frankenthaler and Robert Motherwell Papers relating to David Smith, AAA.

50 Frank O'Hara, 'David Smith: The color of steel', *Art News* 60, No. 8 (December 1961), p. 33. In his catalogue entry for *David Smith: 1906–1965*, O'Hara described Bolton Landing as a 'home, studio, and workshop', set 'in the beautiful mountains above Lake George in northern New York State (near Canada)', and where Smith had 'gradually filled with sculptures which spilled out onto the hill on which the house was situated. In the early days he had begun to place sculptures outdoors in the fields where sculptures became a permanent feature, constantly replaced by newer work. With the hundreds of sculptures and paintings, and some three thousand drawings done in his solitude, Bolton Landing became an extraordinary one-man museum.' Frank O'Hara, 'Introduction', in *David Smith: 1906–1965* (New York: The Museum of Modern Art, 1966), n.p.

51 O'Hara, 'David Smith: The color of steel', p. 32.

52 David Getsy, 'On Not Making Boys: David Smith, Frank O'Hara, and Gender Assignment', in *Abstract Bodies: 1960s Sculpture in the Expanded Field of Gender* (London: Yale University Press, 2015), 43–96 (p. 49). Smith would even gift O'Hara a painting after this visit. Getsy's essay, from the first monograph to address modern American sculpture from the perspective of interdisciplinary transgender studies, is an important intervention in understanding the relationship between O'Hara and Smith.

53 Frank O'Hara, letter to David Smith, 17 August 1961, David Smith Papers, AAA. My emphasis. In the postscript to this letter, O'Hara's identification with Smith's work is complete: 'What I think I mean by the above is I'd like to *be* one of those sculptures!'

54 David Smith, in Frank O'Hara, 'David Smith: Sculpting Master of Bolton Landing', transcript from an interview which appeared in the film *Art New York: The Sculpting Master of Bolton Landing*, 6 November 1964. Reprinted as 'Interview by Frank O'Hara, 1964', in *David Smith: Collected Writings,*

Lectures, and Interviews, ed. by Susan J. Cooke (Oakland: University of California Press, 2018), 422–427 (p. 424).

55 Michael Brenson, *David Smith: The Art and Life of a Transformational Sculptor* (New York: Farrar, Straus and Giroux, 2022), p. 233.

56 David Smith, letter to Kenneth Noland, 26 June 1961, Kenneth Noland Papers relating to David Smith, AAA.

57 In a hostile period that became known as 'The Revolt of the Young Turks', a constellation of younger museum officials in departments outside of the International Program expressed their resentment of McCray's 'empire building' to David Rockefeller. In response, McCray threatened to resign and left the management of the International Program in a state of anxious flux. Eliza Parkinson, who became President of MoMA's Board of Trustees, wrote of 'the Young Turks': 'I think they were awfully jealous because the International Council had become very important and it entailed a lot of travel and they all wanted to travel. He [McCray] represented the Museum and there were all these parties that they'd hear about. But the fact was that he was setting up a little museum within the Museum.' See Russell Lynes, *Good Old Modern: An Intimate Portrait of The Museum of Modern Art* (New York: Atheneum, 1973), pp. 389–390.

58 Frank O'Hara, letter to Clement Greenberg, 1 March 1966, I.A.1390, IC/IP, MoMA Archives, New York.

59 Jane Harrison, letter to Frank O'Hara, 1 April 1966, I.A.1390, IC/IP, MoMA Archives, New York.

60 O'Hara has an important role in the formative years of the *Festival of Two Worlds* in Spoleto. In 1965, he was asked by Gian Carlo Menotti to make the American poetry selection for the Settimana della Poesia. O'Hara chose John Ashbery, Bill Berkson, Gregory Corso, Lawrence Ferlinghetti, Allen Ginsberg, Barbara Guest, Kenneth Koch, Robert Lowell, Charles Olson, Tony Towle, and John Wieners. Lowell declined the invitation, and Ginsberg was disinvited by Menotti because of a scandal he had caused at the Festival in 1962. Invited by Menotti, Ezra Pound held court like an elder statesman – he was not yet *persona non grata* in Italy. While O'Hara could not attend the Festival itself because of curatorial obligations at MoMA he was, according to Berkson, 'there in spirit, having organized a tidy MoMA show of recent landscape painting that featured Alex Katz, Allan d'Arcangelo, Roy Lichtenstein, Jane Freilicher, Richard Diebenkorn, Robert Dash, Christopher Lane, Jane Wilson, and Aristodemos Kaldis'. See Bill Berkson, 'Spoleto '65', *BOMB*, 15 September 2016 <https://bombmagazine.org/articles/spoleto-65> [accessed 12 June 2020].

61 O'Hara, *David Smith*, n.p.

62 Ibid.

63 *David Smith: 1906–1965* travelled to the Tate Gallery in London, where the exhibition opened on 18 August, and it is unclear whether O'Hara had hoped to travel back to Europe for the opening there. As I noted in my Introduction, O'Hara never found his way to England and it is an added tragedy that the likelihood of this visit was foreclosed by his death.

64 Frank O'Hara, letter to Joan Mitchell, Landgoed Hotel Restaurant Groot Warnsborn, 15 May 1966, JMFA. Brad Gooch has speculated that this was the result of an unconfirmed venereal infection.

65 Frank O'Hara, unpublished handwritten speech for the opening of *David Smith 1906–1965*. Kindly reproduced for the author by Maureen Granville-Smith.

66 Erje Ayden, 'From *Seven Years of Winter*', in *Homage to Frank O'Hara*, ed. by Berkson and LeSueur, p. 172.

67 O'Hara, opening speech, *David Smith 1906–1965*.

68 Ibid.

69 Frank O'Hara, letter to Rudi Oxenaar, 21 May 1966, I.A.1390, IC/IP, MoMA Archives, New York.

70 Michael Brenson, *David Smith: The Art and Life of a Transformational Sculptor* (New York: Farrar, Straus and Giroux, 2022), p. 627.

71 Ibid, p. 716.

72 O'Hara, opening speech, *David Smith 1906–1965*.

73 Ibid.

74 Ibid.

75 Frank O'Hara, letter to Joan Mitchell, 15 May 1966, Joan Mitchell Foundation Archives, New York.

76 Greenberg had opposed Smith's use of colour on the grounds that it undermined his doctrine of medium purity and was a nonessential aspect of the sculptural medium. In 1965, Greenberg took the extraordinary step when, as an executor to Smith's works, he stripped paint from five of Smith's sculptures (which had been painted white) and had them rusted and sealed. The critic also let some sculptures deteriorate or fade in colour by not protecting them from the weather, much to the consternation of Rosalind Krauss who documented the custodial negligence of her mentor and criticized him for going against Smith's conception of – and the manner in which he left – his last works. See Sarah Hamill, 'Polychrome in the 1960s: David Smith and Anthony Caro', in *Anglo-American Exchange in Postwar Sculpture, 1945–1975* (Los Angeles: Getty, 2011), 91–104.

77 Brenson, *David Smith*, p. 718.

78 O'Hara, 'David Smith: The color of steel', p. 33.

79 Ibid.

80 Ibid, p. 34.

81 O'Hara, 'David Smith: Sculpting Master of Bolton Landing', pp. 422–427.

Afterword | Living Situations in New York and London

1 Frank O'Hara, 'Art Chronicle I', p. 5.

2 Alex Katz, in 'A Conversation' (2012), interview by Hans Ulrich Obrist, with Vincent Katz, in *Quick Light,* exhibition catalogue (London: Serpentine Galleries and Koenig Books, 2016), p. 11.

3 Frank O'Hara, 'Art Chronicle II', *Kulchur*, No. 6 (Summer 1962), pp. 50–56.

4   Edwin Denby, 'Katz: Collage, Cutout, Cut-Up', *Art News* 63, No. 9 (January 1965), p. 42.

5   David Max Horowitz, 'Realist Illusions: Alex Katz's Cutouts', in *Alex Katz Gathering* (New York: Guggenheim, 2022): 300–304, p. 302.

6   Alex Katz, *Invented Symbols*: *An Art Autobiography*, ed. Vincent Katz (Waterville, Maine: Colby College Museum of Art; Milan: Edizioni Charta, 2012), p. 154.

7   Alex Katz, 'Memoir', in Bill Berkson and Joe LeSueur (eds), *Homage to Frank O'Hara* (Bolinas, CA: Big Sky, 1978), p. 99.

8   Alice Neel, interview with Yetta Groshans and Werner Groshans, 20 March 1979, Yetta and Werner Groshans Papers, Smithsonian Archives of American Art.

9   Alice Neel, referenced in Phoebe Hoban, *Alice Neel: The Art of Not Sitting Pretty* (New York: David Zwirner, 2021), p. 249.

10 Ibid.

11 Ibid.

12 J. S. Marcus, 'The Penetrating Eye', *The Wall Street Journal* (7 November 2008), n.p.

13 John Ashbery, 'In Memory of My Feelings', in *Art News*, January 1968, n.p.